JFK-9/11

50 Years of Deep State

(A deep history of the last fifty years)

Laurent Guyénot

ProgRESSive
Independent Media.
ProgressivePress.com

2014

About the Author

Laurent Guyénot was born in France in 1960. After graduating as an engineer from the École Nationale Supérieure de Techniques Avancées in Paris, and working in the armaments industry in the United States for two years, he turned to the study of religious history and anthropology.

He has earned a PhD in Medieval Studies at La Sorbonne, Paris, and has since authored several groundbreaking books in French on medieval "narrative anthropology," most recently *The Bleeding Spear* (2010) and *Fairy Death* (2011). He has also published an investigation into the psychological and social damage of mass pornography.

He has been researching America's "deep history" for the last five years, and has been a contributor to Voltairenet.org. JFK-911 is his first book in English.

JFK-9/11

50 Years of Deep State

(A deep history of the last fifty years)

by Laurent Guyénot

JFK-9/11 assembles the most significant and well-documented "deep events" of the last fifty years into a coherent narrative of the "deep history" of the United States and its sphere of influence. The result is both a concise introduction for newcomers (a "deep history for dummies"), and an insightful perspective for informed readers.

Relying strictly on documented evidence and state-of-the-art JFK and 9/11 research, the book cuts through the layers of government and mainstream media lies, to expose the hidden powers at work in the Empire's underground foreign policy. It documents the role of undercover and paramilitary operations, psychological warfare and disinformation campaigns, and above all false flag terror, in the course of world politics since the beginning of the Cold War, and increasingly since September 11th.

The book is divided in two parts: the first deals with the underlying forces of the Cold War, the second with the driving forces of the War on Terror. The period investigated begins just before November 22, 1963 and peaks on September 11, 2001, the two deep events that weigh most heavily on the unfolding of American and world history. The author highlights their structural similarities, examines how one made the other possible thirty-eight years later, and follows the underlying thread leading from the one to the other, in the hope of anticipating and circumventing future atrocities.

JFK-9/11

50 Years of Deep State
(A deep history of the last fifty years)

First print edition. Illustrated. List Price: $15.95
ISBN 1-61577-631-1, EAN 978-1-61577-631-3
Length: 84,000 words on 238   pages
Mobi and Epub e-book editions: $4.99. E-book ISBN: 1615776303

Metasubjects: Nonfiction, Politics, History, Biography

Library of Congress Subject Headings
Kennedy, John F. (John Fitzgerald), 1917-1963--Assassination. LC: E842.9, Dewey 364.15
September 11 Terrorist Attacks, 2001. LC: HV6432.7, Dewey 973.931
Conspiracy Theories. LC: HV6275, Dewey 001.9 (Controversial Knowledge)
Zionists--Political activity--United States, E183.8.I7, Dewey 324.4

BISAC Subject Area Codes
BIO011000   Biography & Autobiography / Presidents & Heads of State
HIS036060   History / United States / 20th Century
POL036000   Political Science / Intelligence & Espionage
POL037000   Political Science / Terrorism
SOC049000   Social Science / Jewish Studies
SOC058000   Social Science / Conspiracy Theories

Distribution: Ingram, Baker & Taylor, Gazelle Book Services UK

Version française: JFK, 11 septembre: 50 ans de manipulations

From the Cold War to the "War on Terror," *JFK-9/11* exposes the hidden powers at work in the Empire's foreign policy. Relying strictly on documented evidence and state-of-the-art research on the JFK assassination and 9/11, the book cuts through the layers of government and mainstream media lies. *JFK-9/11* assembles the most significant and well-documented "deep events" of the last fifty years into a coherent narrative of the "deep history" of the United States and its sphere of influence. It highlights the role of undercover and paramilitary operations, psychological warfare and disinformation, and false flag terror.

The author wishes to thank David Mann for sharing his extensive expertise in 9/11 research.

Table of Contents

Introduction

The subject of this book is the "deep history" of the United States and its sphere of influence during the last fifty years. By "deep history" or "deep politics," political scientist Peter Dale Scott refers to the underlying, and often shrouded, decisions and activities that determine major historical events, especially armed conflicts. A deep history relies on declassified secret archives and the testimony of insiders and whistleblowers, rather than merely official pronouncements and public discourse, to explain history's tumult. It includes, but is not limited to, the history of secret services (the United States Intelligence Community includes sixteen government agencies). Considering that the causes of war cited in conventional history are so often rife with false pretense, deep history is necessarily revisionist. Independent investigators study it more often than professional historians. It is also anti-war, since exposing the real causes of war will help prevent wars. Finally, it involves "conspiracy theories," if by that we mean that it openly admits the role of secret pacts and hidden agendas, undercover and paramilitary operations, psychological warfare and disinformation campaigns, in the course of world politics since the beginning of the Cold War, and increasingly since September 11th. In fact, only a deep history can help explain the shift from the world of the Cold War to the world of our amorphous "War on Terror."

An important part of a deep history is devoted to "false flag operations," in which a State feigns an enemy attack in order to wage a war while claiming legitimate defense; that is, framing the country it wants to attack as the aggressor. Conventional history—written by the victors—readily imputes such operations to the defeated nations: we know that in 1931, when the Japanese army decided to invade Manchuria, they dynamited their own railway lines near the military base in Mukden, and then accused the Chinese of the sabotage. We also know that in 1939, when Hitler needed a pretext to invade Poland, he ordered German soldiers and prisoners dressed in Polish uniforms to launch an assault on the Gleiwitz outpost. And we suspect that just prior, in 1933, the Nazis had set fire to the palace of the Reichstag to construct a "Communist conspiracy" and thereby suspend civil liberties. The victorious nations, however, assiduously bury their own lies and war crimes, and it is the role of a deep history to exhume them.

Deep history is the story of the Deep State, meaning the power structures that act behind the scene of political spectacle to set in motion great movements of history. Although it has always existed, the deep state has been strengthened in modern democracies (in a dictatorship it cannot be distinguished from the public state), by those who consider their interests above the people's, and have taken control of the political system without regard to elections or legal principles. Thus the deep state is hostile to the democratic institutions of the republican state. The transparency that is essential to the latter is lethal to the former. But the deep state seeks less to destroy democratic power than to confine and control it. In the United States, it has for fifty years gained almost total control of foreign policy, so much so that almost all direct or indirect actions of the United States in the world have been carried out without the general public's knowledge or understanding.

The exceptional power of the American deep state can be explained by the dual and contradictory nature of that nation, best defined by the oxymoron "imperial democracy." Within its borders, the United States is an ostensible democracy, but outside, it behaves like an empire or colonial power. The deep state is the invisible heart of the Empire, the command and control center of imperial violence. This violence must remain hidden from the eyes and consciences of the American citizenry, who must be satisfied that the government acts only to defend the interests of global freedom and democracy. That is why the deep state constantly needs to blow around itself a screen of humanitarian smoke.

Edward Bernays, a nephew of Freud (on both his mother's and father's side), is considered the father of modern scientific propaganda or "public relations." He was influential in the Committee on Public Information set up by Woodrow Wilson to win over public opinion in favor of entering the war in 1917. His book *Propaganda* (1928) begins with these words: "The conscious and intelligent manipulation of the organized habits and opinions of the masses is an important element in democratic society. Those who manipulate this unseen mechanism of society constitute an invisible government, which is the true ruling power of our country. [...] Propaganda is the executive arm of the invisible government."

While it may occasionally act as an "invisible government," the deep state is not a homogeneous and stable structure, but a polymorphic and changing organism. Some clans are made and unmade with every changing alliance and betrayal. Some of these clans are united by personal ties of blood or money, to which can be added initiation type fraternities. Some are communitarian and, in more than one case, secretly loyal to a foreign government. Other clans are ideological, consumed with visions of global supremacy incompatible with classical republican patriotism and the universal values claimed essential to the public state. Finally, some major players in the deep state appear driven mainly by the thirst for personal power: psychopaths thrive in the deepest workings of the State. It is the task of deep history to bring to light these obscure agendas and loyalties that lie below the shelter of the media's censorship.

Actors within the deep state are not necessarily unknown to the public. Although often engaged in discreet or secret circles, their influence on the world is not completely hidden, and some even boast of it in their later years. The most powerful occupy senior government positions, where they are more often appointed than elected. One of the key positions in the American deep state is the National Security Advisor, because he is protected by institutional secrecy. Recently, it was his/her advisors, acting even more discreetly, who pulled the strings.

For the elite operating at the deep level of power, the world is a battleground where all means are justified. Information is a weapon as important as money in the fight against political opponents, but also for the control of public opinion and the manipulation of democracy. Deep actors create history by telling "stories" to the people, interweaving fact with fiction and fantasy to maintain a continuous national narrative. The phrase "deep state" may therefore also describe the hypnotic sleep into which the deep powers seduce the masses in order to govern them and, most importantly, lead them to approve war.

In 1994, the film *Forrest Gump* received six Oscars. Americans were encouraged to identify with this happy idiot, totally uncritical toward the Vietnam War ("It was nice!"), in fact so incapable of seeing evil that he regards Jenny's alcoholic and incestuous father as "a very loving father." There is a Forrest Gump in each one of us; we would rather not see, hear, or smell evil, and we would rather trust our leaders than suspect them of conspiring behind our back. Unfortunately, this is what allows conspiracies to succeed.

This book is divided into two parts: the first deals with the underlying forces of the Cold War, the second with the driving forces of the War on Terror. The period investigated begins just before November 22, 1963 and peaks with September 11, 2001: these are the two deep events we explore because they weigh most heavily on the unfolding of American history. By "deep events" we mean events whose causality is mostly hidden, and whose functioning emerges only in traces. Their true nature is often different from or contrary to their purported meaning in the media spotlight. It can take fifty years—time for the guilty generation to disappear—for such deep events to gain sufficient transparency to render the "official story" unsustainable, depending on the pace of declassification of archives. The research on the Kennedy assassination is slowly emerging out of the "conspiracy theory" ghetto where it had been locked by institutional culture. The Dallas crime has now become a textbook case, and to anyone willing to take the time, it affords proof of the existence of the deep state, its vital link with war, and its ability to change history and shape public opinion. The main ambition of this book is to examine September 11th through the illuminating lens of November 22nd, highlight their structural similarities, examine how one made the other possible thirty-eight years later, and follow the underlying thread leading from the one to the other, in the hope of anticipating and circumventing future atrocities.

The links between the two cases are structural but also personal. They involve, among others, George H. W. Bush, who was secretly in the CIA and in Dallas on November 22, 1963, long before he became CIA director—then Vice-President, President, and finally a President's father. Those who, like Bush Sr., still fight tooth and nail to defend the government's thesis on Kennedy's death are the same who seek to prevent the emergence of the truth about September 11th. Conversely, denouncing the internal plot of September 11th without elucidating the Kennedy assassination is a bit like telling the story of Noah's Flood without mentioning Adam's Fall.

My goal is brevity; I wanted to present the basic facts and get to the point, so as to make a clear case and give the non-specialist reader the best opportunity to understand what was, and is, a very long and complex history. This book is intended, therefore, not to demonstrate a thesis by accumulation of arguments, but rather to coherently assemble the most meaningful facts, those which give sufficient keys to this deep history; the idea is to paint the big picture from carefully selected elements. Renouncing that which was too obscure or difficult to substantiate, I focus on the surest and most critical episodes, that is to say the minimum needed to understand the genesis and nature of the world in which we live. I am also trying to logically connect the dots, so to speak, as any work of history must. Some illustrated boxes will provide additional details, image-based evidence, revealing quotes, and insights into some personalities whose faces and names deserve a place in the collective memory—deep history has its heroes, martyrs, and villains, rarely mentioned in textbooks.

I have tried to stick to the rules of accuracy and precision. The bulk of the book consists of established facts, and the few interpretations put forward will be clearly stated as such. Any unfounded rumor has been excluded. Most of the data included here is well known to rigorous researchers. In order to help the reader check any statement and seek further information by a search engine, I systematically provide the dates, proper names and other useful keywords. What applies to events also applies to citations, which have been chosen for their informative content; sources are given for quotations. The essential bibliography, from which a great part of this narrative is reconstructed, is given at the end of the work, and information from other sources is referenced in the notes.

BOOK ONE: JFK

1. Dallas, November 22, 1963

November 22, 1963, at half past twelve, while sitting in the back of a converti-ble limousine next to his wife during a parade in Dallas, John F. Kennedy was shot twice. The first bullet pierced his throat; the second caught a rear portion of his skull, splattering with blood and brain the nearest motorcycle policeman, Bobby Hargis. The motorcade had deviated from the originally planned route announced in the *Dallas Morning News*, so the crowd was sparse there, but after a few seconds of confusion, a dozen witnesses rushed to the picket fence atop the little hill (today known as the "grassy knoll"), from which the fatal shots were fired, to the right and front of the limousine at the time of the shots. The first police officer to arrive at the fence, Joe Marshall Smith, testified that he was told to back off by a man showing him an identification of the Secret Service (the security service of the President and White House staff). It would be revealed later that there were in fact no Secret Service agents on foot in Dealey Plaza. In fact, as agent Smith would later reflect, the man was wearing a sports outfit and had dirty nails, and "it didn't ring true for the Secret Ser-vice." More testimonies from eye- and ear-witnesses would confirm that snip-ers had shot from the grassy knoll, while others did spot two men and a gun in the sixth floor of the School Book Depository.[1]

At 1 pm, President Kennedy was pronounced dead at Parkland Hospital in Dallas, but members of the Secret Service prevented the appointed coroner, Earl Rose, from performing the autopsy required by law. Instead, they boarded the body onto the presidential plane Air Force One for an autopsy at the Naval Bethesda Hospital in Washington—an autopsy to be performed by an inexpe-rienced military doctor (James Hulmes), flanked by senior officers and federal agents. The autopsy report would establish that the fatal bullet had entered the back of the skull.

---

[1] James Douglass, *JFK and the Unspeakable: Why He died and Why it Matters,* Touchstone, 2008, p. 261-6.

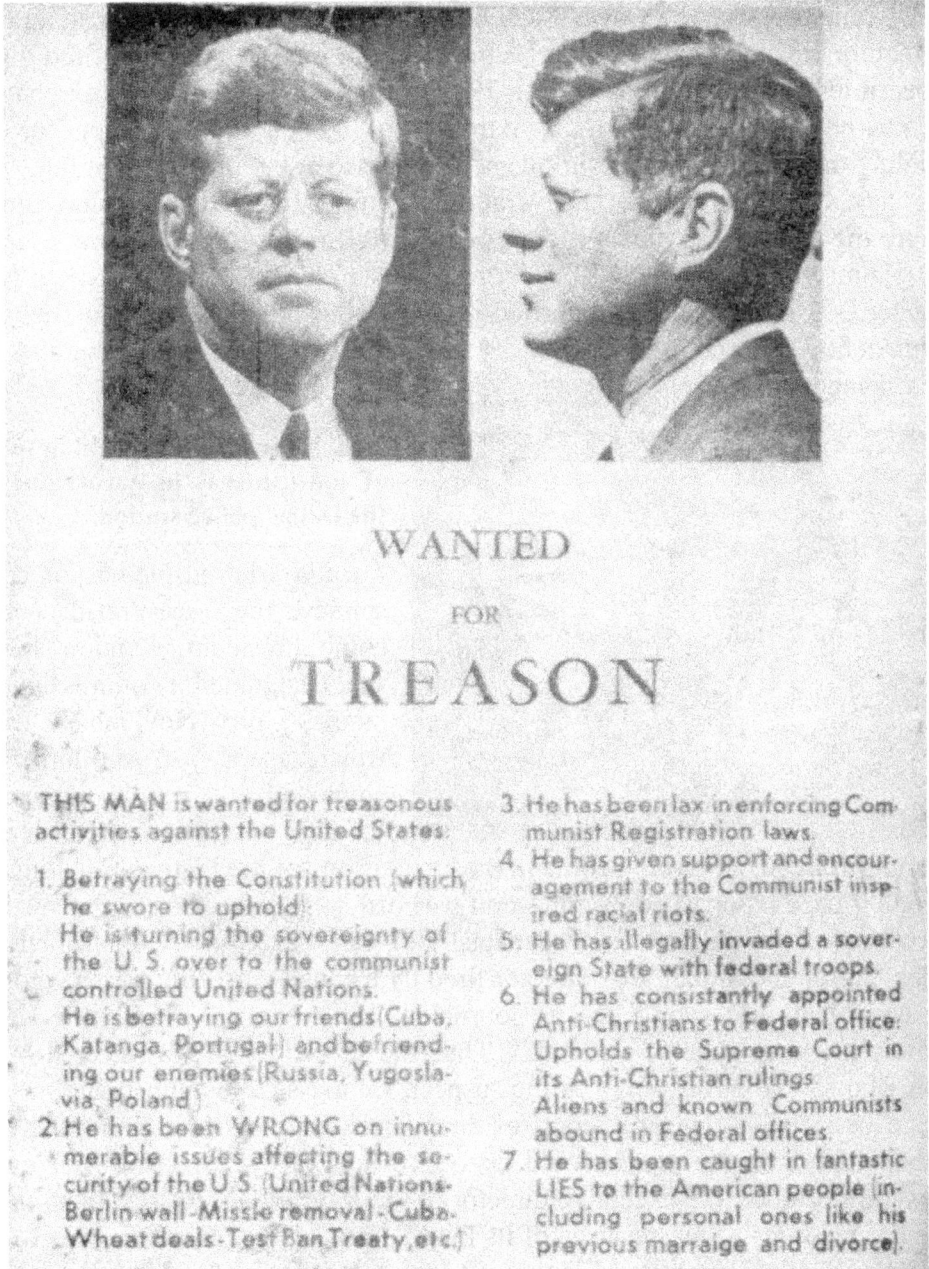

WANTED

FOR

TREASON

THIS MAN is wanted for treasonous activities against the United States:

1. Betraying the Constitution (which he swore to uphold):
   He is turning the sovereignty of the U.S. over to the communist controlled United Nations.
   He is betraying our friends (Cuba, Katanga, Portugal) and befriending our enemies (Russia, Yugoslavia, Poland)

2. He has been WRONG on innumerable issues affecting the security of the U.S. (United Nations-Berlin wall-Missle removal-Cuba-Wheat deals-Test Ban Treaty, etc.)

3. He has been lax in enforcing Communist Registration laws.

4. He has given support and encouragement to the Communist inspired racial riots.

5. He has illegally invaded a sovereign State with federal troops.

6. He has consistantly appointed Anti-Christians to Federal office: Upholds the Supreme Court in its Anti-Christian rulings. Aliens and known Communists abound in Federal offices.

7. He has been caught in fantastic LIES to the American people (including personal ones like his previous marraige and divorce).

"This man is wanted for treasonous activities against the United States," says this poster on the walls of Dallas the day before Kennedy's visit. It illustrates the hostility of certain right-wing circles in the Lone Star state. "We're heading into nut country today," said John to his spouse on departing from Washington DC. "But Jackie, if someone wants to shoot me from a window with a rifle, nobody can stop it, so why worry about it?"[2]

---

[2] David Talbot, *Brothers: The Hidden History of the Kennedy Years,* Simon & Schuster, 2007, p. 242.

Meanwhile, Lee Harvey Oswald had been arrested in a Dallas cinema and immediately broadcast on television as the sole assassin. He allegedly fired three shots in less than 6 seconds, with a 1940 military bolt-action rifle (purchased by mail order), shooting from the sixth floor of the School Book Depository, a building that the presidential limousine had passed at the time of shooting. The next day, Oswald would seize several opportunities to proclaim his innocence before the cameras: "I didn't shoot anybody," "I'm just a patsy,"[3] thus identifying himself as a pawn, a scapegoat manipulated by the real culprits. On November 24th at 11:20 am, in a corridor of the Dallas police department, he was permanently silenced by Jack Ruby, a strip-club owner and former member of the Chicago mob.

Jack Ruby shoots Oswald in front of the cameras in a corridor of the Dallas police station.

To allay the suspicions of conspiracy, the Vice-President become President, Lyndon Johnson, designated a commission of inquiry on November 29th, which spent $10 million and employed 400 people, with unofficial instructions to silence "rumors" of conspiracy and confirm the conclusions of the FBI, culminating in a 16,000 page report. The Commission was officially chaired by Chief Justice Earl Warren (the highest federal magistrate), but was covertly controlled by Allen Dulles, the former CIA director fired by Kennedy in 1961, a man who, at the end of his life, would jeer to journalist Willie Morris: "That little Kennedy... he thought he was a god."[4] Thus the investigation was steered by a man who should have been a prime suspect. En masse, the mainstream media would be satisfied with the report of the Warren Commission. None of Kennedy's friends in the press would denounce the story as a sham—not even Benjamin Bradlee, the executive director of the *Washington Post,* which qualified the report as a "masterpiece of its kind"[5] (Bradlee would publish his *Conversations with Kennedy* in 1975).

A year later, voters confirmed their confidence in Johnson, while still mourning the charismatic young president who had embodied the nation's highest ideals and had dreamed of ending the Cold War.

---

[3] As seen in the documentary film *JFK: 3 Shots That Changed America* produced by The History Channel, 2009.
[4] Willie Morris, *New York Days*, Little, Brown & Co, 1998, p. 35-6.
[5] Talbot, *Brothers, op. cit.,* p. 390.

CE 399
FBI C1
National Archives

The famous "magic bullet" which, according to the Warren Commission, wounded Kennedy twice and John Connally three times, and was later recovered in nearly pristine condition on a gurney in Parkland Memorial Hospital in Dallas. This fantastic claim was indispensable to the preconceived theory of the single shooter, given that: 1) Oswald needed at least 2.3 seconds to reload (without aiming); 2) the Zapruder film showed that all the bullets had been fired in less than 5.6 seconds; 3) one bullet at least missed and hit the tarmac, and one hit Kennedy in the head.

Many have known since the first day that a terrible truth was hidden from them, but the state of trauma, the diffused feeling of a threat to the nation, and the scarcity of dissenting voices in the press, left tongues tied. The testimonies that contradicted the official theory were ignored or suppressed by threat or by violence. Twenty-one members of the hospital staff in Dallas who saw two bullet wounds on the front of Kennedy's body eventually chose to keep quiet. Two doctors, Malcolm Perry and Kemp Clark, who presented these findings in a press conference at the hospital at 3:15 pm, retracted before the Warren Commission. So did Dr. Charles Crenshaw, who would divulge in 1992: "From the damage I saw, there was no doubt in my mind that the bullet had entered his head through the front"—an account which exonerates Oswald, who was behind the president at the time of the shooting. The doctor explains his silence of nearly thirty years in his book *JFK: Conspiracy of Silence*: "I was as afraid of the men in suits as I was of the men who had assassinated the President. [...] I reasoned that anyone who would go so far as to eliminate the President of the United States would surely not hesitate to kill a doctor." At the military hospital near Washington, control was even more complete, as Dr. Pierre Finck explained in 1969: "There were Admirals, and when you are a Lieutenant Colonel in the Army you just follow orders." The medical-aid James Jenkins, who was also present, confirmed: "We were all military, we could be controlled. And if we weren't controlled, we could be punished and that kept us away from the public."[6]

Most of Kennedy's friends and relatives also silenced their doubts, even those whom he mockingly called his "Irish mafia"—"The presidency is not a good

---

[6] Douglass, *JFK and the Unspeakable, op. cit.,* p. 306-13.

place to make new friends," he once said. "I'm going to keep my old friends."[7]
Kenny O'Donnell, who was in the limo directly behind Kennedy, was sure that
at least "two shots" were fired "from behind the fence" on the grassy knoll.
But he explained (to Tip O'Neill, who reported the conversation in his memoirs, *Man of the House*, 1987): "I told the FBI what I had heard, but they said it
couldn't have happened that way and that I must have been imagining things.
So I testified the way they wanted me to. I just didn't want to stir up any more
pain and trouble for the family."[8]

Truth, it seems, never dies altogether. Tirelessly over fifty years, a small but
growing number of researchers carried on the investigation. Some have dedicated their life—some have lost it—in their search for the truth, gathering a
considerable amount of evidence and relevant testimony. Among the investigators of the first critical hour was a young lawyer named Mark Lane: less than
one month after the murder, having formed a Citizens Committee of Inquiry to
interview eyewitnesses of the crime, Lane challenged the official theory in an
article in *The Guardian*, and later in a book, *Rush to Judgment*. Attacks on the
government story became more threatening in 1967, when an investigation
opened by the New Orleans District Attorney Jim Garrison lifted a corner of
the veil cast over the CIA's involvement. Garrison was privileged to see Abraham Zapruder's amateur film, confiscated by the FBI on the day of the assassination, whose images show that the fatal shot came from the grassy knoll
well in front of the President, not the School Book Depository located behind.
Garrison's investigation, however, suffered a smear campaign and the mysterious deaths of his two main suspects and witnesses, Guy Banister and David
Ferrie.

A frame from the Zapruder film, showing Jacqueline Kennedy's desperate attempt to recover the portion of her husband's skull and brain torn apart by the bullet, as the limousine slowly accelerates after a near complete stop. Clint Hill was the only Secret Service agent to rush and climb on the running board, then push Jacqueline back to protect her.

---

[7] Ted Sorensen, *Kennedy* (1965), Harper Perennial, 2009, p. 36.
[8] Peter Janney, *Mary's Mosaic: the CIA Conspiracy to Murder John F. Kennedy, Mary Pinchot Meyer, and Their Vision for World Peace,* Skyhorse Publishing, 2012, p. 239.

In 1968, Robert Kennedy, who under his brother's government held the position of Attorney General, presented his candidacy for the Democratic nomination. Those who still grieved for John Kennedy found hope in the prospect of seeing younger Bobby repossess the White House and, from there, reopen the investigation. Although he kept quiet on the subject, his close friends knew that such was his intention. On a campus in March 1968, Bobby announced, "The archives will be available at the appropriate time."[9] Robert Kennedy was assassinated on June 6, 1968 in Los Angeles, just after winning the California presidential primary that made him the favorite for the Democratic nomination. Republican candidate Richard Nixon, who had been beaten by John Kennedy in 1960, would become President without having to face another Kennedy.

In the 70s, the Watergate scandal precipitated the formation of a Senate committee to investigate the illegal activities of the CIA, the Church Committee, and a House committee on the assassination of John F. Kennedy and Martin Luther King, the House Select Committee on Assassinations (HSCA). Due to legal obstacles, various pressures, and a new wave of deaths among the key witnesses, the reports of these congressional committees resulted only in timid questioning: at least, the HSCA formally established that Oswald was not the only shooter, that "John F. Kennedy was probably assassinated as a result of a conspiracy," that "the Warren Commission failed to investigate adequately the possibility of a conspiracy to assassinate the President," and that "the Central Intelligence Agency was deficient in its collection and sharing of information."[10] In 1975, the American people could see the Zapruder film for the first time on ABC.

In 1991 the Garrison investigation again shook public opinion, thanks to Oliver Stone's hit movie *JFK*, starring Kevin Costner. The ensuing controversy led to the adoption of the President John F. Kennedy Assassination Records Collection Act, intended to declassify the secret archives, and the formation of the U.S. Assassination Records Review Board, which conducted an investigation until 1998, summoning under oath witnesses who had not yet been heard. During all these years, books, articles and websites continued to chip away at the edifice of the official lie. Today, a majority of Americans (70% according to a 2003 ABC News poll) believe in a State cover-up, despite the ridicule hurled at such "conspiracy theories" by the mainstream media, and despite rather paltry efforts to sustain the government's "lone nut" theory. The truth is now available to those who seek.

---

[9] Talbot, *Brothers, op. cit.*, p. 358.
[10] Full text on *National Archives*: www.archives.gov/research/jfk/select-committee-report/summary.html

2. Gambling Johnson

There is hardly any doubt of the complicity of Vice-President Lyndon Baines Johnson (LBJ). Whoever the conspirators were, it is unthinkable that they would act without prior assurance of Johnson's protection, and it is quite plausible that Johnson personally intervened in preparations for the ambush in his home State. After all, Kennedy was assassinated in Texas to bring a Texan to power, and one still sees Texas's enduring sense of foreignness vis-à-vis Washington and the East Coast elite, a century and a half after the Civil War.

From the very first day, Johnson used all the weight of his newly acquired authority to kill the investigation and force Dallas authorities to adopt the "lone gunman" theory. In the afternoon of November 22nd, he ordered the Dallas police to stop investigating, and on November 24th, he even called Dallas Hospital personally to order the surgeon, in the midst of trying to save Oswald's life, to elicit from him "a death-bed confession" instead.[11] In his determination to keep the lid on the truth, Johnson received the full support of FBI chief J. Edgar Hoover, who signed a memo on November 22nd stating his conclusion that Oswald was the sole culprit. He had that conclusion leaked to the press on December 9, before the Warren Commission could get to work—no one would contradict Hoover. This was not Hoover's first cover-up: had he not, as late as 1956, denied the existence of organized crime, even while it dominated the political life of megacities like Chicago?[12]

Johnson maintained a close relationship with certain agents of the Secret Service, who chose the route of the motorcade and were guilty of many of the day's security oversights. One such agent, Joseph Shimon, confided to his daughter in the spring of 1963, "The Vice-President has asked me to give him more security than the President," leading her to believe that, "Something is going to happen and Johnson knows about it."[13]

---

[11] Nelson, *LBJ: The Mastermind, op. cit.,* p. 585.

[12] Hack, *Puppetmaster, op. cit.,* p. 285.

[13] Toni Shimon interviewed in 2007 by Peter Janney, *Mary's Mosaic, op. cit.,* p. 214.

While leaving Love Field airport at Dallas, Secret Service agent Henry Rybka shows his disbelief when asked not to stand on the running board of the presidential limousine, as was standard rule.

Johnson's path to power had been strewn with fraud and even murder ever since his first rigged election to the Senate in 1948, well documented by his biographer Robert Caro.[14] In 1959, Johnson had tried to remove Kennedy from the race for the Democratic nomination by stealing his medical records in order to expose his Addison's disease; at any rate, he was suspected by the Kennedys to have commissioned the break-ins at his two doctors' offices (with no result).[15] Soon afterward, Johnson imposed himself as Kennedy's running mate, thanks to privileged access to the secret files of FBI boss J. Edgar Hoover, his neighbor and friend for 19 years. Hoover, nicknamed *Puppetmaster* by his biographer Richard Hack, was a well-seasoned expert in blackmail: his resources drawn from cabinets of incriminating secrets allowed him to remain at the head of the FBI for 48 years, spanning nine presidents from 1924 until his death at age 72.[16] As soon as Kennedy had become president, Hoover wasted no time in reminding him of his own irreplaceability: in February 1962, for example, feeling the threat of forced retirement, he reported to his supervisor Attorney General Robert Kennedy, that he had stumbled across evidence of sexual relations between his brother, the President, and the mistress of mobster Sam Giancana, Judith Campbell Exner. Earlier in December 1960, he kindly informed Robert that the President's father "had been visited by many gangsters" before the election.[17]

---

[14] Robert Caro, *The Years of Lyndon Johnson,* vol. 1: *The Path to Power,* Alfred A Knopf, 1982.

[15] Richard Mahoney, *The Kennedy Brothers: The Rise and Fall of Jack and Bobby,* Arcade Publishing, 2011, p. 60.

[16] Richard Hack, *Puppetmaster: The Secret Life of J. Edgar Hoover,* New Millennium Press, 2004.

[17] Mahoney, *The Kennedy Brothers, op. cit.,* p. 156, 165.

According to his biographer Robert Caro, Johnson was a man thirsting for power, "for power in its most naked form, for power not to improve the lives of others, but to manipulate and domi-nate them, to bend them to his will [...], a hunger so fierce and consuming that no consideration of morality or ethics, no cost to himself—or to anyone else—could stand before it."

"You know, we had never considered Lyndon" [as a running mate], Kennedy apologized one day to his assistant Hyman Raskin, "but I was left with no choice ... those bastards were trying to frame me. They threatened me with problems and I don't need more problems." Kennedy never said more. To a question on that subject by Pierre Salinger, he replied: "The whole story will never be known. And it's just as well that it won't be." We can, however, trust the account of his personal secretary of twelve years, Evelyn Lincoln: "Jack knew that Hoover and LBJ would just fill the air with womanizing." Kennedy would justify the situation, as his friend Kenneth O'Donnell remembers, by saying: "I'm forty-three years old, [...] I'm not going to die in office. So the vice-presidency doesn't mean anything."[18] Johnson of course saw things dif-ferently: to Clare Boothe Luce, who asked him why he had accepted a post clearly less strategic than Majority Leader in the Senate, which he held prior to his nomination, he replied: "One out of every four presidents has died in of-fice. 'I'm a gamblin man, darling,' and this is the only chance I got."[19] With convincing arguments, some investigators such as Phillip Nelson see Johnson as the *Mastermind of JFK's Assassination* (2010), and believe that when he was taking over the vice-presidency by blackmail, Johnson was already plan-ning to take over the presidency by assassination. Most recently, Roger Stone, a White House insider who served as political aide to Presidents Nixon and Reagan, has also built a case against LBJ in *The Man Who Killed Kennedy: The Case Against LBJ* (2013).[20]

---

[18] Nelson, *LBJ: The Mastermind, op. cit.,* p. 318-20.

[19] Mahoney, *The Kennedy Brothers, op. cit.,* p. 64.

[20] Researcher Robert P. Morrow has assembled a comprehensive file on LBJ, which can be obtained by emailing him to Morrow321@aol.com.

"**Johnson lies all the time. I'm just telling you, he just lies continuously, about everything. In every conversation I have with him, he lies. As I've said, he lies even when he doesn't have to.**" (Robert Kennedy, quoted in Jeff Shesol, *Mutual Contempt: Lyndon Johnson, Robert Kennedy, and the Feud that Defined a Decade,* 1997). [21]

Three years after his election, having repeatedly borne hostility from parts of his administration and threats to his life, Kennedy's greatest fear was to be replaced by Johnson—that "riverboat gambler" as he once described him. [22] In her *Historic Conversations,* recorded in 1964 but only released in 2011, his wife Jackie quoted him: "Jack said it to me sometimes. He said, 'Oh, God, can you ever imagine what would happen to the country if Lyndon was president.'" [23] Likewise, Robert Kennedy remembered his brother complaining about Johnson's incompetence at running the Committee on Equal Employment Opportunity (against racial discrimination) that he had entrusted him with, adding: "Can you think of anything more deplorable than him trying to run the United States? That's why he can't ever be president." [24] John Kennedy was therefore determined to change the vice-presidential name on the ticket for his reelection campaign in 1964. A few days before his fatal trip to Dallas, again confiding in his secretary Evelyn Lincoln, he justified that decision by his desire to work toward "making government service an honorable career." [25]

Indeed, Johnson was implicated in three corruption scandals dating back to his tenure as a Texan senator, between 1949 and 1960. In October 1963, one of Johnson's Texan associates, Navy Secretary Fred Korth, had to resign after the Justice Department implicated him in a fraud involving the Texan company General Dynamics in a $7 billion contract for the construction of TFX military aircrafts. Johnson's personal secretary, Bobby Baker, was charged in the same case, and one of Baker's associates, Don Reynolds, was testifying against him on November 22 before the Senate Rules Committee; he attested to having seen a suitcase with $100,000 in kickbacks intended for Johnson, and further

---

[21] Jeff Shesol, *Mutual Contempt: Lyndon Johnson, Robert Kennedy, and the Feud that Defined a Decade,* WW Norton & Co, 1997, 2012, p. 95.

[22] Benjamin Bradlee, *Conversations with Kennedy,* 1975, Pocket Books, 1976, p. 17.

[23] Jacqueline Kennedy, *Historic Conversations on Life with John F. Kennedy,* Hyperion, 2011.

[24] Shesol, *Mutual Contempt, op. cit.,* p. 73.

[25] Nelson, *LBJ: The Mastermind, op. cit.,* p. 372.

claimed to have been offered bribes for his silence.[26] Baker's indictment took the headlines of the weekly magazine *Life,* just days before November 22: "The Bombshell Bobby Baker: [...] Scandal grows and grows in Washington."[27] A more devastating article was scheduled for the next issue, as James Wagenvoord would reveal as the then Chief Assistant to the Publishing Projects Director of *Life*: "It was going to blow Johnson right out of the water. We had him. He was done [...] Johnson would have been finished and off the 1964 ticket, and would have probably been facing prison time."[28] Instead of the planned article, however, *Life* published 31 images of the Zapruder film, but in a modified order that strategically presented the movement of Kennedy's head as a validation of what would be the official story: that the shooting came from behind.

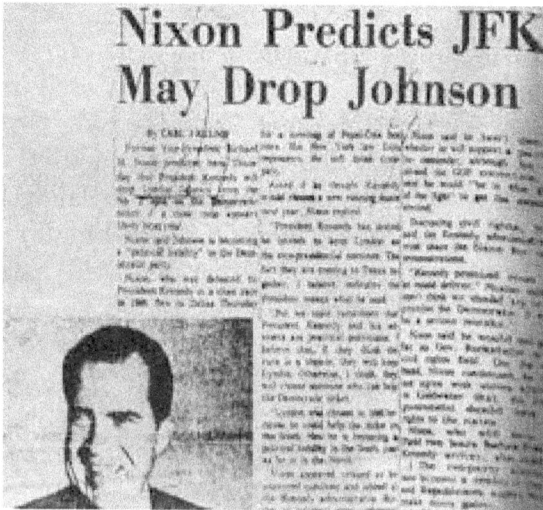

While in Dallas the day before the President's visit, representing Pepsi-Cola at the Soda Bottlers' Convention, Nixon publicized the rumor of Johnson's removal, as the *Dallas Morning News* reported on November 22nd: "Nixon Predicts JFK May Drop Johnson." Instead, Johnson became president that very day.

Kennedy's death propelled Johnson to the head of the State and, in the atmosphere of national crisis thus created, enabled him to bully both the Justice Department and the press, while achieving his life's ambition. Many Americans immediately suspected Johnson's involvement in the assassination, especially in Texas where his methods and character were better known. But the population was somehow reassured by the fact that the new master of the White House kept intact his predecessor's government. Besides, no relatives of the dead president publicly challenged the official story. Who could imagine that all those ministers and advisors, some of them close friends of Kennedy, could have betrayed their hero? They themselves, in fact, could not believe in Johnson's guilt, and were convinced to stand united under the auspices of national interest: "I need you now more than President Kennedy needed you,"

---

[26] Russ Baker, *Family of Secrets: The Bush Dynasty, America's Invisible Government, and the Hidden History of the Last Fifty Years,* Bloomsbury Press, 2009, p. 183.
[27] Nelson, *LBJ: The Mastermind, op. cit.,* p. 370.
[28] Janney, *Mary's Mosaic, op. cit.,* p. 259.

Johnson repeated to each of them.[29] After all, J. Edgar Hoover himself assured the nation that Oswald had acted on his own initiative. The case was closed. It was necessary to ensure the continuity of government, at least until the end of the presidential term, a year later.

Several people directly implicated Johnson in the Dallas crime, starting with Jack Ruby who spoke in slightly veiled terms in a filmed press conference from his prison cell in March 1965: "if [Adlai Stevenson] was Vice-President there would never have been an assassination of our beloved President Kennedy."[30] Ruby was less ambiguous in a letter of sixteen pages that he managed to get out of jail, shortly before being struck down with cancer in 1967.[31] Johnson's mistress of 20 years, Madeleine Brown, wrote about Johnson's foreknowledge of the assassination in her book *Texas in the Morning* (1997) and would repeat to anyone who cared to listen what Johnson had told her on November 21, 1963: "Tomorrow those goddamn Kennedys will never embarrass me again; that's no threat, that's a promise."[32] It is true that some of the key witnesses against Johnson can be deemed unreliable. Included among them was Billie Sol Estes, a Texas businessman who owed his fortune to Johnson and had funneled hundreds of thousands of dollars back to Johnson in the 50s, and who in 1984 tried in vain to negotiate leniency from the Department of Justice in exchange for information on five other killings ordered by Johnson, including Johnson's own sister Josefa.[33] One of the most convincing cases against Johnson has been made by Barr McClellan in his book *Blood, Money & Power: How LBJ Killed JFK* (2003); while working for the law firm of Johnson's attorney Edward Clark, McClellan learned about Johnson's guilt and, in the course of the investigation he secretly conducted, was able to prove that the only unidentified fingerprint found on the sixth floor of the School Book Depository (Warren Commission print 29) belonged to Mac Wallace, known as Johnson's personal hitman. (In 1951, Wallace was convicted for the murder of John Kinser, Johnson's sister's boyfriend, who was probably trying to blackmail Johnson about his rigged 1948 election; and in 1962, he is suspected to have murdered Henry Marshall, a Department of Agriculture inspector who was investigating Billie Sol Estes, leading directly to Johnson).[34]

---

[29] Kenneth O'Donnell and David Powers, *Johnny We Hardly Knew Ye: Memories of John Fitzgerald Kennedy,* Little, Brown & Co, 1970, p. 38.
[30] See on YouTube, "Jack Ruby Talks": www.youtube.com/watch?v=omnpQBa1Euc
[31] Nelson, *LBJ: The Mastermind, op. cit.,* p. 604-7.
[32] Nelson, *LBJ: The Mastermind, op. cit.,* p. 376.
[33] William Reymond and Billie Sol Estes, *JFK. Le Dernier témoin,* Flammarion, 2003.
[34] Nelson, *LBJ: The Mastermind, op. cit.,* p. 271-80, 286-9.

Johnson insisted on being sworn into office right after John Kennedy was declared dead, in the presidential plane Air Force One still on the ground in Dallas. He managed to drag Jacqueline Kennedy by his side, for a picture that strongly contributed to his legitimacy in the public eye. On the next shot, taken seconds after, Lady Bird (Mrs. Johnson) is smiling and Johnson seems to be winking to Senator Albert Thomas.[35]

Johnson's role surrounding the crime of the century raises a more general question about the role of the Vice-President in U.S. policy. That function is so poorly defined and poorly controlled that some analysts see it as a fatal constitutional flaw.

The Vice-President has no official executive role as long as the President is in office, and can, therefore, easily escape direct liability. This has allowed some Vice-Presidents to exert hidden influence without accountability, and use their position as a backdoor to the supreme power. At the outset, the choice of Vice-President largely escapes voters, and is rather a result of backdoor negotiations after the primaries. So, in case of the President's death, the American people find themselves governed by a man not democratically chosen and largely unfamiliar. And if the elected President ends his term, the Vice-President, as a White House insider, has had every opportunity to ensure an advantage in the next presidential race, while securing the blessing of the previous President; it means that the vice-presidency is a position deeply coveted by those seeking expedited avenues to power. It is a historical fact that U.S. Presidents passed through the vice-presidency have all shown a penchant for conspiracy and concealment. Three of them hold key roles in the present narrative: Richard Nixon, George Bush Sr., and Dick Cheney. The first two are linked to the Dallas coup and its repercussions, while the third practically replaced his President without having to kill him. As said Bruce Fein, a former Associate Deputy Attorney General, "Dick Cheney exercises all the power of the Presidency. That has never happened. Ever."[36]

---

[35] Nelson, *LBJ: The Mastermind, op. cit.,* p. 454-5.
[36] Lou Dubose and Jake Bernstein, *Vice: Dick Cheney and the Hijacking of the American Presidency*, Random House, 2006, p. 223.

3. In the Name of National Security

Johnson and Hoover were certainly the masterminds of the cover-up, but probably not of the practical implementation of the murder itself. Many clues direct suspicions towards other enemies of Kennedy, more powerful but less visible. Recent research now tends to confirm what Jim Garrison perceived already in 1968, in a *Playboy* interview: "President Kennedy was killed for one reason: because he was working for reconciliation with the [Soviet Union] and Castro's Cuba. [...] President Kennedy died because he wanted peace." The implications drawn by Garrison were frightening: "In a very real and terrifying sense, our government is the CIA and the Pentagon, with Congress reduced to a debating society. [...] I'm afraid, based on my experience, that fascism will come to America in the name of National Security."[37] "National Security" are the key words here: it is, so to speak, the euphemistic name of the American deep state, housed mainly within the CIA and the Pentagon, but closely linked to the economic elite.

What is commonly called the "National Security State" came to existence in the aftermath of the Second World War, but it had older roots, as can be learned from a little known episode in the history of the United States. In 1933, General Smedley Butler, a hero of the First World War who was immensely popular among veterans for defending their claims for the "soldiers' bonus" in the midst of the Great Depression, was contacted by a representative of a network of businessmen who invited him to lead a coup d'état against President Franklin Roosevelt; he would assume the role of a "knight on a white horse" come to save the nation from the socialist policies of a President in declining health. Butler could have easily mobilized 500,000 men to march on Washington on the occasion of the annual Veterans Convention, and force Roosevelt to appoint him to a position of "Secretary of General Affairs," which would have reduced Roosevelt to a representative role. To support the endeavor, a new lobby of major capitalist entrepreneurs was created, the American Liberty

---

[37] Talbot, *Brothers, op. cit.,* p. 320.

League, and the magazine *Affairs* undertook preparations to sway public acceptance toward the coup. Butler feigned interest in order to accumulate information, and then denounced the plot to Congress and on the radio. A congressional Committee on Un-American Activities (or McCormack-Dickstein Committee) investigated in November 1934 and, in its final report published in February 1935, claimed to have evidence that "certain persons had made an attempt to establish a fascist organization in this country. [...] There is no question that these attempts were discussed, were planned, and might have been placed in execution when and if the financial backers deemed it expedient." Overthrowing or weakening the democratic state by a combination of economic and military power is, indeed, the essence of fascism. To Butler's dismay, however, the report does not name any of the individuals involved—an arrangement probably having been made with Roosevelt, allowing for the implementation of his *New Deal* in exchange for the plotters' impunity.[38]

"War is a racket. It always has been. It is possibly the oldest, easily the most profitable, surely the most vicious. It is the only one international in scope. It is the only one in which the profits are reckoned in dollars and the losses in lives. [...] It is conducted for the benefit of the very few, at the expense of the very many." Thus begins General Smedley Butler's pamphlet *War is a Racket*, published in 1935, after the failed coup against Roosevelt had opened his eyes on the true purpose of American wars.[39]

Even though the attempted coup failed, it foreshadowed an increasing complicity between the financial elite and the military hierarchy, based on a common communist phobia and hostility to the welfare state. Roosevelt's Vice-President and successor, Harry Truman, would be instrumental in allowing that collusion much greater lever on U.S. politics. Propelled to the head of the State by Roosevelt's death in April 1945, after only three months at the vice-presidency, Truman was ill prepared to negotiate this turning point in history. Roosevelt had not informed him of any confidential dossiers, and certainly not of the top secret Manhattan Project. After only four months at the head of the State, during the Potsdam Conference, Truman was notified by a coded telegram that the latest atomic test at Alamogordo, New Mexico was conclusive: "Operated on this morning. Diagnosis not yet complete but results seem satisfactory and

---

[38] Jules Archer, *The Plot to Seize the White* House (1973), Skyhorse Publishing, 2007.
[39] Smedley Butler, *War is a Racket,* CreateSpace, 2012, p. 1.

already exceed expectations."[40] Within days, Truman ordered a uranium bomb dropped on Hiroshima on August 6, 1945, and marveled at the announcement of the result: "This is the greatest thing in history!" Then he ordered a new strike—with a plutonium bomb, for comparison—on Nagasaki.[41]

We now know that this double crime against humanity was not drawn from military necessity, since Tokyo and 66 other Japanese cities had already been reduced to ashes under a barrage of incendiary bombs ordered by Air Force General Curtis LeMay, and that the Japanese emperor had agreed to a conditional capitulation. Hiroshima and Nagasaki were a show of force conceived to make the nuclear threat the instrument of a new world order based on terror. It was the true trigger of the Cold War and the arms race: it only took four years for the Soviets to test their first plutonium bomb. Presumably Roosevelt would have acted differently, who, before Congress January 6, 1941, was calling for a disarmed world that would be "the very antithesis of the so-called new order of tyranny which the dictators seek to create with the crash of a bomb."[42]

Henry Wallace, Roosevelt's Vice-President from 1941 to 1945, would have become President if Roosevelt had died a few months earlier. Would he have unleashed nuclear terror? He challenged Truman in the 1948 presidential race, with a foreign policy program centered on easing the tensions with Communist Russia.

The same Truman who baptized the world in nuclear fire is also responsible for the creation of the National Security State, whose birth certificate is the National Security Act of 1947 (amended in 1949). By this decree, the President wanted to surround himself with command structures adapted to the arising Cold War. First, Truman united the five military commands— Army, Navy, Air Force, Marine Corps and Strategic Command, already co-housed in the Pentagon since 1943—into a permanent committee, the Joint Chiefs of Staff, with an appointed Chairman, thereby giving the military greater influence on foreign policy. Truman simultaneously instituted the National Security Council, which surrounds the President with the main actors of foreign and military affairs, as well as Intelligence. Truman's successor, Dwight Eisenhower, would create a specific position to preside over this structure, the National Security Advisor, who often prevails over the Secretary of

---

[40] Richard Rhodes, *The Making of the Atomic Bomb,* Simon & Schuster, 1987, 2012.
[41] Douglass, *JFK and the Unspeakable, op. cit.,* p. 1.
[42] FDR Library: www.fdrlibrary.marist.edu/archives/significant.html

State in issues of foreign policy (both positions will merge under Henry Kiss-inger, Colin Powell and Condoleezza Rice). Eisenhower also established in 1952, for global espionage, the National Security Agency (NSA), whose exis-tence was kept secret until 1957—which earned it the journalistic nickname "No Such Agency." (In 2013, *The New York Times* would reveal documents provided by NSA whistleblower Edward Snowden, proving NSA's involve-ment in massive illegal spying on U.S. and European soil).[43]

All of the founding texts of the National Security State are characterized by an alarmist exaggeration of the ambitions and power of the Soviet military, which infused into the White House a permanent climate of imminent war. The sup-posed hegemonic policy of the USSR was the justification for the "Truman Doctrine," which affirms the right for the United States to intervene in the in-ternal affairs of any country, near or far, who by leaning slightly to the left could trigger a "domino effect" and cause the collapse on an entire region un-der communist influence. Informed by a quasi-theological and apocalyptic vision of the Cold War, the structures put in place by Truman would be, under the pretext of "national security," a true imperial government, operating under guise to destabilize any insubordinate governments and to prop up dictators willing to remain under its tutelage.

Meeting with the Joint Chiefs of Staff. On the President's right is General Curtis LeMay, com-mander of the U.S. Air Force. Convinced that nuclear war was inevita-ble, and the sooner the better, he had only con-tempt for what he per-ceived as Kennedy's naïve and cowardly pacifism. "I don't want that man near me again," would once say Kennedy to his assistant Charles Daly after having listened to his argument for preemptive nuclear strikes.[44]

The NSC-68 report of April 7, 1950, which had a great influence on the for-eign policy of the United States for twenty years, asserted that the Kremlin posed a threat capable of the "destruction not only of this Republic but of civi-

---

[43] James Risen, "N.S.A. Gathers Data on Social Connections of U.S. Citizens," *New York Times,* September 28, 2013: www.nytimes.com/2013/09/29/us/nsa-examines-social-networks-of-us-citizens.html?pagewanted=all&_r=0

[44] Talbot, *Brothers, op. cit.* p. 68.

lization itself." Its main author, Paul Nitze, considered a preemptive nuclear attack against the USSR desirable, but impractical, "unless it is demonstrably in the nature of a counter-attack to a blow which is on its way or about to be delivered." Unfortunately, "the idea of 'preventive' war—in the sense of a military attack not provoked by a military attack upon us or our allies—is generally unacceptable to Americans." A surprise attack on the Soviet Union "would be repugnant to many Americans. [...] Many would doubt that it was a 'just war' and that all reasonable possibilities for a peaceful settlement had been explored in good faith. Many more, proportionately, would hold such views in other countries, particularly in Western Europe."[45] This report raises an issue quite different from that of deterrence, the official justification of the atomic arsenal: how to strike first, strong enough to crush the striking power of the enemy, while maintaining an air of self-defense? This question obsessed the Pentagon throughout the Kennedy presidency and helped instill a culture of false flag strategy. The idea that the United States should take advantage of their lead in nuclear weapons to strike first under a false pretense, was widely shared and openly advocated by the commander of the Air Force, Curtis Le-May, already responsible for reducing every major Japanese city to ashes.

LeMay was caricatured as the paranoid General Jack D. Ripper in Stanley Kubrick's film *Dr. Strangelove or: How I learned to stop worrying and love the bomb*, which, coincidentally, was scheduled for release on November 22, 1963.

The militarism of the National Security State inevitably came to be encouraged by the arms industry, a market of hundreds of billions of dollars that includes some of the largest industrial groups, and consumes almost half of the National budget without any taxpayer control. Armament firms have permanent delegates at the Pentagon, while almost every retired general serves on the board of one of these companies. The principles of capital accumulation require a constantly growing market demand, and thus the logic of the military industry tends toward steadily increasing military budgets, and periodic consumption of stocks by war. In his *Farewell Address* delivered on January 17, 1961, Eisenhower, a former general, warned the nation against this new phenomenon that he had failed to curtail: "This conjunction of an immense military establish-

---

[45] Truman Library:
www.trumanlibrary.org/whistlestop/study_collections/coldwar/documents/pdf/10-1.pdf

ment and a large arms industry is new in the American experience. The total influence—economic, political, even spiritual—is felt in every city, every State house, every office of the Federal government. [...] In the councils of government, we must guard against the acquisition of unwarranted influence, whether sought or unsought, by the military-industrial complex. The potential for the disastrous rise of misplaced power exists and will persist."[46] The recently discovered draft of this speech warned against "measures which would enable any segment of this vast military-industrial complex to sharpen the focus of its power."[47] To this monstrous military-industrial complex was added in 1958 the NASA (National Aeronotics and Space Administration), whose civilian space program was merely a cover for its military purpose: the development of transcontinental rockets, with the vision of ultimately being able to launch nuclear missiles from orbital stations.[48]

While the democratic state needs transparency to maintain the confidence of citizens, the National Security State, by contrast, thrives on opacity. On behalf of the sacrosanct "National Security Interest," it operates in the utmost secrecy. It assumes the right and duty to conceal all its plans from Congress, but also to hinder by all means the freedom of the press to investigate its actions. This state within the state, controlled by virtually irremovable generals, hostile to the democracy on which it feeds, is rendered largely invisible to Americans, not only by the secrecy surrounding it, but also because its power is exercised outside national borders. The internal history of this shadow government emerges only much later, and always incompletely, at the pace of archive declassification. Advocacy groups must fight for access to these records in order to make them public. It is the mission of the National Security Archive Project at George Washington University, which, since 1985, has already filed 40 suits against the Administration for obstruction under the Freedom of Information Act of 1966.[49]

To get a sense of the pathogenic mind state that came to dominate the U.S. National Security apparatus, it is most helpful to examine the RAND Corporation, a strategic think tank founded in 1945 by the Air Force. In the 1950s, the RAND was searching for scientific models to predict the evolution of the Cold War, and turned toward "game theory," a new field in mathematics meant to model decision-making strategies between individuals or groups motivated solely by self-interest and greed. Among several scientists hired by the RAND was a brilliant mathematician by the name of John Nash, whose research on

---

[46] This televised speech can be watched on YouTube, "Eisenhower Farewell Address": www.youtube.com/watch?v=CWiIYW_fBfY.

[47] Jim Newton, "Ike's Speech," *The New Yorker,* December 20, 2010: www.newyorker.com/talk/2010/12/20/101220ta_talk_newton.

[48] Gerhard Wisnewski, *One Small Step? The Great Moon Hoax and the Race to Dominate Earth From Space,* Clairview, 2007, p. 287-357.

[49] Official website: www.gwu.edu/~nsarchiv/

"non-cooperative equilibriums" would earn him the Nobel Prize in Economy in 1994. Nash's game theory reinforced the cold warriors' opinion that the worst mistake is to trust the enemy in any way, since the strategy of the game relies upon deception; the enemy must be assumed to be cunning and ruthless and will only be defeated by a higher degree of cunningness and ruthlessness. The irony is that John Nash (portrayed by Hollywood in *A Beautiful Mind* staring Russel Crowe in 2001) suffered from "paranoid schizophrenia" for which he was committed in mental hospital in 1958-59 and regularly thereafter.[50] His vision of human relationships, which was transposed into a vision of international relationships by the RAND—the brain of the National Security State—is typical of near-psychopaths with highly narcissistic or paranoid personalities. Fundamentally, the psychopath is incapable of empathy and experiences social life much like poker game, with stakes, wagers, gains and losses, entirely dependent upon the ability to predict, manipulate and deceive.

But empathy, as we shall see, is precisely what will enable Kennedy to avoid nuclear war in the midst of heightened tension. Such is the "Lesson #1" that his Secretary of Defense Robert McNamara will learn from Cuban Missile Crisis: "Empathize with your enemy. We must try to put ourselves under their skin, and look at us through their eyes, just to understand the thoughts that lie beneath their decisions and their actions."[51]

Disgusted by the way McNamara, who had remained Secretary of Defense after Kennedy's death, was now implementing Johnson's war of aggression without

dissent, Adam Walinsky, a friend of the Kennedys, imagined in an essay entitled "Caesar's meat" Johnson's unspoken message to his arch-enemy Robert Kennedy: "You think to challenge me. Then watch carefully what I am about to do. I will take this man—with all he means, all he is, all his power and ability and character—I will take this man and break him into nothing. I will reach in and tear out his spine, and he will say 'thank you, sir.'"[52]

---

[50] See in Adam Curtis's BBC documentary *The Power of Nightmares,* 2005.
[51] McNamara interview by Errol Morris in his film, *The Fog of War: Eleven Lessons from the Life of Robert S. McNamara,* 2003.
[52] Talbot, *Brothers, op. cit.,* p. 350.

4. The CIA and the Bay of Pigs

Within the "military" aspect of "military-industrial complex," "intelligence" must also be included. Eisenhower did not name it in his farewell address, but on leaving the White House, he did complain about it to Allen Dulles, the Director of the Central Intelligence Agency: "The structure of our intelligence organization is faulty. I have suffered an eight-year defeat on this. Nothing has changed since Pearl Harbor. I leave a 'legacy of ashes' to my successor."[53]

Under President Eisenhower, the Dulles brothers dominated Foreign Policy as Wall Street proxies, with Allen heading the CIA and John Foster the State Department.

The CIA is one of the essential weapons endowed to the National Security State since its creation in 1947. Its primary mission is to centralize information for use by the President, but it is also the heir to the Office of Strategic Services (OSS) created during the war, and would integrate the Office of Special Operations during the Korean War in 1952, under the name Directorate of Plans. Known within the Agency as the "Department of Dirty Tricks," the Directorate of Plans controls more than half the CIA's budget. Its specialty is "covert operations," defined by the directive NSC-10/2 of the National Security Council as any activities "which are conducted or sponsored by this Gov-

---

[53] Tim Weiner, *Legacy of Ashes: The History of the CIA,* Doubleday, 2007, p. 167.

ernment against hostile foreign states or groups or in support of friendly foreign states or groups but which are so planned and executed that any US Government responsibility for them is not evident to unauthorized persons and that if uncovered the US Government can plausibly disclaim any responsibility for them."[54]

Designed to absolve the President of all illegal actions in the case of public disclosure, the principle of "plausible deniability" gives the CIA almost complete autonomy, since, in fact, it relieves it of the need to reveal its operations to the President, while still allowing for Presidential protection in the event of failure. It is, in fact, a particular application of the golden rule of every secret service: operate on a need-to-know basis, to make sure that everyone involved knows as little as possible, thus making full exposure of covert operations extremely unlikely. To remain unseen, covert operations (black-ops) will sometimes have to be funded through independent means, resulting in an involvement with arms and drug trafficking. Finally, to maintain secrecy, CIA agents often operate outside of payroll: meaning an agent fired or retired has not necessarily ceased all cooperation with the Agency. By the same logic of "plausible deniability," the CIA has made a habit of calling on professional criminals to carry out its dirty work on American soil, and further upon paramilitary groups to instigate destabilization campaigns abroad, under the guise of civil war. For all these reasons, General George Marshall, former Secretary of State to Truman, saw the birth of something sinister: "The powers of the proposed agency seem almost unlimited and need clarification," he wrote in a memo to Truman in February 1947.[55] George Kennan, who prepared the document NSC-10/2, later saw it as "the greatest mistake [he] ever made."[56]

One of the inherent problems with the CIA was its leadership. Among its seven founding directors, only one was not a banker or lawyer on Wall Street. The head position was ultimately awarded to Allen Dulles, who with his brother John Foster, soon to be Secretary of State under Eisenhower, had worked for one of the largest law firms on Wall Street, Sullivan & Cromwell, before entering politics; hence the CIA was said to be directed from New York rather than Washington. In this context, national interest merged with the private interests of large industrial groups. Although created under the National Security Act in 1947, and thus dedicated to the struggle against the communist threat, the CIA would prioritize the interests of global financial stakeholders. Designed in theory to inform the President, in practice the CIA acted as a me-

---

[54] National Security Archive:
www.gwu.edu/~nsarchiv/NSAEBB/NSAEBB52/docXXXIII.pdf.
[55] "Marshall's Doubts About the CIA," *New York Times,* July 26, 1973:
jfk.hood.edu/Collection/White%20%20Files/Security-CIA/CIA%200743.pdf.
[56] Douglass, *JFK and the Unspeakable, op. cit.,* p. 33.

dium and means through which the financial class could steer U.S. foreign policy to its own profit.

Eisenhower had attempted to initiate détente with the Soviet Union, and intended to reduce drastically the Defense budget before leaving office. Two days before his *Peace Summit* with Khrushchev on May 16th, 1960, the CIA managed to have one of its U-2 spy planes shot down in Soviet airspace. Tensions immediately heightened and the Congress voted an increase in military budget.

On three continents, the CIA overthrew democratically elected governments and replaced them with dictatorships under U.S. tutelage. Its first major success was the 1953 coup against the Iranian Prime Minister Mohammad Mossadegh who was about to nationalize the Anglo-Iranian Oil Company (AOIC, renamed British Petroleum in 1954). The AOIC was British and not American, but the Dulles brothers happened to have served as its legal counsels and had developed vested interests in the company. Under the joint CIA-MI6 Operation Ajax, mosques were bombed, religious leaders killed, and civilians machine gunned, while phony handbills were distributed claiming these acts in the name of Mossadegh, leading to his arrest and imprisonment for life. After that, the CIA flew the Shah Mohammad Pahlavi into Tehran, and proceeded to train his dreaded secret police, the SAVAK—including in methods of torture.[57] In the late Eisenhower years, the CIA and other European secret services oversaw the assassination of the first elected president of the Republic of Congo, Patrice Lumumba, and transferred power to the bloodthirsty Mobutu who terrorized the country (renamed Zaire) for 32 years. That Lumumba was assassinated three days before Kennedy's inauguration speaks volumes to the CIA's disregard for elected government. The Agency's leadership had reasons to worry about the incoming President, who had clearly proclaimed his anti-colonialist stances in his famous "Algerian speech" in 1957, then again in 1959: "Call it nationalism, call it anti-colonialism, call it what you will, Africa is going through a revolution. [...] The word is out—and spreading like wild-

---

[57] Stephen Kinzer, *All the Shah's Men: An American Coup and the Roots of Middle East Terror,* John Wiley and Sons, 2003. On National Security Archive: "The Secret CIA History of the Iran Coup, 1953," ed. Malcolm Byrne:
www.gwu.edu/~nsarchiv/NSAEBB/NSAEBB28/index.html

fire in nearly a thousand languages and dialects—that it is no longer necessary to remain forever poor or forever in bondage."[58]

Honored as "Man of the Year" by *Time* magazine in 1951, Mohammad Mossadegh was then overthrown by a CIA-orchestrated coup two years later. Charged with treason in a military trial, he pronounced: "My greatest sin is that I nationalized Iran's oil industry and discarded the system of political and economic exploitation by the world's greatest empire. [...] I am well aware that my fate must serve as an example in the future throughout the Middle East in breaking the chains of slavery and servitude to colonial interests."[59]

In Central America, CIA began harassing President Jacobo Arbenz of Guatemala, elected in 1951. By his plan to redistribute a portion of land to 100,000 poor farmers, Arbenz threatened the interests of the multinational United Fruit Company, the giant banana corporation that held more than 90% of the land. The Dulles brothers were shareholders of United Fruit, for whom they had written capital contracts in the '30s; John Foster even sat on its board of directors. Therefore the Dulles brothers orchestrated, financed and armed the coup against Arbenz by a military junta responsible for more than 200,000 civilian deaths from 1954 to 1996, especially among the Mayan population. A CIA manual entitled *A Study of Assassination*, written in 1953 and declassified in 1997, contains detailed instructions on the various methods of murder by weapons, bombs or simulated accidents. In some cases, it is recommended that assassins be "clandestine agents or members of criminal organizations." Always in keeping with the "need-to-know" basis and the principle of "plausible deniability,""it is desirable that the assassin be transient in the area. He should have an absolute minimum of contact with the rest of the organization and his instructions should be given orally by one person only."[60]

What makes the CIA particularly effective as an arm of the U.S. Empire is its capacity to act behind a curtain, and when possible, even don the mask of its enemies in order to blame them for its own acts of terror. It is necessary that its covert wars in foreign lands remain hidden to the American public, who might object. This is why in the 50s the CIA initiated a massive propaganda opera-

---

[58] Arthur Schlesinger Jr., *A Thousand Days: John Kennedy in the White House* (1965), Mariner Books, 2002, p. 554.
[59] The Mossadegh Project: www.mohammadmossadegh.com/biography/
[60] National Security Archive: www.gwu.edu/~nsarchiv/NSAEBB/NSAEBB4/ciaguat2.html

tion, orchestrated from the Directorate of Plans under the codename Mocking-bird. The operation allowed the collusion of dozens of respected directors and journalists from CBS, *Newsweek, The New York Times, The Washington Post* and twenty other institutions, by providing them with classified information and sometimes ready-made releases, while punishing over-independent investigators. It was revealed in 1977 that one of the journalists "owned" by the CIA was Joseph Alsop, whose foreign policy articles appeared in 300 different newspapers. Manipulation of public opinion with Operation Mockingbird has as its immediate corollary the surveillance Operation Chaos, by which, in violation of statutes that prohibit domestic spying, the CIA can actively monitor those who know too much, and silence them if necessary.[61]

When Kennedy succeeded Eisenhower in January 1961, the CIA had set a goal to overthrow Fidel Castro in Cuba. Castro's socialist revolution, which replaced the corrupt dictatorship of Fulgencio Batista in 1959, in no way threatened the security of the United States but deeply conflicted with American economic interests by increasing the price of sugar and tobacco. After his success in Guatemala, Dulles had no doubt that he could overthrow Castro with the same team. From late 1959, an anti-Castro group was organized by the Deputy Director of Plans (head of the Directorate of Plans) Richard Bissell, which included: officers from the Guatemalan operation such as David Atlee Phillips and Howard Hunt; and opponents of Castro like Felix Rodriguez (a nephew of a minister of Batista) and Frank Sturgis (a former companion to Castro turned anti-communist). The group was named the Cuban Task Force, or Operation 40 (because it initially consisted of forty men). In Nicaragua, paramilitary training camps were set up for Cubans who had fled Castro's revolution, joined by other mercenaries from Latin America. The plan was to land these supposedly autonomous Cuban counter-revolutionaries in Cuba, then send to their aid the U.S. Air Force and Navy under the pretext of supporting a popular uprising, and thereby invade Cuba without ethical controversy—a method of disguising imperialist wars behind civil wars, that today rings familiar. Simultaneously, the CIA began plans to contact Mafia leaders interested in reclaiming control over their lucrative casinos and whorehouses (such as Santo Trafficante), in order to subcontract assassination jobs against Castro, in the hope of depriving the Cuban people and army of leadership.

Eisenhower is less involved in these preparations than his Vice-President Richard Nixon, a corporate lawyer like Dulles. It was he who, mandated by the businessmen expropriated by Castro (including his client Pepsi Cola, dependant on Cuban sugar), coordinated the funding of Operation 40. However, in late 1960, Nixon was in line to become Eisenhower's successor, and postponed the risky campaign until after the election, assuming a win. Kennedy, of

---

[61] Spartacus Educational: www.spartacus.schoolnet.co.uk/JFKmockingbird.htm

course, would win with a narrow margin. Dulles wasted no time in selling the operation to the new President at a National Security Council meeting, leading him to believe that the invasion by Cuban exiles would be sufficient to trigger a popular uprising. Kennedy agreed, but warned clearly that he would not allow any participation of the U.S. Army—which would amount to an act of war. Dulles was convinced that once put before the impending crisis, the President would concede, and the operation was launched April 15, 1961: a contingent of 1,500 armed Cuban exiles boarded seven boats from the Nicaraguan coast and landed in the Bahia del Cochinos (Bay of Pigs) on the Zapata Peninsula of Cuba. They were quickly surrounded by Castro's army and, as expected, called the United States for help. Five U.S. destroyers and aircraft carrier Essex were just less than 2 miles from the Cuban coast. But Kennedy understood that he had been deceived and refused to engage his ships, personally telephoning the captain of the fleet to forbid any movement. About 200 Cuban rebels were killed and 1,300 captured by Castro's forces.

Howard Hunt. "He was perfect for the CIA. He never felt guilt about anything," said his son Saint John.[62] In 1985, Hunt lost his libel suit against the magazine *Spotlight*, which had stated, in its August 16, 1978 issue, that he was in Dallas on the day of Kennedy's assassination. *Spotlight*'s lawyer, Mark Lane, could convincingly prove that Hunt had lied under oath about his whereabouts that day.

Kennedy took public responsibility for the failure of the operation, but was furious with the CIA: "I want to splinter the CIA in a thousand pieces and scatter it to the winds," Mike Mansfield heard him say. An internal document at the CIA, dated November 15, 1960 and declassified in 2005, proves that Dulles lied to the President when he led him to believe that the operation was likely to succeed without overt U.S. intervention: "our concept […] to secure a beach with airstrip is now seen to be unachievable, except as joint Agency/DOD [Department of Defense] action." Dulles himself explains in notes published posthumously: "We felt that when the chips were down— when the crisis arose in reality, any action required for success would be authorized rather than permit the enterprise to fail." Kennedy understood, and commented to his aides Kenneth O'Donnell and David Powers (who told it in their book *Johnny We Hardly Knew Ye*, 1970): "They were sure I'd give in to

---

[62] *Rolling Stone*, April 5, 2007.

them and send the go-ahead order to the Essex. They couldn't believe that a new President like me wouldn't panic and try to save his own face. Well, they had me figured all wrong." Kennedy fired the chief instigators of the operation, the Director Allen Dulles and his two Deputy Directors Charles Cabell and Richard Bissell.[63]

But the CIA is more a family than an organization, united by a code of honor not unlike an ethnic mafia. The remaining members of the management team, almost all recruited by Dulles, remained loyal to their former boss and took a violent resentment toward Kennedy; they no longer sought Presidential assent and effectively transformed the CIA into a parallel power. The grudge was even stronger among Cuban exiles, a diaspora of nearly one million people concentrated around Miami, mostly composed of political refugees that had fled Castro's revolution. The United States is for them a temporary haven and they are not concerned with its national or imperial interests, but primarily want to regain their rights and property in Cuba. These Cuban patriots are organized around the Cuban Revolutionary Council, which serves as umbrella organization for many militant groups. Although financed by American institutions to the tune of $ 2 million per year, the Council defines itself as the legitimate government to replace that of Castro, thus similar to an allied foreign power acting in concert with the United States against a common enemy, communism. From their point of view, the Council and other representative organizations of Cuban exiles are not involved in the Cold War as much as in a civil war. They need American support to get back their political and economic power, while the CIA uses them to restore an American protectorate. Since the botched operation, both harbored a fierce hatred against Kennedy. In April 1963, a leaflet circulated among Cuban exiles, with the message: "Only through one development will you Cuban patriots ever live again in your homeland as freemen: if an inspired Act of God should place in the White House within weeks a Texan known to be a friend of all Latin Americans."[64] It's obvious that these Cuban patriots didn't have the means to kill Kennedy with impunity, but it is no less obvious that anyone who wanted to assassinate Kennedy could find plenty of volunteers among them.

---

[63] Douglass, *JFK and the Unspeakable, op. cit.,* p. 14-5; Talbot, *Brothers, op. cit.,* p. 47; O'Donnell et Powers, *Johnny, We Hardly Knew Ye, op. cit.,* p. 274.
[64] Mahoney, *The Kennedy Brothers, op. cit.,* p. 267.

5. *The Northwoods Pattern*

The military, not just the CIA, misled Kennedy, and he did not forget that "those sons-of-bitches with all the fruit salad just sat there nodding, saying it would work."[65] In an attempt to end the collusion between the Pentagon and the CIA, and the power granted the CIA to initiate military operations, Kennedy signed a National Security Action Memorandum (NSAM-55) establishing "the Joint Chiefs of Staff as my only military advisors [...]. I expect their advice to come to me direct and unfiltered."[66] A year later, March 13, 1962, advice came from General Lyman Lemnitzer, Chairman of the Joint Chiefs of Staff, under the name "Operation Northwoods." It was a false flag operation designed to orchestrate a *casus belli* against Cuba. The project consisted of a wave of terrorist acts falsely attributed to Cuba, culminating in the explosion of a plane allegedly carrying vacationing American students over Cuban waters. The explosion would have been preceded by distress radio communications indicating an attack by a Cuban fighter. The actual passengers would be secretly transferred to another plane, and a state funeral would be held in their remembrance. Below is an excerpt of the project, from the copy kept by McNamara, declassified in 1997 and published by James Bamford in *Body of Secrets* (2001):

"3. A 'Remember the Maine' incident could be arranged in several forms: We could blow up a US ship in Guantanamo Bay and blame Cuba. We could blow up a drone (unmanned) vessel anywhere in the Cuban waters. We could arrange to cause such incident in the vicinity of Havana or Santiago as a spectacular result of Cuban attack from the air or sea, or both. The presence of Cuban planes or ships merely investigating the intent of the vessel could be fairly compelling evidence that the ship was taken under attack. The nearness to Ha-

---

[65] Talbot, *Brothers, op. cit.,* p. 51.

[66] www.ratical.org/ratville/JFK/USO/appE.html#NSAM55#NSAM55

vana or Santiago would add credibility especially to those people that might have heard the blast or have seen the fire. The US could follow up with an air/sea rescue operation covered by US fighters to 'evacuate' remaining members of the non-existent crew. Casualty lists in US newspapers would cause a helpful wave of national indignation.

"4. We could develop a Communist Cuban terror campaign in the Miami area, in other Florida cities and even in Washington. The terror campaign could be pointed at Cuban refugees seeking haven in the United States. We could sink a boatload of Cubans en route to Florida (real of simulated). We could foster attempts on lives of Cuban refugees in the United States even to the extent of wounding in instances to be widely publicized. Exploding a few plastic bombs in carefully chosen spots, the arrest of Cuban agents and the release of prepared documents substantiating Cuban involvement also would be helpful in projecting the idea of an irresponsible government."[67]

NAVAL OFFICERS THINK THE MAINE WAS DESTROYED BY A SPANISH MINE.

The expression "Remember the Maine" refers to the explosion of the USS Maine "by a Spanish mine" in Havana harbor on February 15, 1898. It was hammered as a slogan in favor of U.S. intervention against Spain to gain control of its colony, under the false pretext of assisting the Cubans' struggle for freedom. When the USS Maine was refloated in 1910, its hull was found to have exploded from inside. As no officer was on board on that fatal day, it smells of false flag.

---

[67] National Security Archive: www.gwu.edu/~nsarchiv/news/20010430/. James Bamford, *Body of Secrets: How America's NSA and Britain's GCHQ Eavesdrop on the World,* Century, 2001, p. 84-90.

Kennedy rejected the Northwoods plan. But a month later, on April 10, 1962, General Lemnitzer returned with a memorandum on behalf of the Joint Chiefs of Staff, recommending "a national policy of early military intervention in Cuba [...] to overthrow the present communist regime." The Joint Chiefs, states the document, "believe that the intervention can be accomplished rapidly enough to minimize communist opportunities for solicitation of UN action." Kennedy responded by dismissing General Lemnitzer, sending him away as Supreme Commander of NATO forces in Europe, and replacing him by Maxwell Taylor at the head of the Joint Chiefs.

As Richard Cottrell has shown in *Gladio, NATO's Dagger at the Heart of Europe*, Lemnitzer brought a curse on Europe, where his enthusiasm for "black warfare" was given free rein. It was Lemnitzer who launched the false flag terror campaign known as "Operation Gladio," diverting the stay-behind cells of NATO from their original purpose—organizing and arming the resistance in case of Soviet invasion of Western Europe—to instead setting up assassinations and bomb attacks to be blamed on left-wing revolutionaries, in a "strategy of tension" meant to hinder the democratic progression of communism. In Italy, the NATO-sponsored *Brigate Rosse* (Red Brigades) bombed trains, buses and schools, and assassinated political leaders, such as former Prime Minister Aldo Moro, who had befriended the Communist Party. When a bomb killed 85 people and wounded 200 in the central station of Bologna on August 2, 1980, some officials started to distance themselves from this synthetic terror campaign, leading to public disclosure. In France, NATO cells under Lemnitzer's command are responsible for most of the failed assassinations of De Gaulle, who had determined in 1960 to disengage France from NATO. "The penumbra of Lemnitzer's madness clings to Europe like a nightmare," writes Cottrell, who also suspects Lemnitzer of having planned the assassination of Kennedy.[68]

In Washington, the removal of Lemnitzer was a change with little effect: most of the generals shared the belief that they had already entered into the Third World War, which could only be won or lost. The President failed to reform their perspective, and kept receiving recommendations for Machiavellian schemes to start a war against Castro. One memo sent by the Assistant Secretary of Defense Paul Nitze on May 10, 1963, recommended that the U.S. "undertake various measures designed to stimulate the Cubans to provoke a new incident," for example "an attack on a United States reconnaissance aircraft [that] could be exploited toward the end of effecting the removal of the Castro regime."[69] According to his Special Assistant Arthur Schlesinger, Kennedy

---

[68] Richard Cottrell, *Gladio, NATO's Dagger at the Heart of Europe: the Pentagon-Nazi-Mafia Terror Axis*, Progressive Press, 2012, p. 23.
[69] Bamford, *Body of Secrets, op. cit.*, p. 87-9.

feared the Pentagon more than the Kremlin because he knew that if nuclear war broke out, it would be by his own camp. He tried to listen patiently to these high-ranking officials, but he sometimes would leave meetings of the National Security Council, sickened by their impatience to trigger nuclear Apocalypse: "These people are crazy!" Deputy Secretary of Defense Roswell Gilpatric heard him comment on one such occasion.[70] "The first advice I'm going to give my successor," Kennedy confided to his friend and journalist Ben Bradlee, "is to watch the generals and to avoid feeling that just because they are military men, their opinions on military matters are worth a damn." For their part, the generals despised Kennedy and the young East Coast generation around him, and they believed that the country's security rested squarely on their own shoulders.[71]

It was during the Cuban Missile Crisis that the tension reached its peak. The failed invasion of the Bay of Pigs had convinced Fidel Castro to officially declare himself a communist and place his country under the protection of the Soviet Union. In October 1962, the CIA's U-2 spy planes flying over Cuba reported the installation of Soviet nuclear warheads pointed at the United States. During a meeting of the National Security Council that lasted 13 straight days, Kennedy resisted the generals' vehement requests for an air attack against the Cuban missiles' launch sites, an attack that would probably not destroy all missiles before they could be fired, and would amount to a declaration of war against the Soviet Union. Kennedy simply enforced "a strict quarantine on all offensive military equipment under shipment to Cuba," and instructed his brother Robert to enter into negotiations with the Soviet Commander in Chief Nikita Khrushchev through the ambassador to Washington Anatoly Dobrynin.[72] According to an account given by Khrushchev's son, Robert Kennedy's message was: "If the situation continues much longer, the President is not sure that the military will not overthrow him and seize power. [...] The situation might get out of control, with irreversible consequences. [...] I don't know how much longer we can hold out against our generals." Khrushchev would comment to his Foreign Affairs Minister Andri Gromyko, "We have to let Kennedy know that we want to help him... Yes, help. We now have a common cause, to save the world from those pushing us toward war." Kennedy and Khrushchev would emerge from the crisis with a secret agreement in which Kennedy promised not to invade Cuba and to dis-

---

[70] Douglass, *JFK and the Unspeakable, op. cit.,* p. 109.

[71] Bradlee, *Conversations with Kennedy, op. cit.,* p. 117.

[72] Robert Kennedy recounted that crisis in *Thirteen Days: A Memoir of the Cuban Missile Crisis,* released in 1969 (W.W. Norton & Co, 2000). Robert, however, remains discreet on the veiled threat of coup that his brother was under.

mantle the American missiles in Turkey, in exchange for the withdrawal of Soviet missiles in Cuba.[73]

"Naturally, the common people don't want war; neither in Russia nor in England nor in America, nor for that matter in Germany. That is understood. But, after all, it is the leaders of the country who determine the policy and it is always a simple matter to drag the people along, whether it is a democracy or a fascist dictatorship or a Parliament or a Communist dictatorship. Voice or no voice, the people can always be brought to the bidding of the leaders. That is easy. All you have to do is tell them they are being attacked, and denounce the peacemakers for lack of patriotism and exposing the country to danger. It works the same in any country" (Hermann Goering, quoted in Gustave Gilbert, *The Nuremberg Diary*, 1947).[74]

Kennedy had thus deprived the Joint Chiefs a historic opportunity to engage with communist powers. The generals, however, did not relent. A month later, on November 20, 1962, they handed Defense Secretary Robert McNamara a memorandum advocating an increase in nuclear capacity in order to tip the balance between the two powers and grant the ability to strike the USSR with a surprise attack so devastating, that the risk of retaliation would be sufficiently low: "The Joint Chiefs of Staff consider that a first-strike capability is both feasible and desirable." It was an obsession: July 20, 1961 during a meeting of the National Security Council, the generals had presented to Kennedy, a plan for a nuclear attack on the Soviet Union "in late 1963, preceded by a period of heightened tensions." On this occasion, after raising questions about the expected casualties, Kennedy got up and walked right out of the meeting, directing at his Secretary of State Dean Rusk, "and we call ourselves the human race."[75]

In avoiding disaster the two Heads of State were brought closer; Khrushchev sent Kennedy a private letter in which he expressed his hope that, in the eight years of Kennedy's presidency, "[they] could create good conditions for peace-

---

[73] Sergei Khrushchev, *Nikita Khrushchev and the Creation of a Superpower*, Pennsylvania State University, 2000, quoted in Douglass, *JFK and the Unspeakable, op. cit.*, p. 174-5.
[74] Gustave Gilbert, *The Nuremberg Diary* (1947), Da Capo Press, 1995.
[75] Douglass, *JFK and the Unspeakable, op. cit.*, p. 236-8.

ful coexistence on earth and this would be highly appreciated by the peoples of [their] countries as well as by all other peoples." This was the second letter of their back-channel correspondence, which would include a total of twenty-one. The first had been written by Khrushchev during the Berlin Crisis, September 29, 1961: wrapped in newspaper and discreetly handed to Kennedy's Press Secretary Pierre Salinger by Georgi Bolshakov, the KGB agent loyal to Khrushchev and operating under the cover of a press editor. Kennedy responded positively to Khrushchev's proposal to bypass their respective bureaucracies "for a personal, informal but meaningful exchange of views," that "must be kept wholly private, not be hinted at in public statements, much less disclosed to the press."[76] Through such secret dialogues, the two men worked cooperatively to avoid catastrophe. "One of the ironic things about this entire situation," Kennedy commented to journalist Norman Cousins, "is that Mr. Khrushchev and I occupy approximately the same political positions inside our governments. He would like to prevent a nuclear war but is under severe pressure from his hard-line crowd, which interprets every move in that direction as appeasement. I've got similar problems."[77]

The only encounter between Kennedy and Khrushchev, in Vienna two months after the Bay of Pigs failed invasion, was ice-cold. But Khrushchev changed his opinion on Kennedy after the happy ending of the Cuban Missile Crisis. He was despondent after the news of Kennedy's death, the only time when his collaborators saw him cry, then withdraw into a shell for several days, according to what a high official of the Soviet Embassy in Washington told Pierre Salinger.[78]

It should be remembered that Nikita Khrushchev was not only Stalin's successor; he was the architect of the "de-Stalinization" taking place in the USSR. His denunciation of Stalin's crimes to the Communist Party Congress in 1956

---

[76] Janney, *Mary's Mosaic, op. cit.,* p. 205 ; Douglass, *JFK and the Unspeakable, op. cit.,* p. 220.
[77] Douglass, *JFK and the Unspeakable, op. cit.,* p. 344.
[78] Douglass, *JFK and the Unspeakable, op. cit.,* p. 378.

brought a breath of hope to the West when published by the *New York Times*, and his policy of détente had begun to loosen the grip of repression in the satellite countries. Given their secret correspondence, there is little doubt that if Kennedy had lived and had been reelected in 1964, he and Khrushchev would have normalized relations between their governments and put an end to the Cold War in the 1960s. Kennedy's friend Bill Walton remembers that on November 19, 1963, after signing the first treaty limiting nuclear testing, Kennedy told him that, "he intended to be the first U.S. President to visit the Kremlin, as soon as he and Khrushchev reached another arms control agreement."[79] Kennedy was killed three days later.

His successor Johnson never responded to Khrushchev's repeated pleas for exchange, and Khrushchev himself would soon be plagued by problems from his own camp, later to be overthrown by a bloodless coup in September 1964 and placed under house arrest. Forced to sidelines throughout the Vietnam War and watching the Soviet invasion of Czechoslovakia in 1968, Khrushchev lamented in his memoirs: "What kind of socialism is it when you have to keep people in chains?"[80] Khrushchev died in 1971.

---

[79] Douglass, *JFK and the Unspeakable, op. cit.,* p. 378.
[80] *Memoirs of Nikita Khrushchev, vol. 2: 1945-1964,* edited by Sergei Khrushchev, Pennsylvania State University Press, 2007, p. 232.

6. Poisonous Diplomacy

As a continuation of his relationship with Khrushchev, in 1963 Kennedy tried to establish dialogue with Fidel Castro, in an attempt to resolve disputes and develop diplomatic relations. The CIA, however, worked to sabotage his efforts. It would be a disciple of Dulles, Richard Helms, who would replace Richard Bissell as Deputy Director of Plans. Taking counsel from his former bosses, Helms kept the new Director John McCone away from sensitive issues. At the end of 1960, Bissell contacted Chicago's Sam Giancana and Miami's Santos Trafficante via the emissary of the Mafia Johnny Roselli, in order to place a $150,000 contract on Castro's head. Helms pursued this arrangement without McCone's knowledge, as he admitted in 1975 before the Church Committee. The President, of course, was also kept in the dark, on the grounds, said Helms, that "Nobody wants to embarrass a president of the United States by discussing the assassination of foreign leaders in his presence."[81]

In an attempt to poison the Cuban leader, Helms also tried to use some of Castro's companions who, though turned off by his conversion to communism, still had access to his person. He charged his Technical Services Staff, a division under the direction of Dr. Sidney Gottlieb, to develop an arsenal of poisons and gadgets for this purpose. October 29, 1963, for example, Helms connected his Deputy Desmond Fitzgerald with Cuban Rolando Cubela, who had secretly contacted the CIA to betray Castro—but was perhaps, in reality, commissioned by Castro himself to inform him of attempts against his life. It was agreed between Helms and Fitzgerald that, "Fitzgerald should hold himself out as a personal representative of Attorney General Robert Kennedy," but that, "it was not necessary to seek approval from Robert Kennedy for Fitzgerald to speak in his name."[82] This confession by Helms given before the Church

---

[81] Church Committee, *Alleged Assassination Plots Involving Foreign Leaders,* 1975 : www.archive.org/stream/allegedassassina00unit#page/n7/mode/2up, p. 150.
[82] Douglass, *JFK and the Unspeakable, op. cit.,* p. 252.

Committee illustrates how the principle of "plausible deniability," rather than protecting the government in case of failure, could be used to bypass legitimate authorities altogether. After having long spread the rumor that plans to assassinate Castro had been ordained by Robert Kennedy, and having insinuated that he was therefore responsible for the death of his brother when these plans backfired against John in 1963, Helms was forced to admit to the Church Committee that he had never received Robert's consent, but had only "the feeling that [RFK] would not be unhappy if [Castro] had disappeared off the scene by whatever means."[83]

Richard Helms is described by his biographer as a "gentlemanly planner of assassinations."[84] He supervised the MK-ULTRA research into mindcontrol, and destroyed nearly all record of it in 1975. Convicted of lying under oath to Congress, he received a suspended sentence of two years in prison, but then was awarded the National Security Medal by Ronald Reagan. He is buried in Arlington National Cemetery, like Kennedy. Brazilian journalist Claudia Furiati, author of *ZR Rifle: The Plot to Kill Kennedy and Castro* (1994), sees him as the ultimate author of Kennedy's assassination.

A particularly sinister manipulation took place in April 1963, when Helms tried to use a peace ambassador of the American President to poison Castro. In August 1962, the Kennedy brothers sent to Havana a young lawyer named James Donovan to negotiate the release of 1,113 Bay of Pigs prisoners (in exchange for $53 million in food, medicine and equipment). Donovan travelled to Cuba three times and established a very friendly relationship with Castro, who often invited him to long nighttime discussions, baseball games and fishing trips; he was often accompanied by John Nolan, another lawyer loyal to Kennedy. Donovan and Nolan contributed to the resumption of relations between Kennedy and Castro, but in their last trip to Cuba in April 1963, Helms arranged for Donovan and Nolan to bring a gift for Castro: a diving suit contaminated by Dr. Gottlieb with a fungus known to cause chronic skin disease.

---

[83] Talbot, *Brothers, op. cit.,* p. 111.
[84] Thomas Powers, *The Man who Kept the Secrets: Richard Helms and the CIA,* Random House, 1979.

In 1975, Donovan and Nolan would learn through the findings of the Church Committee that the CIA had tried to make them commit a political assassination without their knowledge.[85]

Meanwhile, the CIA-trained armed groups of Cuban exiles tried to poison relations between the U.S. and the Castro government. The most active of these groups was called Alpha 66; it was led by Antonio Veciana and overseen by CIA officer David Atlee Phillips, who, according to Veciana, "kept saying Kennedy would have to be forced to make a decision, and the only way was to put him up against the wall." From October 1962, Alpha 66 staged raids along the Cuban coast, attacking both commercial and military Russian ships and leaving dozens dead. On the 19th of March 1963, the group announced they had attacked a Russian ship off the coast of Cuba, with the aim, Veciana would explain, "to publicly embarrass Kennedy and force him to move against Castro." Kennedy responded by ordering the Florida Coast Guard to intercept the raids and seize the boats. He further cut funds going to the Cuban Revolutionary Council, lowering the $2 million to less than one. The head of the Council, Jose Miro Cardona, complained in protest to the *New York Times* that "the struggle for Cuba was in the process of being liquidated by the Government." Again, the Cuban exile community was acting as though they were a foreign power seeking to provoke a war and draw the United States into it for their own account.[86]

During this time, Kennedy sought to restore diplomatic ties with Castro while remaining discreet within a growing atmosphere of paranoid anti-communism. He made the most of his relations among journalists, a profession he had practiced before entering politics. He asked Lisa Howard, a TV host who had interviewed Fidel Castro and was close to Che Guevara, to arrange a quiet meeting between Carlos Lechuga, the Cuban ambassador to the United Nations, and William Attwood, a former journalist who had also met Castro in 1959, before being promoted by Kennedy as UN diplomat. The first informal meeting took place at Howard's residence on September 23, 1963, and led to the idea of a meeting between Castro and Attwood in Cuba: the project would be aborted by the death of Kennedy.[87]

Che Guevara had made the first step toward the Kennedy Administration when initiating, four months after the Bay of Pigs, a secret meeting in Montevideo (Uruguay) with Dick Goodwin, one of Kennedy's most liberal aides. Goodwin's report to Kennedy (with a box of the best Havana cigars as a gift from Che Guevara) marked the beginning of Kennedy's fascination for the Che and Fidel, whom he saw as two intellectuals devoted to social justice, who had

---

[85] Talbot, *Brothers, op. cit.,* p. 114-8.
[86] Douglass, *JFK and the Unspeakable, op. cit.,* p. 342, 58.
[87] Douglass, *JFK and the Unspeakable, op. cit.,* p. 70.

simply taken a wrong path. That was also the opinion of Guevara and Castro, who had greeted positively Kennedy's economic program *Alliance for Progress* designed to "cast off the chains of poverty" in Latin America, although they considered it doomed to fail as long as the dictatorships were not overthrown.[88]

After the assassination of Kennedy, journalist Lisa Howard refused to cut her contacts with Castro, despite a CIA threat. In December 1964, she had a long conversation with Guevara at the United Nations. In a top-secret memorandum, her former contact at the CIA, Gordon Chase, mentioned the necessity to "remove Lisa from direct participation" in dealings with Cuba. She was fired from the ABC TV network and died on the 4th of July 1965, at 33, officially by suicide, after having swallowed a hundred pills of phenobarbital.[89]

Kennedy also called upon French journalist Jean Daniel. Learning that Daniel planned to go to Cuba to interview Castro, Kennedy invited him to the White House October 24th: officially to give him an interview, unofficially to ask him to be his messenger to Castro. In his message, Kennedy expressed not only his desire for reconciliation, but furthermore his empathy for the people of Cuba: "I believe that there is no country in the world, [...] where economic colonization, humiliation and exploitation were worse than in Cuba, in part owing to my country's policies during the Batista regime. [...] I will even go further: to some extent it is as though Batista was the incarnation of a number of sins on the part of the United States. Now we shall have to pay for those sins." While Daniel waited in Cuba for Castro's consent to grant him an interview, Kennedy sent the latter an indirect message on November 18, 1963, declaring in a speech to the Inter-American Press Association in Miami that he was ready "to work with the Cuban people in pursuit of those progressive goals which a few short years ago stirred their hopes and the sympathy of many people throughout the hemisphere." The next day, November 19th at 10 pm, Castro rushed to

---

[88] Talbot, *Brothers,* p. 55-6.
[89] National Security Archive: www.gwu.edu/%7Ensarchiv/NSAEBB/NSAEBB103/.

Daniel's hotel for an interview that would last until four o'clock in the morning. Castro received enthusiastically Kennedy's message of sympathy, commenting: "He still has the possibility of becoming, in the eyes of history, the greatest president of the United States, the leader who may at last understand that there can be coexistence between capitalists and socialists, even in the Americas." Daniel was having lunch with Castro when they were interrupted with news of the assassination. "Everything is changed," commented Castro, dejectedly. "You watch and see, I know them, they will try to put the blame on us for this thing." Like clockwork, the radio would soon announce that the culprit was a "pro-Castro Marxist."[90]

In light of all available evidence, the most prominent and respected Kennedy historians such as David Talbot and James Douglass agree that the Kennedy assassination was an undercover coup planned by a clan of generals and CIA officers, with the active cooperation of Cuban exiles. For his commitment to restraint and disarmament and for his determination to further diplomacy and dialogue with Khrushchev and Castro, Kennedy was perceived by warmongers not only as a weak link in the chain of command, but also as a traitor in collusion with the enemy. We don't know who fired the shots on Dealey Plaza, but the CIA had the means as well as the motive for the assassination: the Agency could have easily found volunteers among Cuban exiles who believed that the United States owed them a "debt of blood" from the days of the Bay of Pigs. Mafia hitmen could also be hired for a good price. And after all, coups d'états and political assassinations were the CIA's specialty. As for the mastermind of the operation, Richard Helms, the head of the Directorate of Plans, comes out as a prime suspect. But Allen Dulles, his mentor, is not far behind, especially given his leadership role in the Warren Commission cover-up. Suspicion also falls of course on the other two CIA directors fired by Kennedy after the Bay of Pigs: Richard Bissell and Charles Cabell. Jim Garrison had intended to charge Cabell with conspiracy, but gave up for lack of evidence, and it is noteworthy that Charles's brother, Earl Cabell, was at the time the Mayor of Dallas and thus could facilitate the ambush of Kennedy.

---

[90] Jean Daniel, "Unofficial Envoy: An Historic Report from Two Capitals," *New Republic,* December 14, 1963, quoted in Douglass, *JFK and the Unspeakable, op. cit.,* p. 73, 251 and Talbot, *Brothers, op. cit.,* p. 252-3. A French version was published in *L'Express,* November 28, 1963: www.lexpress.fr/informations/avec-castro-a-l-heure-du-crime_590917.html?xtmc=Jean_Daniel,_Kennedy&xtcr=7

Of Mexican origin and nicknamed El Indio, CIA agent David Sanchez Morales gained the reputation of chief assassin in Guatemala during the operation against Arbenz, before participating in the training of the Cuban exiles as chief of JW/WAVE unit. After his retirement in 1975, alcoholism made him dangerously talkative. Speaking of Kennedy, for example, he once confided to his friend Ruben Carbajal, "Well, we took care of that SOB, didn't we?" In May 1978, as he was scheduled to testify in front of the HSCA, he came back sick from a reunion with former colleagues and died within a week. No autopsy was performed.[91]

It is not trivial that precisely one month after Kennedy's assassination, on December 22, 1963, former President Harry Truman published an editorial in the *Washington Post* titled "U.S. Should Hold CIA to Intelligence," in which he said he was "disturbed by the way CIA has been diverted from its original assignment. It has become an operational and at times a policy-making arm of the Government." "I never had any thought when I set up the CIA that it would be injected into peacetime cloak and dagger operations," and at the point of becoming across the globe "a symbol of sinister and mysterious foreign intrigue [...] there are now some searching questions that need to be answered." The article appeared in the morning edition, and subsequently disappeared from those following.[92] No other newspaper made comment. This silence only confirms the serious implications of the message, which, given the timing, can be read as indicting the CIA for its complicity in the Kennedy assassination. As Kennedy researcher Ray Marcus says, "If that wasn't what he meant, then I can't imagine he would have written and/or released it then for fear of having it read that way."[93]

---

[91] Spartacus Educational: www.spartacus.schoolnet.co.uk/JFKmorales.htm
[92] Mark Lane, *Last Word: My Indictment of the CIA in the Murder of JFK*, Skyhorse Publishing, 2011, p. 246.
[93] Quoted in Janney, *Mary's Mosaic, op. cit.,* p. 253.

7. Assassination under False Flag

In July 1961, the Joint Chiefs presented Kennedy with a plan for a nuclear attack on the Soviet Union to take place "in late 1963, preceded by a period of heightened tensions." Kennedy was assassinated in late 1963, and there is every reason to believe that his assassination had as secondary purpose to generate such "tensions" with the Soviet bloc. The same day, *United Press International* revealed that the alleged offender, Lee Harvey Oswald, had Marxist convictions and connections with the pro-Soviet regime in Cuba: "The assassin of President Kennedy is an admitted Marxist who spent three years in Russia trying to renounce his U.S. citizenship... After changing his mind and returning to the United States last year, Oswald became a sympathizer of the Cuban prime Minister, Fidel Castro."[94] This news release strategically casts suspicion outside American borders, keeping attention fixed on foreign threats and communist conspiracy—away from the vipers' nest. Moreover, it made the Kennedy assassination look like an act of war requiring retaliation, in the form of the invasion of Cuba.

To strengthen the suspicion, much was made of a statement by Castro during the summer of 1963, in relation to recent assassination attempts on his life: "U.S. leaders should think that if they are aiding terrorist plans to eliminate Cuban leaders, they themselves will not be safe." The militant groups of anti-Castro Cuban exiles were quick to promote the "Castro" conspiracy theory and call for vengeance. Immediately after the assassination, the Directorio Revolucionario Estudiantil (DRE), better known as the Cuban Student Directorate, released a special edition of their newspaper: the front page linking photos of Oswald and Castro under the heading, "Presumed Assassins." The DRE was funded by the CIA, up to $25,000 per month, and was supervised by George Joannides under the command of Richard Helms. According to a re-

---

[94] See footage in the documentary *JFK: 3 Shots That Changed America,* The History Channel, 2009.

port by the HSCA, "the DRE was, of all the anti-Castro groups, one of the most bitter toward President Kennedy."[95]

Oswald holding the supposed murder weapon, as well as the motive in the form of two communist newspapers—the perfect proof presented to the public on the front cover of *Life* magazine.

Ironically, these alleged links between Oswald and Cuba provide conclusive evidence of the CIA's and perhaps FBI's guilt, once we recognize them as a fabricated "legend." Oswald enlisted in the Marines in 1956 at the age of 17, and, two years later, received training at the military base at Atsugi in Japan, one of the outposts of the CIA. He learned Russian. Back in the United States, he subscribed to the journal of the Communist Party and in 1959 went to the USSR with a 60-day visa. Upon his arrival in Moscow, he went to the U.S. Embassy, where he solemnly declared wanting to renounce his American nationality: "My allegiance is to the Union of Soviet Socialist Republics." He further expressed his intention to hand over to the Soviets any information known to him as a specialist in radar operations in the Marines. He spent two and a half years in the USSR, where he married Marina Prusakova. According to Victor Marchetti (a CIA agent from 1955 and assistant to Richard Helms for three years before his resignation in 1969), the CIA launched in 1959 a program of false defectors comprising "three dozen, maybe forty, young men who were made to appear disenchanted, poor American youths who had become turned off and wanted to see what communism was all about."[96] It was hoped that these young men, apparently lost to the USSR, would be recruited by the KGB and serve as double agents for the CIA. Yuri Nosenko, a soviet diplomat who defected in Geneva in 1964 after eight years as a KGB agent (two of which as a double agent), said that the KGB determined Oswald too mentally fragile to recruit.

It was then, in all likelihood, that Oswald's mission changed. In June 1962, he appears again at the U.S. Embassy in Moscow, this time for a return visa. Far from being arrested or harassed, he is granted a loan to cover his relocation expenses. Upon his return, he settled in Fort Worth, Texas with his Russian wife and their child, but soon moved to Dallas, to be chaperoned by George de Mohrenschildt. De Mohrenschildt was the son of a tsarist officer, consultant

[95] Douglass, *JFK and the Unspeakable, op. cit.,* p. 69, 63.
[96] Douglass, *JFK and the Unspeakable, op. cit.,* p. 40.

and marketing agent for Texan oilmen, occasionally rendering his services to the CIA in exchange for foreign contacts. Four days after his installation in Dallas, Oswald is hired by Jaggars-Chilles-Stovall, a graphic arts company under contract with the Army Map Service. In April 1963, he moves alone to New Orleans, where he works for the Reily Coffee Company, whose owner William Reily has CIA ties. From June, Oswald is often seen—and twice filmed—handing out leaflets for the pro-Castro Fair Play for Cuba Committee on the streets. He even attracts enough attention to be interviewed by a local television crew, expressing to them his Marxist convictions.[97] During this time, Oswald is in frequent contact with Guy Banister, a former FBI agent turned private detective. Banister's address would later be found stamped on one of the Fair Play for Cuba Committee leaflets distributed by Oswald. In October 1963, Oswald returns to Dallas and takes a job in the School Book Depository, the building where he'll be on November 22 at 12:30.

On March 29, 1977, while expecting to be summoned by the HSCA, De Mohrenschildt gave an interview to journalist Edward Epstein. On his return, he learnt that an investigator for the HSCA wanted to talk to him, which made him apparently upset. A few hours later, he was found dead in his home with a bullet through his head. His death was ruled a suicide. The investigation established that his mental health had seriously deteriorated, as evidenced by his repeated complaints that "the Jews" and "the Jewish Mafia" were out to get him.[98]

Oswald probably believed that his mission in New Orleans was to infiltrate pro-Castro groups, and perhaps discredit them. But unbeknownst to him, he was being prepared for his role as a scapegoat. Placed in memorable situations pre-fit to construct the identity of a political enemy, Oswald was set up to be pinned as a conspirator. His "legend" as the pro-Soviet defector and Castro-friendly activist that he believes to be his undercover protection, would actually be his assassin backstory. It was a narrative not intended to deceive the communist circles he had infiltrated, but rather the American public. Six months before the Kennedy assassination, or maybe as early as his return from the USSR, Oswald was selected as potential patsy (perhaps among several candidates), and exhibited to the press in a tailor-made communist suit that would implicate him as the

---

[97] See footage in Matthew White's documentary *Murder of JFK: A Revisionist History,* 2006.
[98] Read the Sheriff's Office report: mcadams.posc.mu.edu/death2.txt

instrument of a Cuban conspiracy. With a cynicism that goes beyond measure, the conspirators, who hated Kennedy for his sympathy for Castro, hoped to blame Castro for Kennedy's assassination, and thus construct the pretext for the invasion of communist Cuba, risking to make real the nuclear nightmare Kennedy had once prevented.

The plan was thwarted by Lyndon Johnson and J. Edgar Hoover, who chose instead to impose the theory of the disturbed solitary gunman. They forced the CIA to abandon plan A by threatening to make public vulnerabilities in the plot that might expose the Agency's complicity in the assassination. In staging the Oswald patsy scheme, the CIA had indeed been overzealous; it had manufactured evidence that Oswald had stayed in Mexico City between September 27 and October 2, 1963, to visit the Soviet Embassy (twice) and Cuban Embassy (three times), to which he would have also placed calls (seven to the first, three to the second). The object of his calls and visits would be to obtain a Cuban and a Russian visa, in order to fly to Moscow via Havana. At the Soviet Embassy, Oswald had met, telephoned, and later written Valery Kostikov, a KGB officer known to the CIA as "the officer-in-charge for Western Hemisphere terrorist activities—including and especially assassination." The CIA claimed to have photographs of Oswald entering the Soviet Embassy, and a recording of his telephone conversation with an employee at that embassy. This was meant to substantiate that Oswald had acted with the support of Cuba and the Soviet Union, and that he had prepared his escape in advance. It could have worked if Hoover and Johnson had gone along and not decided otherwise. But seven FBI agents who listened to the CIA's recording after interviewing Oswald on the 22nd and 23rd of November agreed, according to a memorandum signed by Hoover, that the person identifying himself on the phone as "Lee Oswald" "was NOT Lee Harvey Oswald"; the voices did not match. In a recently declassified recorded telephone conversation with Johnson, Hoover said that the photo was also not a match: "that picture and the tape do not correspond to this man's voice, nor to his appearance. In other words, it appears that there is a second person who was at the Soviet embassy down there." He added, without finishing his sentence: "Now if we can identify this man who was at the Soviet embassy in Mexico City…" Seven weeks later, Hoover handwrites in the margin of a report a note about the CIA's "false story regarding Oswald's trip to Mexico."[99] Oswald had in fact never been to Mexico, just as his wife had consistently asserted. The Agency's fabricated evidence against Oswald had backfired. The connections were too obvious, and an investigation of the relationship between Oswald, Cuba and the Soviet Union would risk their disclosure.

---

[99] Douglass, *JFK and the Unspeakable, op. cit.,* p. 80-1, 228-9.

In 1977, the House Select Committee on Assassination established that Oswald's false visit to Mexico City was staged by the CIA, and suspected David Atlee Phillips, who worked under the direction of Richard Helms as Chief of Covert Action of the Northern Hemisphere, headquartered in Mexico.[100] Phillips has always denied his participation to the fraud, which might have been orchestrated, in his opinion, by "some CIA guy that I never saw [who] did something that I never heard of."[101]

David Atlee Phillips left, after his death in 1987, the synopsis of a novel titled *The AMLASH Legacy* where he offered a peculiar version of the backfire theory, as an antidote to Oswald's CIA links. One character, representing Phillips himself, explains: "I was one of the two case officers who handled Lee Harvey Oswald. After working to establish his Marxist bona fides, we gave him the mission of killing Fidel Castro in Cuba [...]: in Havana Oswald was to assassinate Castro with a sniper's rifle from the upper floor window of a building on the route where Castro often drove in an open jeep. Whether Oswald was a double-agent or a psycho I'm not sure, and I don't know why he killed Kennedy. But I do know he used precisely the plan we had devised against Castro."[102]

While Hoover compromised CIA plans by neutralizing the links they'd forged between Oswald and communism, Johnson enacted another blackmail, intended to curb the combat ambitions of a fervent military, which was more than eager to consider the Kennedy assassination a declaration of war by the Soviets. As a master player in Machiavellian deep politics, Johnson actually used the CIA's fabricated rumor of communist plot to thwart the CIA's plan. Beginning the afternoon of November 22nd, he invoked the threat of national destabilization to coerce the authorities at Dallas to cease the investigation and expedite confirmation that Oswald had acted alone. Dallas District Attorney Henry Wade, Texas Attorney General Waggoner Carr, and Police Chief Jesse Curry all received phone calls from Johnson's aide Cliff Carter (Johnson's flunky ever

---

[100]Full text on *National Archives*: www.archives.gov/research/jfk/select-committee-report/summary.html

[101] Michael Collins Piper, *Final Judgment: The Missing Link in the JFK Assassination Conspiracy,* American Free Press, 6th ed., 2005, p. 284.

[102] Spartacus Educational: www.spartacus.schoolnet.co.uk/JFKphillips.htm

since he had helped him steal his first Senate election in 1948), issued directly from Air Force One and then the White House. According to Wade, "[Carter] said that President Johnson felt any word of a conspiracy—some plot by foreign nations—to kill President Kennedy would shake our nation to its foundations. [...] Washington's word to me was that it would hurt foreign relations if I alleged conspiracy, whether I could prove it or not. I was just to charge Oswald with plain murder and go for the death penalty. Johnson had Cliff Carter call me three or four times that weekend."[103] Johnson continued to use the specter of nuclear war to silence the "rumors" of a communist conspiracy: "40 million American lives hung in the balance," he kept repeating.[104]

Johnson used the same argument to direct the hand of the members of the Warren Commission: "We've got to be taking this out of the arena where they're testifying that Khrushchev and Castro did this and did that and check us into a war that can kill 40 million Americans in an hour," he explained to senator Richard Russell in a telephone conversation on November 29, in an effort to persuade him to join the Commission.[105] An internal memo dated February 17, 1964 refers to the first meeting of the Warren Commission on January 20, 1964, during which Warren, after being briefed by the CIA and the President, explained to all members that their mission was to destroy all the "rumors" that, "if not quenched, could conceivably lead the country to war which would cost forty million lives." "No one could refuse to do something which might help prevent such a possibility," Warren insisted, parroting Johnson's leitmotiv.[106]

So, immediately after the Dallas coup, we see Johnson, a master player in Machiavellian deep politics, playing a threefold game: to the public, he expressed his absolute confidence in the Warren Commission's conclusion that Oswald was a deluded lone gunman. To his administration and Texas authorities, he hinted at a possible Communist plot and urged them not to investigate for fear of triggering World War III. But in his conversation with Hoover, he shows knowledge that the Communist plot is phony, which supposes awareness that Oswald was a patsy. Johnson would keep playing this game until his death. In September 1969, he admitted during a CBS interview that he has "not completely discounted" the possibility that "there might have been international connections" in Kennedy's assassination.[107]

[103] Nelson, *LBJ: The Mastermind, op. cit.,* p. 513-4.
[104] Nelson, *LBJ: The Mastermind, op. cit.,* p. 619.
[105] Listen on YouTube, "Phone call: Lyndon Johnson & Richard Russel: www.youtube.com/watch?v=YE6i2vYbY3I
[106] Lane, *Last Word, op. cit.,* p. 209.
[107] This part of the interview was broadcast on April 24, 1975 on CBS Nightly News. See on YouTube: "LBJ Speaks on a conspiracy in JFK Murder," www.youtube.com/watch?v=oF4_7_Emzy0

How are we to make sense of the arm-twisting game between Johnson and the CIA? Researchers like James Douglass and David Talbot believe Johnson to be fundamentally innocent of the assassination of Kennedy; after the fact, he could not expose the plotters for fear of plunging the country in a fatal crisis, but at least he thwarted their plan to launch WWIII by keeping Kennedy's promise not to invade Cuba. This hypothesis ignores the obvious motive Johnson had to see Kennedy dead, and the opportunity he had to plan the ambush in Texas. It ignores his psychological profile as a ruthless murderer of anyone standing in his way to the White House. The second possible interpretation is that Johnson (and maybe Hoover) conspired together with the CIA to assassinate Kennedy, but then double-crossed the CIA. Any plot like this one necessarily involves several players with differing agendas, holding each other hostage: by killing Kennedy, the CIA wanted to eliminate an obstacle to its imperialistic black warfare, while Johnson simply wanted to eliminate the only remaining obstacle to his presidential ambition. Johnson may have outsmarted the CIA and frustrated them of their false flag, with the help of his buddy Hoover.

There is a third hypothesis, which has been elaborated by Gary Wean, a detective sergeant for the Los Angeles Police Department, in his book *There's a Fish in the Courthouse* (1987). Relying on a well-informed source in Dallas (later identified as Republican Senator John Tower), Wean raises the possibility that the Dallas shooting had originally been planned by the CIA as a fake failed assassination, meant to spare Kennedy's life but force him to retaliate against Castro, but that the operation had been hijacked by another faction who wanted Kennedy dead; this other faction could be Johnson and Hoover. Real snipers would have been added to the CIA's staged assassination. Veteran JFK researcher Dick Russel has reached the same conclusion is his book *The Man Who Knew Too Much* (1992), after interviewing Cuban exiles who believe they had been used. This likely double-cross scenario is comparable to a drill exercise being diverted into a real attack.

Whatever the case may be, a complex blackmail involving Johnson, Hoover and the CIA forms the background of November 22 and its aftermath. Douglass, Talbot and most authors defending the "CIA-did-it" thesis before them ignore not only the evidence against Johnson, but also the FBI's obscure role and its deep-seated rivalry with the CIA. Much has been made, for example, of De Mohrenschildt's statement that he had been introduced to Oswald by J. Walton Moore, assumed to be a CIA agent; however, Moore started his career as an FBI officer and De Mohrenschildt knew him as such, according to his testimony to the Warren Commission.[108] The theory of the CIA's responsibility in framing Oswald rests for a large part on conjectures about who was se-

---

[108] William Kelly quoting the HSCA report, volume XI, p. 77-8, on: educationforum.ipbhost.com/index.php?showtopic=8515&page=2

cretly working for the CIA. By contrast, the evidence that Oswald was also an FBI informant is as hard as you can get, and it comes with the proof that the Warren Commission deliberately suppressed it. In a closed-door session on January 27, 1964, whose "top secret" transcript was declassified after a legal battle (by Harold Weisberg, who published in his *Whitewash IV,* 1974), the commissioners discussed evidence received by general counsel J. Lee Rankin that "Oswald was an undercover agent for the FBI, [...] employed by the F.B.I. at $200 per month from September of 1962 up to the time of the assassination." Rankin called that information "a dirty rumor that is very bad for the Commission," and said "it must be wiped out insofar as it is possible to do so by this Commission."[109] From April to September 1963, while exhibiting himself as a Marxist in New Orleans, Oswald was in close contact with Guy Banister, a former FBI agent turned private detective. Banister's address would later be found stamped on one of the Fair Play for Cuba Committee leaflets distributed by Oswald. Even the phony Mexico City appearances of Oswald in the Soviet and Cuban embassies could very well have been fabricated by the FBI to mislead the CIA and create a trail leading from Oswald to the Agency.[110] One reason to believe that the FBI was pulling the ropes is the fact that on October 9, 2013, one day before the CIA informed the FBI that Oswald had just contacted the Soviet Embassy in Mexico City, a FBI officer named Marvin Gheesling had just disconnected Oswald from a federal alarm system, thus making sure that the patsy would be left unwatched in Dallas on the President's visit.[111]

Finally, consideration must be given to the fact that the Texas Book Depository where Oswald got a job in October 1963, belonged to David Harold Byrd, a business friend of Johnson, to whom he was much obliged. Byrd was the co-founder of Ling Temco Vought (LTV), which had become one the largest government contractors thanks to Senator Lyndon Johnson. After Johnson's hit-man Mac Wallace had been convicted in Austin, Texas of first degree murder and gotten away with a five-year suspended sentence, Byrd had hired him as a Purchasing Manager of LTV. Wallace's fingerprint would be found in the sniper's nest on the sixth floor of the Book Depository.[112]

[109] Douglass, *JFK and the Unspeakable, op. cit.,* p. 65.
[110] Piper, *Final Judgment, op. cit.,* p. 284.
[111] Douglass, *JFK and the Unspeakable, op. cit.,* p. 177.
[112] Tague, pos. 4846-4992

8. Vietnam Instead

The invasion of Cuba that the CIA and Cuban exiles hoped for never materialized. Instead, Cuba was sanctioned with drastic trade embargos designed to cause the regime's internal collapse. In fact, they did little but galvanize the Castro regime into an attitude of self-defense and tighten its links with the Kremlin. This U.S. policy of economic sanctions would survive the end of the Cold War, and remains unchanged today. That unlikely anachronism is due to the intense lobbying of the Cuban American National Foundation (CANF), the second most powerful lobby in the United States after AIPAC, founded in 1981 by a veteran of the Bay of Pigs, Jorge Mas Canosa.

In lieu of invasion, Johnson offered to the generals the Vietnam War. This was another betrayal of the late President. Kennedy had resisted the urging of the Joint Chiefs of Staff to send troops to Vietnam, resolving only to maintain a force of 15,000 men, who were officially deemed "military advisors." General Douglas MacArthur, who knew Asia, had told Kennedy: "Anyone wanting to commit American ground forces to the mainland of Asia should have his head examined." Kennedy would then quote him in response to the advice of the Joint Chiefs: "Well, now, you gentlemen, you go back and convince General MacArthur, then I'll be convinced." General Taylor remembers: "I don't recall anyone who was strongly against [sending ground troops], except one man and that was the President. The President just didn't want to be convinced that this was the right thing to do [...]. It was really the President's personal conviction that U.S. ground troops shouldn't go in." In late 1963, Kennedy decided to evacuate all U.S. military personnel in Vietnam. Knowing that his decision would be exploited by his enemies in the coming 1964 campaign, he decided to keep it quiet until his second term. "The first thing I do when I'm re-elected," he confided to Tip O'Neill, "I'm going to get the Americans out of Vietnam. [...] that is my number one priority—get out of Southeast Asia."[113] From the 11th of November, he paved the way for the withdrawal by directive

---

[113] Douglass, *JFK and the Unspeakable, op. cit.,* p. 102-5, 181-2.

NSAM-263, which included removing "1,000 U.S. military personnel by the end of the 1963," and "by the end of 1965 [...] the bulk of U.S. personnel."[114] Just before leaving the Oval Office for Texas, November 21, and after reading a report on the latest casualties, he repeated his resolution to his Assistant Press Secretary Malcolm Kilduff: "After I come back from Texas, that's going to change. There's no reason for us to lose another man over there. Vietnam is not worth another American life."[115]

The car bomb in front of the Opera in Saigon on January 9, 1952 contributed to justifying the U.S. military involvement in Vietnam. Ho Chi Minh was blamed, although he condemned the attack. In his memoirs entitled *Ways of Escape*, journalist and novelist Graham Greene, once a collaborator of the CIA, suggests that the photographer dispatched by *Life* magazine, who immortalized the event with this photo taken seconds after the explosion, had been tipped in advance. *Life* was strongly anti-Communist and close to the CIA. Its precedent issue had warned in front page, "Indo-China is in danger," and called for U.S. military intervention.

Meanwhile in Vietnam, the attitude of the CIA reflected the same deliberate sabotage of presidential politics as in Cuba, taking parallel methods. Evidenced by the bombing in Saigon on May 8, 1963, which left eight dead and fifteen wounded among the Buddhist monks who were protesting against their oppression by the Catholic President Ngo Dinh Diem. The CIA at once accused Diem, claiming "the weight of evidence indicates that government cannon-fire caused the death." Diem, for his part, accused the Viet Cong. But his brother Ngo Dinh Can confided to an investigator at a Catholic newspaper *Hoa Binh* that he was "convinced the explosions had to be the work of an American agent who wanted to make trouble for Diem": it indeed appeared that the explosion was due to American-made plastics.[116] In 1970, the same newspaper obtained the confession of a certain Captain Scott of the CIA, who detailed the operation. Why this criminal action? In 1963, the CIA decided, with the help of Ambassador Henry Cabot Lodge, a longtime Republican enemy of Kennedy, to destabilize Diem's government and support a military coup. It was in direct opposition to the explicit orders of Kennedy, who relied on the stability of the country and had personally assured Diem of his support. The Saigon

---

[114] JFK Library: www.jfklibrary.org/Asset-Viewer/w6LJoSnW4UehkaH9Ip5IAA.aspx
[115] Nelson, *LBJ: The Mastermind, op. cit.,* p. 638.
[116] Douglass, *JFK and the Unspeakable, op. cit.,* p. 129-31, 148.

attack contributed significantly to delegitimizing Diem in the eyes of the mainly Buddhist population, and paved the way for what was to follow: October 30, 1963, with approval of the CIA, four generals took power, arrested Diem, his brother and sister-in-law, and, after promising them safe exile, shot them dead in a truck. The insubordination of the CIA had reached its tipping point, with the assassination of Diem as a fateful prelude to the assassination of Kennedy himself. Senator George Smathers remembers Kennedy's reaction when hearing about Diem's overthrow and death: "I've got to do something about those bastards… they should be stripped of their exorbitant power." He was talking, of course, about the CIA.[117]

October 2, 1963, Richard Starnes, *Washington Daily News* correspondent in Saigon, exposed the insubordination of the CIA, who was working against the President's efforts to stabilize the country. "The story of the Central Intelligence Agency's role in South Vietnam is a dismal chronicle of bureaucratic arrogance, obstinate disregard of orders, and unrestrained thirst for power. […] They represent a tremendous power and total unaccountability to anyone." Arthur Krock quoted Starnes' investigation the next day in his daily column in the *New York Times*, addressing "The Intra-Administration War in Vietnam." He wrote that according to an unnamed "high United States source," "The CIA's growth was 'likened to a malignancy' which the 'very high official was not sure even the White House could control any longer.'" "If the United States ever experiences a *'Seven Days in May'*, it will come from the CIA."[118] Krock was a friend to Kennedy, and it is likely that the "very high official" is none other than Kennedy himself, who wanted to warn the American people through the press of the imposing threat to both his life and the democratic fabric of his country.

Seven Days in May is a political thriller published in 1962, which details a military coup for control of the White House. Kennedy's opinion on that novel was known to his friends. Having read it in the summer of 1962, he declared it a credible scenario. "It's possible. It could happen in this country," he said, "if, for example, the country had a young President, and he had a 'Bay of Pigs'." If this "Bay of Pigs" was followed by one or two other clashes with the military, he added, "the military would almost feel that it was their patriotic obligation to stand ready to preserve the integrity of the nation, and only God knows what segment of democracy they would be defending if they overthrew the elected establishment."[119] Nearing the end of 1963, after having refused the generals more than three times, Kennedy felt the threat closing in, and most likely used his contacts in the media to send a message, one that *a posteriori* sounds like a

---

[117] Douglass, *JFK and the Unspeakable, op. cit.,* p. 211.
[118] Douglass, *JFK and the Unspeakable, op. cit.,* p. 186, 196.
[119] Douglass, *JFK and the Unspeakable, op. cit.,* p. 12-3.

posthumous accusation of the CIA. According to Fletcher Prouty, who served as Chief of Special Operations for the Joint Chiefs under Kennedy, the President's decision to withdraw all military personnel from Vietnam by the end of 1965, "may well have been the ultimate pressure point that created the climate in which the decision was reached to do away with the President."[120]

Seven Days in May **is a political thriller by Fletcher Knebel, based on his investigation into right-wing militarism. Interested in getting its prophetic message across, Kennedy encouraged movie director John Frankenheimer to adapt the novel (after his successful adaptation of** *The Manchurian Candidate*) **and offered him access to the White House for filming.**[121] **The film was shot in 1963 with Burt Lancaster, Kirk Douglas and Ava Gardner, but its release was delayed till February 1964 because of the President's death.**

Kennedy's decision to withdraw U.S. troops from Vietnam would be reversed after his death. On November 24, barely installed in the Oval Office, Johnson summoned Ambassador Henry Cabot Lodge and told him: "I am not going to lose Vietnam. I am not going to be the President who saw Southeast Asia go the way China went."[122] On November 26, the day after Kennedy's funeral, Johnson buried the NSAM-263 directive and replaced it with another, NSAM-273, which requires the military to develop a plan "for the United States to begin carrying the war north," including "different levels of possible increased activity," and "military operations up to a line up to 50 kilometers inside Laos"—which violated the 1962 Geneva Accords on the neutrality of Laos.[123] The draft of this memo, identified by code OPLAN-34A, is dated the 21st of November, and states: "The President has reviewed the discussions of South Vietnam which occurred in Honolulu, and has discussed the matter further with Ambassador Lodge."[124] The statement is untrue, since the "President," who was still Kennedy at that time, could not have been materially informed of the discussions taking place at the Conference of the Joint Chiefs, ended in Honolulu on November 21st. The draft therefore betrays a bureaucratic trick: if

---

[120] Fletcher Prouty, *The CIA, Vietnam, and the Plot to Assassinate John F. Kennedy*, Skyhorse Publishing, 2011.
[121] Douglass, *JFK and the Unspeakable, op. cit.*, p. 13.
[122] Janney, *Mary's Mosaic, op. cit.*, p. 260.
[123] LBJ Library: www.lbjlib.utexas.edu/johnson/archives.hom/nsams/nsam273.asp
[124] JFK Library: www.jfklibrary.org/Asset-Viewer/w6LJoSnW4UehkaH9Ip5IAA.aspx

the date of OPLAN-34A is authentic, it gives credence to the premeditated nature of Johnson's NSAM-273, and furthermore implicates the Joint Chiefs in a certain foreknowledge of the President's imminent death. All ambiguities cleverly laid out in the NSAM-273 directive would be lifted by another memo signed on January, 1964 by General Maxwell Taylor, which said: "National Security Action Memorandum n° 273 makes clear the resolve of the President to ensure victory over the externally directed and supported communist insurgency in South Vietnam [...]. To do this, we must prepare for whatever level of activity may be required." It is no longer a question of stopping the war, but rather to win at any cost. Robert McNamara, continuing as Secretary of Defense, acceded to Johnson's agenda, recommending the mobilization of 50,000 soldiers and a program of "graduated overt military pressure" against North Vietnam, a policy which Johnson rubberstamped in March 1964 by memorandum NSAM-288.[125]

"Why are we in Vietnam?" Arthur Goldberg recalls that, in response to this recurring question during an informal conversation with journalists, **"LBJ unzipped his fly, drew out his substantial organ and declared, 'This is why!'"**[126] Kennedy's libido was of another kind.

A suitable pretext was still needed for aggression: it would be in the Gulf of Tonkin on the 2nd and 4th of August 1964, when torpedoes were allegedly launched by the North Vietnamese against the American destroyers USS Maddox and USS Turner Joy. It was proven in 2001, and became public knowledge in 2005, that the August 4th attack was imaginary, made up out of falsified NSA data.[127] With that faked event, Johnson could announce on national television a "retaliatory" bombing of the North Vietnamese navy, and pass through Congress on August 7, 1964, the Gulf of Tonkin Resolution which gave him full powers to send up to 500,000 soldiers into North Vietnam. With that, Johnson plunged the Vietnamese people into a decade of unspeakable suffering, taking the lives of more than a million civilians. From 1965 to 1968, as part of Operation Rolling Thunder, 643,000 tons of bombs were dropped— three times more than during the entire Second World War—on a mostly rural country, and about 500,000 American soldiers were sent to Vietnam, where 50,000 perished.

---

[125] LBJ Library: www.lbjlib.utexas.edu/johnson/archives.hom/nsams/nsam288.asp
[126] Quoted in Janney, *Mary's Mosaic, op. cit.,* p. 262, from Robert Dallek, *Flawed Giant,* 2005.
[127] Scott Shane, "Vietnam Study, Casting Doubts, Remain Secret," *New York Times,* October 31, 2005: www.nytimes.com/2005/10/31/politics/31war.html?pagewanted=all&_r=0.

9. The Peace Race

At the time the National Security State was born, John Kennedy was a young lieutenant recently returned from the Pacific with a severe back injury, the Navy and Marine Medal for "extremely heroic conduct," and a deep distaste for modern warfare. Hailed a hero by the press, he understood the limits of the cult of the warrior, and noted in his diary: "War will exist until that distant day when the conscientious objector enjoys the same reputation and prestige that the warrior does today."[128] "The war makes less sense to me now than it ever made and that was little enough—and I would really like—as my life's goal—in some way at home or some time to do something to prevent another."[129] In 1945, he began a career as a journalist for the *Chicago Herald-American* covering the founding conference of the United Nations in San Francisco. This experience convinced him that the world of journalism was not for him: "you can't make changes. There's no impact. I'm going to go into politics and see if you can really do anything," he confided to his longtime Irish friends Dave Powers and Kenny O'Donnell.[130] In announcing his candidacy for Congress on April 22, 1946 in Boston, Kennedy declared: "The days which lie ahead are most difficult ones. Above all, day and night, with every ounce of ingenuity and industry we possess, we must work for peace. We must not have another war."[131]

For Kennedy, the nuclear weapon was the negation of all historical efforts to restrain war and spare civilians: this military abomination had to be eradicated. On the 25th of September 1961, after less than a year in power, he declared before the United Nations General Assembly: "Today, every inhabitant of this planet must contemplate the day when this planet may no longer be habitable. Every man, woman and child lives under a nuclear sword of Damocles, hanging by the slenderest of threads, capable of being cut at any moment by accident or miscalculation or by madness. The weapons of war must be abolished before they abolish us. [...] It is therefore our intention to challenge the Soviet

---

[128] Douglass, *JFK and the Unspeakable, op. cit.*, p. 6, 322.
[129] Christ Matthews, *Jack Kennedy, Elusive Hero,* Simon & Schuster, 2011, p. 72.
[130] Matthews, *Jack Kennedy, op. cit.*, p. 76.
[131] Douglass, *JFK and the Unspeakable, op. cit.*, p. 5.

Union, not to an arms race, but to a peace race—to advance together step by step, stage by stage, until general and complete disarmament has been achieved." The program he outlined did not stop at nuclear disarmament: "It would achieve under the eyes of an international disarmament organization, a steady reduction in force, both nuclear and conventional, until it has abolished all armies and all weapons except those needed for internal order and a new United Nations Peace Force."[132] It was the speech that would inspire Khrushchev's first private letter to Kennedy—a letter of 26 pages.

A teenage friend of John Kennedy, Mary Pinchot Meyer holds a unique place among his extra-marital love affairs. A peace activist, she encouraged Kennedy to think in the same line. Having divorced a CIA officer, Cord Meyer, she knew what Kennedy was against. After the President's death, she determined to produce evidence of a CIA plot, but was found dead near her home on October 12, 1964, while her journal was stolen by CIA official James Jesus Angleton. Her story has been told by Peter Janney, the son of a CIA officer involved in her murder (*Mary's Mosaic*, 2012).

In 1963, Kennedy vigorously engaged his country in the direction of disarmament. May 6, he addressed directive NSAM-239 entitled "U.S. Disarmament Proposals" to all government administrations, both military and civilian, inviting them to cooperate with the Arms Control and Disarmament Agency created in 1961, by making proposals towards the goal of "general and complete disarmament." This phrase, which recurs as a leitmotif throughout the document, is repeated in his famous "Peace Speech" of June 10, 1963, delivered at the American University of Washington before a crowd of students: "Our primary long-range interest is general and complete disarmament—designed to take place by stages, permitting parallel political developments to build the new institutions of peace which would take the place of arms." Rejecting the goal of a "*Pax Americana* enforced on the world by American weapons of war," he invited citizens to deeply question the dangerous Manichean ideology that lay buried in anti-communism. "Some say that it is useless to speak of world peace or world law or world government—and that it will be useless until the leaders of the Soviet Union adopt a more enlightened attitude. I hope they do. I believe we can help them do it. But I also believe that we must reexamine our own attitude—as individuals and as a Nation—for our attitude is as

---

[132] JFK Library: www.jfklibrary.org/Asset-Viewer/DOPIN64xJUGRKgdHJ9NfgQ.aspx

essential as theirs. […] Every graduate of this school, every thoughtful citizen who despairs of war and wished to bring peace, should begin by looking inward—by examining his own attitude toward the possibilities of peace, toward the Soviet Union, toward the course of the cold war and toward freedom and peace here at home." Kennedy was addressing the deeper, spiritual cause of all wars, which was the dehumanization and demonization of the enemy: "No government or social system is so evil that its people must be considered as lacking in virtue. […] For, in the final analysis, our most basic common link is that we all inhabit this small planet. We all breathe the same air. We all cherish our children's future. And we are all mortal."[133] His words had the power to inspire American youth to a new ideal. But paradoxically, they received less coverage in the American press than in the Soviet Union, where Khrushchev translated and published the full speech in *Pravda*, and broadcast it on radio, calling it "the greatest speech by any American President since Roosevelt."

In that speech, Kennedy made public his intention to establish a direct communication line with Khrushchev, in order to avoid "dangerous delays, misunderstandings, and misreadings of other's actions which might occur at a time of crisis," implicitly referring to the Cuban Missile Crisis, which Arthur Schlesinger has deemed "the most dangerous moment in all human history."[134] He also announced his negotiations towards global disarmament, which would lead to the first treaty that limited nuclear testing: "While we proceed to safeguard our national interests, let us also safeguard human interests. And the elimination of war and arms is clearly in the interest of both."

On June 11, 1963, one day after his "Peace Speech," Kennedy pronounced his "Civil Rights Address." It appealed again to his fellow Americans' conscience

and capacity for empathy after the attempt by Governor George Wallace to prevent two Afro-Americans from registering in the University of Alabama. "I hope every American, regardless of where he lives, will stop and examine his conscience about this and other related incidents […] We are confronted with a moral issue. It is as old as the Scriptures and it is as clear as the American Constitution."[135]

To have his Test Ban Treaty accepted by a rather reluctant Congress, he launched an ambitious communication campaign

[133] JFK Library: www.jfklibrary.org/Asset-Viewer/BWC7I4C9QUmLG9J6I8oy8w.aspx

[134] Schlesinger, *A Thousand Days, op. cit.,* p. 7.

[135] JFK Library : www.jfklibrary.org/Asset-Viewer/LH8F_0Mzv0e6Ro1yEm74Ng.aspx

and spoke directly to the nation on television on July 26, 1963, building the people's awareness of the urgency of stopping an arm race that could lead to "a full-scale nuclear exchange" after which "the living would envy the dead"—a direct quote from Khrushchev.[136] The treaty, which prohibited nuclear testing in the atmosphere and under water, was signed in August 1963 by the Soviet Union, the United States and the United Kingdom. "No other single accomplishment in the White House ever gave Kennedy greater satisfaction," according to Ted Sorensen, who helped craft the treaty.[137] Six weeks later, on the 20th of September, Kennedy expressed his pride and hope to the United Nations: "Two years ago I told this body that the United States had proposed and was willing to sign, a limited test ban treaty. Today that treaty has been signed. It will not put an end to war. It will not remove basic conflicts. It will not secure freedom for all. But it can be a lever, and Archimedes, in explaining the principles of the lever, was said to have declared to his friends: 'Give me a place where I can stand—and I shall move the world.' My fellow inhabitants of this planet, let us take our stand here in this Assembly of nations. And let us see if we, in our own time, can move the world to a just and lasting peace." Again, he invited the USSR "to compete in a host of peaceful arenas, in ideas, in production and ultimately in service to all mankind. And in the contest for a better life all the world can be a winner."[138] In his last letter to Kennedy, delivered to the U.S. Ambassador Roy Kohler but never making its final destination, Khrushchev was clearly proud of this first historic treaty, which had "injected a fresh spirit into the international atmosphere"; he put forward other propositions, and, echoing the language of Kennedy, hoped that "Their implementation would clear the road to general and complete disarmament, and, consequently, to the delivering of peoples from the threat of war."[139]

In the sixties, nuclear disarmament was an achievable goal, since only four countries had nuclear weapons. There was a historic opportunity, and Kennedy was determined not to let it pass. "I am haunted by the feeling that by 1970, unless we are successful, there may be ten nuclear powers instead of four, and by 1975, fifteen or twenty," he said prophetically during his press conference on March 21, 1963.[140] Following the USA and USSR, all NATO countries and the communist bloc were making a first step towards nuclear disarmament. All countries but one: Israel. By the early 1950s, David Ben Gurion, both Prime Minister and Defense Minister, entrusted Shimon Peres to stir Israel toward the secret manufacture of atomic bombs, diverting from its pacific aim the coop-

---

[136] JFK Library : www.jfklibrary.org/Asset-Viewer/ZNOo49DpRUa-kMetjWmSyg.aspx

[137] Sorensen, *Kennedy, op. cit.,* p. 740.

[138] Audio file on JFK Library: www.jfklibrary.org/Asset-Viewer/Archives/JFKWHA-218.aspx www.jfklibrary.org/

[139] Douglass, *JFK and the Unspeakable, op. cit.,* p. 269.

[140] Audio file on JFK Library: www.jfklibrary.org/Asset-Viewer/Archives/JFKWHA-169.aspx

eration program Atoms for Peace, launched naively by Eisenhower. Informed by the CIA in 1960 of the military aim pursued at the Dimona complex in the Negev desert, Kennedy would do his utmost to force Israel to renounce it. He asked Ben Gurion for regular inspections of Dimona, first verbally in New York in 1961 and later through more and more insistent letters. In the last letter dated June 15, 1963, Kennedy demanded Ben Gurion's agreement for an immediate visit followed by regular visits every six months, otherwise "this Government's commitment to and support of Israel could be seriously jeopardized."[141] The result was unexpected: Ben Gurion resigned June 16, thereby avoiding receiving the letter. As soon as the new Prime Minister Levi Eshkol took office, Kennedy sent him a similar letter, dated July 5, 1963, to no avail.

Kennedy and his son John Jr. (John-John) at the White House. "I keep thinking of the children, not my kids or yours, but the children all over the world," the President said to his friend and assistant Ken O'Donnell, while working on his Test Ban Treaty.[142] He urged the American people to share his concern in his televised elocution on July 26, 1963: "This treaty is for all of us. It is particularly for our children and our grandchildren, and they have no lobby here in Washington."[143]

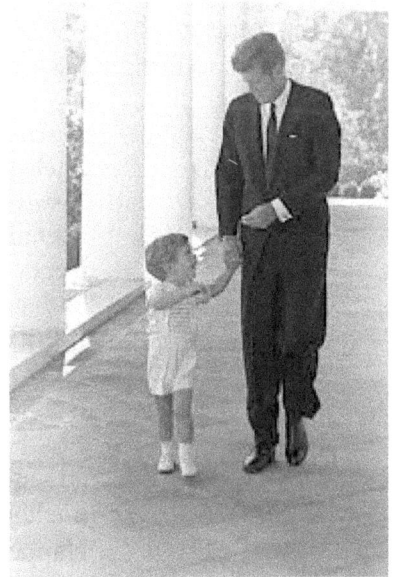

Kennedy's death released the pressure on Israel, as Johnson chose to turn a blind eye. John McCone, CIA Director appointed by Kennedy, resigned in 1965 complaining about the lack of interest by Johnson on this subject. Under Johnson, Israel's first nuclear bombs were made with material and expertise stolen from the U.S., as Seymour Hersh has documented in his best-selling book *The Samson Option* (1991). Zalman Shapiro, who was running a publicly owned nuclear fuel processing firm in Apollo, Pennsylvania, known as NUMEC (Nuclear Materials and Equipment Corporation), managed to smuggle hundreds of pounds of weapons-grade uranium to Israel, despite being on a CIA watch list. He was the son of an Orthodox rabbi from Lithuania, a member of the Zionist Organization of America, a partner with the Israeli government in some business ventures, and a frequent traveler to Israel.[144]

[141] Warren Bass, *Support any Friend: Kennedy's Middle East and the Making of the U.S.-Israel Alliance,* 2003, p. 219.
[142] O'Donnell and Powers, *Johnny We Hardly Knew Ye, op. cit.,* p. 285.
[143] LBJ Library : www.jfklibrary.org/Asset-Viewer/ZNOo49DpRUa-kMetjWmSyg.aspx
[144] Seymour Hersh, *The Samson Option: Israel's Nuclear Arsenal and American Foreign Policy*, Random House, 1991, p. 202-4.

Under Johnson, military aid to Israel reached $92 million in 1966, more than the total of all previous years combined. Johnson even allowed the delivery of Phantom missiles capable of carrying nuclear warheads. Israel developed its first nuclear bomb in 1967, without ever giving public acknowledgement. Nixon took no more interest than Johnson, while his National Security Advisor Henry Kissinger privately expressed his satisfaction at the idea of Israel as a nuclear power ally. Nixon would play a double game: while publicly support-ing the Non-Proliferation Treaty of 1968 (which wasn't an American initia-tive), to his cabinet he authored a contrary message, as part of a top-secret Na-tional Security Decision Memorandum (NSDM-6), stating: "there should be no efforts by the United States government to pressure other nations [...] to fol-low suit. The government, in its public posture, should reflect a tone of opti-mism that other countries will sign or ratify, while clearly disassociating itself from any plan to bring pressure on these countries to sign or ratify."[145]

It was not until 1986 that the world realized Israel's nuclear capability, with the publication in the *Sunday Times* of photographs taken by Israeli technician Mor-dechai Vanunu inside the Dimona Complex in the Negev Desert. Vanunu was abducted by the Mossad, and convicted of treason in Israel. He has spent 18 years in prison, including 11 in solitary confinement.

Kennedy's peace initiatives were a declaration of war against the arms industry—an industry eager to take advantage of the huge opportunity represented by nuclear development. "If Peace Does Come—What Happens to Business?" the *U.S. News and World Re-port* cynically headlined on August 12, 1963, a week after the signing of the Test Ban Treaty. Their worries would be put to rest with Kennedy's death, so too "disarmament" from American election agendas. According to 2011 SIPRI (Stockholm International Peace Research Institute) figures, world military ex-penditure stands at $1,738 trillion per year, or 4.7 billion per day, with the United States far out in front producing 41% of the world's total arms.

What makes the war business so profitable is its mimetic, addictive, and self-feeding quality: everybody needs to match his neighbors' weapons. As Middle East expert Stephen Zunes writes: "every major arms transfer to Israel creates a new demand by Arab states," and *vice versa*. So when, in 2007, Bush ac-cepted the sale of $20 billion of military equipment to Saudi Arabia, he simul-taneously raised the sales to Israel by $30 billion, to help her keep the advan-

---

[145] Hersh, *The Samson Option, op. cit.,* p. 175.

tage.[146] The vicious but lucrative circle is especially efficient with nuclear weapons. Spending in that field is estimated at $100 billion per year. Throughout the world there are now about 20,000 nuclear bombs with an average destructive power 30 times greater than the Hiroshima bomb, which adds up to 600,000 Hiroshimas. Among these bombs, 1,800 are ready to be launched in minutes.

That doesn't include the growing arsenal of "mini-nukes." Sixty years after Manhattan Project, nano-technology has combined with nuclear physics to create much smaller and "cleaner" bombs (in terms of residual radioactivity). Miniaturization was already advanced in 1962, with the test of the M29 Davy Crockett bomb, which was no bigger than a watermelon and could be launched from a tripod. By the end of the 1980s, the military-industrial complex was advocating the abolishment of the distinction between conventional and nuclear weapons. Zbigniew Brezinski argued in that sense in a 1988 *Foreign Affairs* article, while serving as co-chairman of President Bush's National Security Advisory Task: "Technological changes have wrought a revolution in the way nuclear weapons may be used in the future. They are no longer just crude instruments for inflicting massive societal devastation but can be used with precision for more specific military missions, with relatively limited collateral societal damage."[147]

In October 2009, the newly elected President Obama received the Nobel Peace Prize for his "vision and work for a world without nuclear weapons or Zero Nukes," a vision he had expressed some months earlier in Prague and London, then at the United Nations on September 23rd—but never at home.[148] His words, which had raised the hopes of the jury, were never put into effect.

[146] Stephen Zunes, *Tinderbox: US Middle East Policy and the Roots of Terrorism*, Common Courage Press, 2002, p. 40.

[147] Zbigniew Brezinski, "America's New Geostrategy," *Foreign Affairs*, Spring 1988, quoted in Robert Malcolmson, *Beyond Nuclear Thinking*, McGill-Queen's University Press, 1990, p. 100.

[148] Official Nobel Prize website:
www.nobelprize.org/nobel_prizes/peace/laureates/2009/press.html

10. The Last of the Kennedys

November 29, 1963, Bill Walton, a close friend of the Kennedy family, went to Moscow and handed to Georgi Bolshakov (the agent who had already carried communications between Khrushchev and Kennedy) a message for Khrushchev from Robert and Jacqueline Kennedy; according to the memo found in the Soviet archives in the 90s by Alexandr Fursenko and Timothy Naftali (*One Hell of a Gamble*, 1998), they wanted to inform the Soviet Premier that they believed John Kennedy had been "the victim of a right-wing conspiracy." Furthermore, "Walton, and presumably [Robert] Kennedy, wanted Khrushchev to know that only RFK could implement John Kennedy's vision and that the cooling that might occur in U.S.-Soviet relations because of Johnson would not last forever."[149]

Jack and Bobby in 1957, during a session of the Select Committee on Improper Activities in Labor and Management (or Rackets Committee), set up on the initiative of Robert. With 253 investigations between 1957 and 1960, and 138 convictions, it revealed the scale of criminal networks that FBI boss Hoover persisted in denying.

Ostensibly ignored overnight by Hoover and Johnson, despite still serving as Attorney General, Robert Kennedy would be without resources against the forces that killed his brother, not to mention his being monitored closely. After

---

[149] Talbot, *Brothers, op. cit.,* p. 25-7.

a period of deep mourning, during which, says his first biographer Jack New-field, he seemed to "will himself into an avatar of his martyred brother," unconsciously adopting his familiar gestures and wearing his oversized overcoat, Robert opted for political survival.[150] He refused to testify before the Warren Commission and stated that he did not intend to read its final report, but instead accepted to sign the following statement: "I would like to state definitely that I know of no credible evidence to support the allegations that the assassination of President Kennedy was caused by a domestic or foreign conspiracy." To those close friends who criticized him for it, Robert replied (for example to Dick Goodwin in July 1966): "there's nothing I can do about it. Not now." He also said: "If the American people knew the truth about Dallas, there would be blood in the streets."[151]

Robert Kennedy had planned to run for the American Presidency in 1972, but two things rushed his decision to run in 1968: first, Johnson's renunciation of a second term due to his unpopularity, and secondly, the opening of Jim Garrison's investigation in 1967. When talks of the investigation began, Kennedy asked one of his closest advisors, Frank Mankievitch to follow its developments: "I want you to look into this, read everything you can, so if it gets to a point where I can do something about this, you can tell me what I need to know." He confided to his friend William Attwood, then editor of *Look* magazine, that he, like Garrison, suspected a conspiracy, "but I can't do anything until we get control of the White House."[152] He refrained from openly supporting Garrison, believing that since the outcome of the investigation was uncertain, it could jeopardize his plans to reopen the case later, and even weaken his chances of election by construing his motivation as a family feud. Instead, Robert focused his campaign around the struggle against poverty and criticism of the Vietnam War. He had already taken a clear stand on Vietnam on the 2nd of March, 1967, in a speech to the Senate calling everyone to deeply reflect on the "horror" of war: "All we say and do must be informed by our awareness that this horror is partly our responsibility. [...] It is our chemicals that scorch the children and our bombs that level the villages. We are all participants [...] we must also feel as men the anguish of what it is we are doing."[153]

April 4, 1968, Reverend Martin Luther King was killed in circumstances not unlike those of the late President Kennedy: the name, portrait and profile of the alleged lone sniper were broadcast almost instantly. As William Pepper, King's friend and attorney, has shown in *An Act of State* (2003), the mentally deficient James Earl Ray had been handled by some unidentified "Raul," who had arranged for his housing in a room overlooking King's balcony at the

[150] Jack Newfield, *RFK: A Memoir* (1969), Nation Books, 2003, p. 31.
[151] Talbot, *Brothers, op. cit.,* p. 278-80, 305, 268.
[152] Talbot, *Brothers, op. cit.,* p. 312-4.
[153] Newfield, *RFK, a Memoir, op. cit.,* p. 137.

Lorraine Motel in Memphis, and for a gun to be found under his window with his fingerprints on it. The court-appointed lawyer to defend Ray had no trouble in convincing him to plead guilty in hopes of receiving mercy from the jury. Nobody paid attention when he recanted three days later, maintaining his innocence thereafter until his death in 1998. Reverend King had embarrassed Johnson's government through his stance against the Vietnam War, and further through his project to gather "a multiracial army of the poor" in a "Poor People's Campaign" that would march on Washington and set camp before Capitol Hill until Congress signed a "Declaration of the Human Rights of the Poor."[154]

District Attorney Jim Garrison tried to convince Robert Kennedy into supporting his investigation. Garrison claims that Robert sent him a message through a mutual friend: "Keep up the good work. I support you and when I'm president I am going to blow the whole thing wide open." But Garrison rightly feared that Robert would not live long enough, and thought that speaking out publicly would have protected him.[155]

Robert Kennedy supported the "Poor People's Campaign" of Martin Luther King Jr., and both men took an identical stance against the Vietnam War. On the 4th of April 1968, Robert was on his way to a poor neighborhood of Indianapolis when he heard of King's death, and proceeded to announce it to a mostly Black crowd, standing on top of his car.

Robert Kennedy was assassinated two months later in Los Angeles on June 6, 1968, just after the announcement of the results of the California primaries that made him the favorite for the Democratic ticket. Inscribed on his tomb in Arlington Cemetery is an excerpt from his speech at the University of Cape Town (South-Africa) in June 1966, where he challenged the moral legitimacy of the apartheid: "Each time a man stands up for an ideal, or acts to improve the lot of others or strikes out against injustice, he sends forth a tiny ripple of hope, and crossing each other from a

---

[154] On King's murder, read William Pepper, *An Act of State: The Execution of Martin Luther King,* Verso, 2003.
[155] Garrison, quoted in Talbot, *Brothers, op. cit.,* p. 333.

million different centers of energy and daring, those ripples build a current which can sweep down the mightiest walls of oppression and resistance."[156]

Once Robert Kennedy was eliminated from the Presidential race, the victory came to the Republican Richard Nixon, against Vice-President Hubert Humphrey. The torch of political antimilitarism was taken up by George McGovern, who in May 1963, had pleaded for the open recognition of the Cuban revolution, as a condition to prioritize the fight against poverty in Latin America. McGovern ran for office in 1972 on a program advocating withdrawal from Vietnam. He beat the militarist Henry Scoop Jackson at the Democratic primaries, but was severely beaten by Republican candidate Richard Nixon. The political movement he represented, in the wake of the Kennedys, never recovered in American Presidential politics.

Robert Kennedy was shot by a young Palestinian man described by some witnesses as being in a trance. Although he was also convinced to plead guilty by his court-appointed lawyer, Sirhan Sirhan has continued to claim for 45 years that he has never had any recollection of his act: "I have never been able to remember what happened in that place at that time. And I have not been able to remember many things and incidents which took place in the weeks leading up to the shooting," he said again in a parole hearing in 2011, failing to convince the judges for the fourteenth time.[157] Sirhan believes he was drugged and/or hypnotized. Psychiatric experts and lie detector tests confirm his amnesia. In addition, Dr. Thomas Noguchi, the coroner who conducted the autopsy of Robert Kennedy, concluded (and confirmed in his memoirs in 1983)[158] that the fatal bullet was fired a few inches behind the right ear of Kennedy, following an upward angle. Yet all the witnesses confirmed that Robert had never turned his back on Sirhan and that Sirhan was several meters away from his target when he fired. Finally, ballistics reports found evidence of twelve bullets, while Sirhan's gun carried only eight. Strong suspicion falls upon Thane Eugene Cesar, a security guard hired for the evening, who was set behind Kennedy at the time of shooting, and seen with his pistol drawn by several witnesses. Cesar was never investigated, even though he did not conceal his hatred for the Kennedys, who according to him had "sold the country down the road to the commies."[159]

The mystery of Sirhan was partially clarified with the findings of the Church Committee and the ensuing declassification of over 18,000 pages of CIA documents, detailing extensive mind control programs such as Bluebird or Arti-

---

[156] Talbot, *Brothers, op. cit.,* p. 338.
[157] Watch on YouTube, "Sirhan Sirhan Denied Parole":
www.youtube.com/watch?v=nsm1hKPI9EU
[158] Thomas Noguchi, *Coroner,* Simon&Schuster, 1983.
[159] Talbot, *Brothers, op. cit.,* p. 374.

choke in 1950-51, that were later rolled over into the larger MKULTRA project (for *Mind Kontrolle ultra-secret*) in 1953—a project highly secretive even within the CIA. According to the documents, experiments in mental manipulation were conducted on hundreds of unknowing subjects using drugs—including heroin, opium, mescaline and the recently synthesized LSD; hypnosis, electroshock and permanent electrodes in the brain.

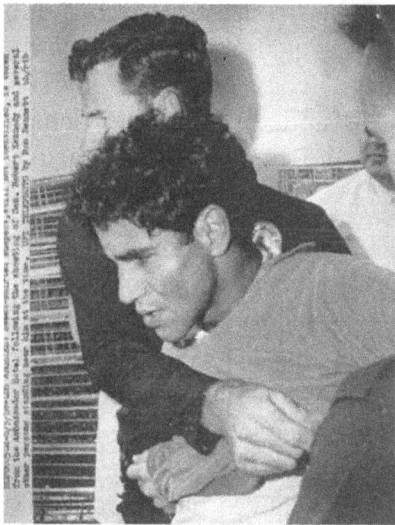

Sirhan Sirhan has never remembered shooting Robert Kennedy, nor wishing to kill him. Raised in a pious Christian family, he was known as fundamentally non-violent, and cannot explain his act to himself: "My own conscience doesn't agree with what I did. It's against my upbringing: my childhood, my family, church, prayers, the Bible. And here I go and splatter this guy's brain. It's just not me."[160]

During the Korean War, the justification for Project MKULTRA was the need to unravel the mystery of "brainwashing" allegedly practiced by the Communists, and thereby obtain "a thorough knowledge of the enemy's theoretical potential, thus enabling us to defend ourselves against a foe who might not be as restrained in the use of these techniques as we are" (according to a memo addressed by Helms to Dulles on April 3, 1953);[161] in other words, beat the (imaginary) devil at his own evil game. On prisoners in Germany, Japan, Korea, and later in Vietnam, Dr. Sidney Gottlieb and his associates experimented with forceful interrogation techniques combining drugs, hypnosis, and electroshock, together with traditional torture methods such as sleep deprivation. At home, the CIA hired secret collaborators in 3 prisons, 12 hospitals, and 44 universities, where inmates, patients, and students served as guinea pigs.

Although Helms illegally destroyed almost all MKULTRA archives in 1975, some documents related to Project Bluebird, reproduced by Colin Ross in *Bluebird: Deliberate Creation of Multiple Personality by Psychiatrists* (2000), show the extent of the CIA's mind control experiment. One document dated May 1951 instructed Bluebird teams to answer the questions: "Can a man be made to commit acts useful to us under post-hypnotic suggestion?" and "Can a person under hypnosis be forced to commit murder?"

---

[160] In Shane O'Sullivan's documentary, *RFK Must Die: the Assassination of Bobby Kennedy,* 2007.
[161] Gordon Thomas, *Secret & Lies: A History of CIA Mind Control & Germ Warfare,* Konecki & Konecki, 2007.

Sidney Gottlieb encouraged and financed doctor Ewen Cameron, a renowned psychiatrist (president of the American Psychiatric Association, pictured here), to apply brutal treatments on unknowing patients at his Montreal clinic which were designed to thoroughly erase and reprogram their personality.[162]

A document from May 1955 outlines the goal of the Chemical Division of the Technical Services Staff of the CIA: "the discovery of [...] materials and methods" allowing to "alter personality structure in such a way that the tendency of the recipient to become dependent upon another person is enhanced"; and, to "produce amnesia for events preceding and during their use." A document dated September 25, 1951 described a successful experiment, in which a female subject was programmed to enter into a hypnotic state when hearing a code word, and, in that state, set up a bomb and place it according to instructions. Another declassified CIA report dated January 7, 1953 describes the experimental creation of multiple personalities in two 19-year old girls: "These subjects have clearly demonstrated that they can pass from a fully awake state to a deep hypnotic state by telephone, by receiving written matter, or by the use of code, signal, or words, and that control of those hypnotized can be passed from one individual to another without great difficulty." Another report dated February 10, 1954, describes an experiment regarding the creation of unsuspecting assassins: a young lady who had previously expressed a fear of firearms was programmed under hypnosis to "pick up a pistol and fire it at Miss [deleted]. She was instructed that her rage would be so great that she would not hesitate to 'kill' [deleted]. Miss [deleted] carried out these suggestions including firing the (unloaded) gun at [deleted], and then proceeded to fall into a deep sleep. After proper suggestions were made, both were awakened. Miss [deleted] expressed absolute denial that the foregoing sequence had happened."[163]

---

[162] See Don Gillmor, *I Swear by Apollo: Dr. Ewen Cameron and the CIA-Brainwashing Experiment,* Eden Press, 1987.
[163] Colin A. Ross, *Bluebird: Deliberate Creation of Multiple Personality by Psychiatrists,* Manitou Communications, 2000. A good summary on: www.wanttoknow.info/bluebird10pg.

11. Tricky Dick's Revenge

Having spent eight years as Vice-President under Dwight Eisenhower, Nixon was the natural choice for a Republican candidate in 1960, even though Eisenhower was unable to name a single idea Nixon had contributed: "If you give me a week, I might think of one," he once answered a reporter. Nixon himself later confided to Bob Haldeman: "I saw Dwight Eisenhower alone about six times in the whole deal."[164]

As Eisenhower's Vice-President, Nixon had been busy in clandestine operations. He supervised with the CIA the overthrow of Iran's democratic government and its replacement by the unpopular Shah Mohammad Reza Pahlavi, whom he called his "personal friend" in his memoirs,[165] without mentioning the Shah's generous contributions to his two presidential campaigns.

On the day of his victory over Nixon in 1960, a man he had known from their political beginnings, John Kennedy commented to a friend: "If I've done nothing for this country, I've saved them from Dick Nixon." John couldn't foresee, of course, that Nixon would be back in 1968 to win the Presidency after his brother's assassination. History would cruelly repeat itself, the murder of one Kennedy after another yielding the power each time to a man with a danger-

---

[164] Anthony Summers, *The Arrogance of Power: The Secret World of Richard Nixon,* Penguin Books, 2001, p. 159, 114.
[165] *The Memoirs of Richard Nixon,* volume 2, Warner Books, 1979.

ously disordered personality, both contributing to the insanity of the Vietnam War. While Johnson is, to this day, the only American President to forgo a second term due to unpopularity, Nixon would become the only President to resign under the threat of impeachment. The Watergate scandal and the subsequent release of conversation recordings made the public aware of Nixon's paranoia, hypocrisy and cynicism, fully documented in Anthony Summers's biography, *The Arrogance of Power* (2001). After his resignation, Nixon's psychiatrist since 1952, Dr. Arnold Hutschnecker, who had so far expressed his concerns over the President's mental health only privately, suggested in a *New York Times* article that from then on Presidential candidates be subjected to a psychiatric evaluation.[166]

In 1968, Nixon won by a narrow margin over the Democratic candidate Hubert Humphrey, Johnson's Vice-President. Humphrey would probably have won if Johnson had managed to put an end to the Vietnam War, as he was trying to do in the last months of his term, to salvage his legacy. In October, his Administration had announced a "bombing halt" and convinced the leaders of South Vietnam, North Vietnam and the Viet Cong to enter into negotiations. The peace talks, planned for November, would have given Humphrey a decisive advantage in the elections. But Nixon sabotaged the plan by secretly promising a better deal to South Vietnam's President Nguyen Van Thieu, if he boycotted the talks. At the same time, he told the American people: "If in November this war is not over, I say that the American people will be justified in electing new leadership, and I pledge to you that new leadership will end the war and win the peace in the Pacific." Nixon's secret emissary to the South Vietnamese Ambassador Bui Diem was a Chinese-born diplomat named Anna Chennault (the widow of a Lieutenant General and a member of Nixon's campaign team), who acknowledges her role in her 1980 autobiography, *The Education of Anna*, as does Bui Diem in his 1987 memoir, *In the Jaws of History*. In a book co-written by Jerrold Schecter (*The Palace File*, 1986), Nguyen Tien Hung, advisor to President Thieu, quotes Thieu outlining Nixon's assurances to him in 1968: "He promised me eight years of strong support: four years of military support during his first term in office and four years of economic support during his second term" ("economic support" meaning military arms).[167]

Johnson found out about Nixon's maneuver; on his request, Hoover had wiretapped conversations between Chennault and Bui Diem. When leaving the White House, Johnson entrusted Walt Rostow, his Special Assistant for National Security Affairs, with a file chronicling Nixon's Vietnam gambit, consisting of scores of "secret" and "top secret" documents. Rostow labeled the file "The X Envelope" and kept it secret until after Johnson's death on January 22, 1973 (two days after Nixon was sworn in for a second term). Rostow then

---

[166] Summers, *The Arrogance of Power, op. cit.,* p. 168, 248-9.
[167] Summers, *The Arrogance of Power, op. cit.,* p. 239.

gave the file to the LBJ Library, who started declassifying its content in July 1994, three months after Nixon's death. Journalist Robert Parry gathered the pieces in his book *America's Stolen Narrative* (2012), from which the following summary can be drawn.[168]

Shortly after taking office in 1969, Nixon was told by FBI Director J. Edgar Hoover about the wiretaps that Johnson had ordered against his campaign team. So Nixon knew there was a classified file somewhere containing the evidence against him, but was unable to locate it. When the *New York Times* began publishing the *Pentagon Papers* in June 1971, Nixon's mind turned again to that file. *The Pentagon Papers,* compiled under the order of McNamara before leaving office, and leaked to the press by RAND Corporation whistleblower Daniel Ellsberg, chronicled many government public lies relating to the Vietnam War until 1968. Nixon feared that his prolonging the war for electoral purpose would also be leaked. The first transcript in Stanley Kutler's *Abuse of Power*, a book on Nixon's recorded White House conversations relating to Watergate, is of an Oval Office conversation on June 17, 1971, in which Nixon orders his Chief of Staff Bob Haldeman, in the presence of Henry Kissinger, to break into the Brookings Institution, a Washington think tank where he believes the 1968 file ("the bombing halt stuff") might be: "God damnit, get in and get those files. Blow the safe and get it." In a June 30, 1971 conversation on the same subject, Nixon again berated Haldeman about the need to break into Brookings and "take [the file] out." Nixon even suggested using former CIA officer Howard Hunt: "You talk to Hunt, I want the break-in. Hell, they do that. You're to break into the place, rifle the files, and bring them in. […] Just go in and take it."[169] One year later, Hunt was convicted for having planned the break-in into the headquarters of the Democratic Party in the Watergate building, by a team of burglars led by a member of the Committee for the Re-Election of the President (CREEP) and four former CIA Bay of Pigs participants (Frank Sturgis and three Cuban exiles). So the Watergate scandal, which would ultimately cause Nixon's downfall, appears linked to Nixon's desperate effort to suppress proof of his sabotage of Johnson's Vietnam peace talks.

In the three-page "Memorandum for the record" that he attached to Johnson's secret file on Nixon's Vietnam peace-talk sabotage, Rostow expressed regret that Johnson had chosen, for "the good of the country," to keep quiet about what he considered Nixon's high treason—as unauthorized secret dealings with a foreign power in times of war must be considered. But the reason for Johnson's silence may have had less to do with "the good of the country"—

---

[168] Robert Parry, *America's Stolen Narrative: From Washington and Madison to Nixon, Reagan and the Bushes to Obama,* Media Consortium, 2012, kindle, pos. 1107-2728.
[169] Conversations transcribed by Stanley Kutler in *Abuse of Power: The New Nixon Tapes,* S&S International, 1999, quoted Parry, *Stolen Narrative, op. cit.,* pos. 2168-2247.

what good could possibly come from a prolonged Vietnam War?—than with Nixon's ability to blackmail Johnson back about how *he* had become President. For Nixon certainly knew that the truth of Kennedy's assassination had been smothered by Johnson himself. After all, the Vice-President that Nixon would appoint in 1973 before resigning, Gerald Ford—with the mission to grant Nixon absolute and complete pardon after his resignation—had participated directly in the cover-up as a member of the Warren Commission.

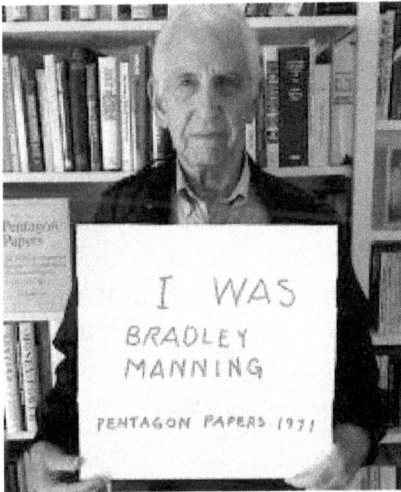

Daniel Ellsberg, the whistleblower who leaked to *The New York Times* the top-secret document *United States-Vietnam Relations, 1945-1967: A Study by the Department of Defense* (known as the *Pentagon Papers*), supports today the campaign to free Bradley Manning, the young soldier who risks life sentence after leaking to Wikileaks the video *Collateral Murder* showing the murder of civilians by a U.S. Apache crew in Iraq in 2007.

Was Nixon himself involved in any way in the 1963 Dallas coup? For one thing, he was in Dallas in the morning of November 22, 1963. And by another strange coincidence, Jack Ruby had worked for Nixon: a recently declassified FBI memo dated November 24, 1947 states that "one Jack Rubenstein of Chicago [...] is performing information functions for the staff of Congressman Richard Nixon, Republican of California," and that he should "not be called for open testimony" by a congressional committee investigating organized crime.[170] Shortly after, Rubenstein moved to Dallas and shortened his name into Ruby. Those two coincidences do not prove any direct involvement of Nixon in the assassination of his nemesis John Kennedy, but they reinforce the probability that he knew enough to make Johnson think twice before revealing Nixon's dirty trick. At the end of his life, according to his former aide Roger Stone who conducted a series of interviews with him, Nixon "never flatly said who was responsible [for Kennedy's death]. But he would say, 'Both Johnson and I wanted to be president, but the only difference was I wouldn't kill for it.' When pressed on who he thought killed Kennedy, Nixon "would shiver and say, 'Texas.'"[171]

---

[170] Copy at www.jfkmurdersolved.com/nixonruby.htm.
[171] Stone's book *The Man Who Killed Kennedy: The Case Against LBJ*, Skyhorse, 2013, was not yet available when the present book went to press. This information is borrowed from a

Nixon did not possess any secret file on the Kennedy assassination, but he knew where to look for one. The man from whom he tried to get such valuable information was Richard Helms, who was heading the CIA since 1966. Testimonies from two of Nixon's close assistants, Bob Haldeman and John Ehrlichman, indicate that Nixon asked Helms for the secret file on Dallas from his very first year in office, but that Helms—*The Man who Kept the Secret* as his biographer Thomas Powers calls him (1979)—never gave in. Four years later, when Nixon became entrapped in the Watergate scandal, he tried to use what he knew about Kennedy's assassination to pressure Helms into taking responsibility for the failed burglary. He directed his Chief of Staff Bob Haldeman to tell Helms that, "if it gets out, […] it's likely to blow the whole Bay of Pigs, which we think would be very unfortunate for the CIA." Haldeman is convinced, like Ehrlichman, that the "Bay of Pigs" was actually a code phrase between Nixon and Helms: "in all those Nixon references to the Bay of Pigs, he was actually referring to the Kennedy assassination."[172] It appears, therefore, that Nixon was threatening to reveal the CIA's involvement in the Kennedy assassination, though he never really had the means to do it. Helms refused to yield and was ousted in 1972, while Nixon, trapped by his own recording system within the Oval Office, fell in turn two years later.

The exposure and coverage of the Watergate scandal still passes today as proof of the independence of the American media and their effectiveness against anti-democratic power. In reality, it illustrates the role of the media in deep political warfare. The Church Committee has shown that since the inception of Operation Mockingbird twenty years earlier, the CIA had accumulated considerable hidden power over the media, through a network of friendly or fully owned directors, editors and journalists. Bob Woodward, the journalist who broke the Watergate scandal, had a rather curious background, which was revealed by Len Colodny and Robert Gettlin in *Silent Coup* (1991): he had been hired by the *Washington Post* on a government recommendation, relayed by the President of the *Washington Post* himself—none other than the former Navy Secretary to President Johnson, Paul Ignatius. Woodward had no experience in journalism; rather, after graduating from Yale, he had worked five years for the Navy in the communications sector with top-secret security clearance. It was Woodward who pointed at the link between Watergate and Nixon by revealing that the burglars were in possession of a check signed by Hunt, who was then working for the White House Counsel Charles Colson. Woodward never revealed the name of his informant, famously known as Deep Throat, but some suspect Richard Helms to be the source of the leaks. Helms could be as well the origin of the poorly planned Watergate operation itself,

---

preview in *The Daily Beast*: www.thedailybeast.com/articles/2013/05/14/roger-stone-s-new-book-solves-jfk-assassination-johnson-did-it.html

[172] Baker, *Family of Secrets, op. cit.*, p. 181-2.

which, as Nixon writes in his *Memoirs* (1979), "was so senseless and bungled that it almost looked like some kind of setup."[173]

Nixon had been elected in 1968 on the premise that he had a secret plan to end the war. He was instead making a secret deal to carry on the war. But when in office, he did develop a plan, which he once explained to Bob Haldeman: "I call it the 'Madman Theory', Bob. I want the North Vietnamese to believe I've reached the point where I might do anything to stop the war. We'll just slip the word to them that, 'for God's sake, you know Nixon is obsessed about Communists. We can't restrain him when he's angry—and he has his hand on the nuclear button'—and Ho Chi Minh himself will be in Paris in two days begging for peace."[174] In fact, not only Nixon prolonged the war for four years after his election, adding to the toll 21,000 American deaths, 110,000 among Allied South Vietnam soldiers, and 500,000 among their enemies, but two months after his election, he secretly and illegally expanded the war into Cambodia, triggering a massive bombardment under the codename Breakfast, followed by Lunch, Dessert, Snack, Dinner and Supper—all of which leading to the rise of the Khmer Rouge, an exceptionally bloody, tyrannical regime responsible for the extermination of one third of the Cambodian population.

Nixon: "I'd rather use the nuclear bomb."
Kissinger: "That, I think, would just be too much."
Nixon: "The nuclear bomb? Does that bother you? I just want you to think big, Henry, for Christ's sake" (a conversation recorded in the White House in 1972).[175]
"If the President had his way, there would be a nuclear war each week," Kissinger would later say. As early as the '50s, Nixon had been recommending to Eisenhower the use of the nuclear bomb in Indochina and North Korea.[176]

Nixon's legacy in Latin America is no better: as Vice-President to Eisenhower and working with the CIA, Nixon had overseen the operations in Guatemala, and the preparations for the invasion of Cuba that led to the fiasco of the Bay

---

[173] Baker, *Family of Secrets, op. cit.,* p. 176, 205-9.
[174] Summers, *The Arrogance of Power, op. cit.,* p. 230.
[175] Audio recording appears in John Pilger's documentary *The War you Don't See,* 2010.
[176] Summers, *The Arrogance of Power, op. cit.,* p. 289.

of Pigs. As President, he decided with his National Security Advisor Henry Kissinger and under the influence of the corporate lobby Council on Latin America, to overthrow the president of Chile, Salvador Allende, elected in 1970. In 1976, the Select Committee on Intelligence established that, before the inauguration of Allende, the CIA had tried to bribe the commander in chief of the Chilean Army, René Schneider Chereau, into leading a military coup. But the general was faithful to the Constitution of his country and eventually became an obstacle to the planned coup. In response, a CIA team led by David Atlee Phillips assassinated the general and then orchestrated a disinformation campaign designed to blame the murder on Allende. $10 million was spent in efforts to corrupt other army officers in preparation for the coup, which materialized in September 11, 1973, when Allende was attacked in his presidential palace, and "committed suicide." The United States would help maintain for seventeen years the fascist dictatorship of General Pinochet.

In 1974, the new president Gerald Ford asked his new CIA director William Colby to clean up the Agency. Colby fired a number of officers and agents and, in late December, submitted to the Attorney General a 693-page document (colloquially called the "Family Jewels") on the illegal operations of the CIA. Ford then found himself forced to appoint a Presidential commission headed by Vice-President Nelson Rockefeller; the Rockefeller Commission revealed various abuses, but was mostly tasked with damage control; unsurprisingly, its report concluded that there was "no credible evidence" of CIA involvement in the assassination of President Kennedy.[177] Ford's initiative, however, was soon overtaken by the Senate, which created its own commission led by Democrat Frank Church, to investigate the "Governmental Operations with Respect to Intelligence Activities." The Church Committee published between 1975 and 1976 fourteen separate reports on the abuses perpetrated by intelligence agencies. Meanwhile, the House of Representatives also headed up its own commission, under the direction of Otis Pike. The reports of the Church and Pike Committees demonstrated the CIA's involvement in assassinations or attempted assassinations of foreign leaders like Patrice Lumumba, Fidel Castro, Rafael Trujillo and Ngo Dinh Diem. The findings led to a swell of public outcry, and forced Ford to issue an Executive Order prohibiting operations "involved in the murder of a political leader for political purposes."[178] Now aware of the Agency's assassination activities, the American public began to suspect that such activities could be linked to the Dallas murder. Abraham Zapruder's film, broadcast on television in March 1975, would further help to raise an urgent request to reconsider the conclusions of the Warren Commission, leading the House of Representatives in 1976 to create the

---

[177] Ford Presidential Library:
www.fordlibrarymuseum.gov/library/document/0005/7288238.pdf
[178] Baker, *Family of Secrets, op. cit.*, p. 251-62.

House Select Committee on Assassinations (HSCA) to reopen the investigation into the assassination of John F. Kennedy and Martin Luther King (Robert Kennedy was not officially included).

The HSCA, however, met with fierce political opposition. Its General Counsel Richard Sprague, who had refused to sign a confidentiality clause on all documents provided by the CIA, became the target of a violent defamation campaign and was forced to resign; he was then replaced by Robert Blakey, who accepted the rules of the CIA and the lone gunman narrative. Robert Tannenbaum, Sprague's Deputy Counsel in charge of the investigation into Kennedy, resigned in turn stating that the HSCA was now engaged in the construction of a "false history," as he explained in 1995. Simultaneously in January 1976, CIA director William Colby, who was proving too cooperative with the Church Commission, was replaced by George H. W. Bush. Together Bush and Blakey would kill the investigation by agreeing to appoint George Joannides as the intermediary between the CIA and the HSCA; the press did not realize until much later that Joannides had been in 1963 the CIA agent charged with the management and financing of the Directorio Revolucionario Estudiantil (DRE) or Cuban Student Directorate—the group of Cuban exiles most virulently against Kennedy. The HSCA could never break the surface of the plot, and contented itself only to conclude a "probable conspiracy."

At the same time new books were published—and praised by corporate medias—to debunk "conspirationist" inquiries and defend the Warren Commission's lone gunner theory. First came *The Search for JFK*, by Joan and Clay Blair Jr (1976), then Edward Jay Epstein's *Legend: The Secret World of Lee Harvey Oswald* (1978), commissioned by *The Reader's Digest*.[179] The information war goes on until today, and every new breakthrough in the quest for JFK Truth is counter-attacked. Gerald Posner's *Case Closed* appeared just after Oliver Stone's film motivated the *President John F. Kennedy Assassination Records Collection Act* in 1992. Fifteen years later, we had *Reclaiming History* by Vincent Bugliosi (2007), and again in 2012, Bill O'Reilly's *Killing Kennedy*. More importantly and more efficiently, at the time of the Church Committee and the HSCA started what James DiEugenio calls the second or the posthumous assassination of JFK, through a constant flow of anti-Kennedy books aiming at destroying the Kennedy "myth" or "mystique," by attacking his character and vilifying his family. For "assassination is futile if a man's ideas live on through others," so it is necessary for Kennedy's assassins to "smother any legacy that might linger."[180]

---

[179] Baker, *Family of Secrets, op. cit.,* p. 264.

[180] James DiEugenio, "The Posthumous Assassination of JFK", in *The Assassinations: Probe Magazine on JFK, MLK, RFK, and Malcolm X,* edited by Jim DiEugenio and Lisa Pease, Feral House, 2003.

12. "Mr. George Bush of the CIA"

George H. W. Bush would remain only a year at the head of the CIA, but under his leadership it took on profound changes, resulting in its being further removed from Congress' oversight. Additionally, the power of the Agency would be reinforced by an executive order from Ford that reorganized the intelligence community by increasing the authority of the CIA over all other agencies of military intelligence. Bush's successor, Stanfield Turner (appointed by Carter in 1976), would again, like William Colby, try to discipline the CIA by removing 600 CIA agents involved in covert operations. But instead of ending covert operations, these measures would simply shift temporarily their control from the CIA to the National Security Council; this is illustrated by the close collaboration between Carter's National Security Advisor Zbigniew Brzezinski and his assistant Robert Gates, a CIA veteran who would then return as CIA director under President Reagan. Besides, firing a CIA agent does not mean that he is suddenly out of the loop; it may just provide him with better coverage under covert financing. As Reagan's Vice-President, Bush maintained close ties with some of his former CIA colleagues, whom he employed to carry out secret and illegal operations in Central America. Under Bush's discreet supervision, as Vice-President then as President, covert activities abroad would also be partly outsourced to foreign military or intelligence services, and self-financed by revenues from weapons and drugs trafficking.

But who really is George H. W. Bush? Unlike Johnson and Nixon, both of middle-class origin, he comes from a family two generations into the political and economic upper spheres. The Bush saga is inseparable from that of the Harrimans, who are themselves associated with the Rockefellers since Edward H. Harriman took control of the Union Pacific Railroad in 1898 (for his ruthless ways akin to John D. Rockefeller's, Harriman was declared an "undesirable citizen" by Theodore Roosevelt and sentenced under the anti-trust laws in 1904). Thanks to the United States' entry into war in 1917, Samuel Bush made himself useful to Percy Rockefeller, owner of Remington Arms, while acting as member of the War Industries Board (the market-place of the military-industrial complex, so to speak). In 1919, Rockefeller rewarded Samuel Bush by introducing him into the bank Harriman & Co, founded by Averell Harriman. Prescott Bush, son of Samuel, in his turn would join Harriman & Co after graduating from Yale and being initiated into Yale's secret society Skull & Bones — in the same class as Roland Harriman, Averell's brother. In 1921, Prescott married the daughter of the president of Harriman & Co, George Herbert Walker (also a member of Skull & Bones), and three years later named his firstborn son: George Herbert Walker Bush. In 1926, Prescott became Vice-President of Harriman & Co; in 1928, Harriman & Co bought Dresser Industries, a tech producer for the energy and natural resources field, and, shortly after the stock market crash of 1929, Harriman's bank merged with Brown Brothers to form Brown Brothers Harriman (whose lawyers would include the Dulles brothers). Prescott Bush developed Dresser into an emergent force in the military-industrial complex during the 1930s, through the acquisition of several arms companies. His son, George H. W. would join with Dresser as well, after graduating from Yale and Skull & Bones in 1948. When Dresser moved its headquarters to Dallas in 1950, the reins of the company were entrusted to another Skull & Bones member, Neil Mallon, who would take George under his wing. In 1954, George ventured into the petroleum business with the creation of Zapata Offshore, a provider of offshore platforms in the Caribbean, headquartered in Houston, Texas.

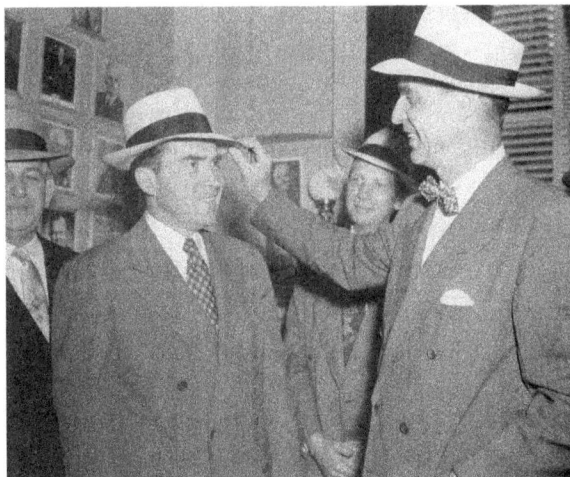

Nixon is a creature of Wall Street and an appointee of Prescott Bush. Prescott, however, resented him for not choosing his son George H. W. as Vice-President, and Russ Baker thinks he is not without responsibility in Nixon's downfall. Prescott was an unforgiving man, as appears in his letter of consolation to Allen Dulles's widow in January 1969, where he mentions John Kennedy's firing of Dulles: "I have never forgiven them."[181]

The Bush family belongs to the capitalist aristocracy, heir of the *robber barons* emerged in the late nineteenth century thanks to transportation industries, oil extraction and weapons manufacturing, and deep ties with international banks. Even better than the Rockefellers and Harrimans, and better still than the Dul-

---

[181] Baker, *Family of Secrets, op. cit.,* p. 47.

les, the Bushes managed the merger between finance and politics, bridging Wall Street and Washington. They also typify the influence of the Skull & Bones secret society, whose exclusively WASP membership is influential in a range of networks such as the Bilderberg Group.[182] For George H.W. Bush, Skull & Bones was a family heritage: his father, his brother Jonathan, his uncles John Walker and George Herbert Walker Jr., his cousins George Herbert Walker III and Ray Walker, his sons George W. and Neil Mallon are all "skullbonians," as are many of the family's friends such as the Harriman brothers or Percy Rockefeller.

Finally, the Bush legacy embodies the anti-democratic tendencies of this handful of super-rich families from the 20th Century. In 1930, Prescott Bush opposed Roosevelt's New Deal. In 1942, the Union Banking Corporation, a subsidiary of Harriman & Co, co-directed by Prescott and his stepfather George Herbert Walker, was seized by the Roosevelt administration under the Trading with the Enemy Act, for its links with Fritz Thyssen, the main financier of the Third Reich (as Thyssen boasts in his book, *I Paid Hitler*). With such a controversial family history, George H. W. Bush probably could never have become President without first flying under the democratic radar as Vice-President.

George H. W. Bush on a Skull & Bones photo. Was this secret society, whose influence grew in the 60s, targeted by Kennedy in his enigmatic speech to the American Newspaper Publishers Association, on April 27, 1961: "The very word 'secrecy' is repugnant in a free and open society; and we are as a people inherently and historically opposed to secret societies, to secret oaths and secret proceedings."[183]

In addition to his membership in the world of high finance, George Bush represents another aspect of U.S. deep politics after the war: its ties with the Intelligence underworld and the CIA in particular. Before becoming Vice-President under Reagan in 1984, Bush had been Director of the CIA during the brief presidency of Gerald Ford, as mentioned above. In order to get this position, he swore before Congress to have never previously worked for the CIA. He was lying: a note from November 29, 1963 by J. Edgar Hoover with the subject line "Assassination of President Kennedy" mentions that a certain "Mr. George Bush of the Central Intelli-

---

[182] See the list of members in Anthony Sutton, *America's Secret Establishment: Introduction to the Order,* Research Publishings, 1983.

[183] Audio recording on JFK Library: www.jfklibrary.org/Search.aspx?nav=N:4294871658

gence Agency" was warned orally by the Agency of the risk that "some mis-guided anti-Castro group might capitalize on the present situation and under-take an unauthorized raid against Cuba, believing that the assassination of President John F. Kennedy might herald a change in U.S. Policy." The "anti-Castro group" in question was probably the Directorio Revolucionario Estudi-antil (DRE), or another group armed by the CIA. George H. W. Bush, faced with this note in 1985, denied being the "George Bush" mentioned, but there is more evidence of his secret collaboration with the CIA from 1953 on. One can assume he had been introduced in the Agency by Neil Mallon, whom he con-sidered his "favorite uncle," and whose name he would give to his first son, Neil Mallon Bush; according to a letter from his father Prescott Bush dated March 26, 1953, Mallon was providing services to the CIA, "especially in the procurement of individuals to serve in that important agency." George Bush was also associated, through his Zapata venture, with Thomas Devine, a man described in a 1975 internal report to the CIA (declassified in 1996) as "a for-mer CIA Staff Employee."[184] It appears as well that Zapata Offshore was in-strumental in facilitating the 1961 invasion of the Bay of Pigs — located, as it happens, in the Zapata Peninsula — with Bush contributing to the recruitment and financing for Operation 40, in partnership with another Texan oil industry tycoon, Jack Crichton, and in conjunction with Felix Rodriguez, a Cuban offi-cer deeply involved in the Bay of Pigs.

Even though George Bush has always maintained his faith in the conclusions of the Warren Commission, he could not have been fooled by such a fable. He was 38 years old when Kennedy was assassinated. He had just launched his first campaign for the Senate, violently attacking Kennedy and his policy, and calling for "a new government-in-exile invasion of Cuba." Curiously, just like Johnson and Nixon, he was in Dallas on the morning of November 22, 1963, after attending a night meeting of the American Association of Oil Drilling Contractors at the Sheraton-Dallas Hotel, where members of the Secret Service were also housed. Furthermore, at 1:45 pm, an hour and 15 minutes after Ken-nedy was shot, Bush did something odd: he made a phone call to the FBI, pre-tending to be in the city of Tyler (a hundred miles from Dallas). His call was immediately recorded in a memo (declassified in 1993, but disclosed by the *San Francisco Examiner* in 1988), stating that: "Mr. GEORGE H. W. BUSH, President of the Zapata Off-shore Drilling Company, Houston, Texas" has called—requesting his call to "be kept confidential"—to report that he had heard that a certain James Parrott "has been talking of killing the President."

---

[184] Baker, *Family of Secrets, op. cit.,* p. 7, 78, 12.

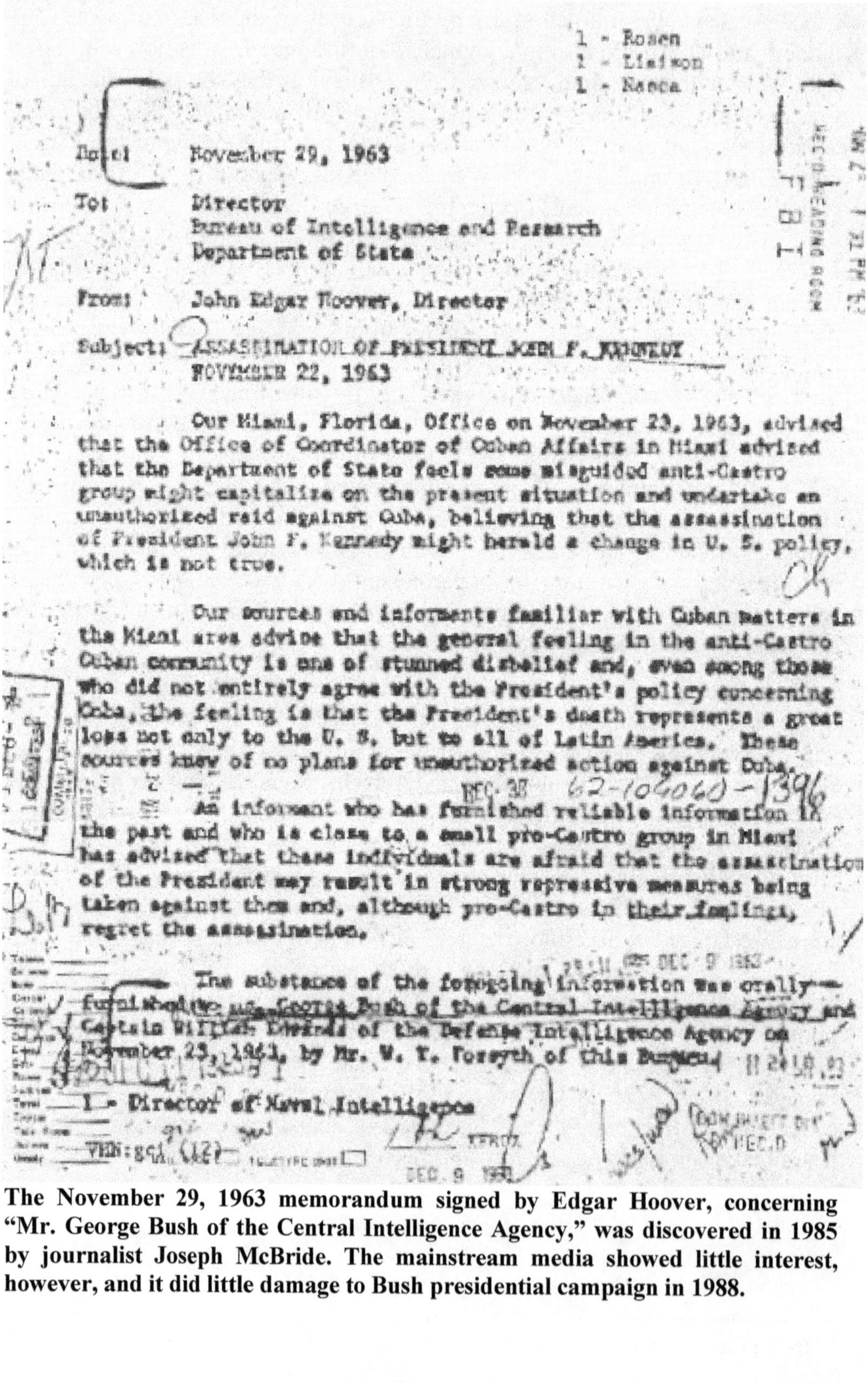

1 - Rosen
1 - Liaison
1 - Nasca

Date: November 29, 1963

To: Director
Bureau of Intelligence and Research
Department of State

From: John Edgar Hoover, Director

Subject: ASSASSINATION OF PRESIDENT JOHN F. KENNEDY
NOVEMBER 22, 1963

Our Miami, Florida, Office on November 23, 1963, advised that the Office of Coordinator of Cuban Affairs in Miami advised that the Department of State feels some misguided anti-Castro group might capitalize on the present situation and undertake an unauthorized raid against Cuba, believing that the assassination of President John F. Kennedy might herald a change in U. S. policy, which is not true.

Our sources and informants familiar with Cuban matters in the Miami area advise that the general feeling in the anti-Castro Cuban community is one of stunned disbelief and, even among those who did not entirely agree with the President's policy concerning Cuba, the feeling is that the President's death represents a great loss not only to the U. S. but to all of Latin America. These sources knew of no plans for unauthorized action against Cuba.

An informant who has furnished reliable information in the past and who is close to a small pro-Castro group in Miami has advised that these individuals are afraid that the assassination of the President may result in strong repressive measures being taken against them and, although pro-Castro in their feelings, regret the assassination.

The substance of the foregoing information was orally furnished to Mr. George Bush of the Central Intelligence Agency and Captain William Edwards of the Defense Intelligence Agency on November 23, 1963, by Mr. W. T. Forsyth of this Bureau.

1 - Director of Naval Intelligence

The November 29, 1963 memorandum signed by Edgar Hoover, concerning "Mr. George Bush of the Central Intelligence Agency," was discovered in 1985 by journalist Joseph McBride. The mainstream media showed little interest, however, and it did little damage to Bush presidential campaign in 1988.

The memo proceeds: "BUSH stated that he was proceeding to Dallas, Texas, [and] would remain in the Sheraton-Dallas Hotel and return to his residence on 11-23-63." Parrott, a harmless young activist of the Houston Republican Club that Bush attended, was quickly exonerated. Given the circumstances, it is difficult to ignore the impression that the true purpose of Bush's telephone call was to give himself an alibi. As investigator Russ Baker has it: "By telling the FBI he was planning to go there [Dallas], he created a misleading paper trail suggesting that his stay in Dallas was many hours after Kennedy's shooting, rather than a few hours before."[185] What was George H. W. Bush trying to hide? Did he know the CIA was involved in the assassination, and did he fear being suspected as a CIA agent connected to one of the anti-Castro groups most hostile to Kennedy? Or was he afraid to have been picked as the patsy? The answer, of course, is blowing in the wind.

The last disturbing element linking George H. W. Bush to the Kennedy assassination is a letter addressed to him by George De Mohrenschildt on September 5, 1976, while he was Director of the CIA. De Mohrenschildt felt he was being harassed ever since he had sent a few pages of his biography to the Danish journalist Willem Oltmans, as he explained to George Bush, to whom he had already a previous letter signed, "Your old friend G. DeMohrenschildt." "Dear George, You will excuse this hand-written letter. Maybe you will be able to bring a solution into the hopeless situation I find myself in. My wife and I find ourselves surrounded by some vigilantes; our phone bugged; and we are being followed everywhere. [...] We are driven to insanity by this situation. I have been behaving like a damn fool ever since my daughter Nadya died from cystic fibrosis over three years ago. I tried to write, stupidly and unsuccessfully, about Lee H. Oswald and must have angered a lot of people—I do not know. But to punish an elderly man like myself and my highly nervous wife is really too much. Could you do something to remove the net around us? This will be my last request for help and I will not annoy you anymore." Two months later, De Mohrenschildt was admitted to a psychiatric hospital, and six months later, in March 1977, he was found dead in his office with a bullet in his head, the same day that a HSCA investigator had contacted him through his daughter.[186]

---

[185] Baker, *Family of Secrets, op. cit.*, p. 50, 65.
[186] Baker, *Family of Secrets, op. cit.*, p. 262-4.

13. Secret Dirty Wars of Vice-President Bush

Ousted from the CIA by President Carter, George H. W. Bush would return to the center of national politics as vice-presidential candidate on Ronald Reagan's ticket in 1980. The lesson of Nixon's secret sabotage of Johnson's peace plan to steal the presidency from the Democrat candidate had not been lost on the Republicans, particularly on a deep-political animal like Bush. Not unlike Johnson in 1968, Carter was hoping to tip the balance in his favor and win a second term by securing the release in October 1980 of 52 hostages who had been captured in Tehran's U.S. Embassy one year prior, in retaliation for Carter's unhappy decision to grant political asylum to the Shah fleeing the Islamic Revolution. Negotiations with Iran were about to succeed, and the return of the hostages was imminent, but Carter's "October Surprise" was sabotaged by a team of Republicans including George Bush and Robert Gates, with the help of an Israeli intelligence officer named Ari Ben-Menashe who acted as intermediary with Iran, and set a meeting in Paris in October 1980.[187] The Bush team presented Iran with an overbid on Carter's deal, which included illegal arms sales, and thereby reached a secret agreement to delay the release of the hostages. Iran was then at war with Iraq, which was armed by 24 U.S. arms firms legally exporting weapons to Baghdad (including biological weapons). Deprived of his October Surprise like Johnson before him, Carter lost his reelection. The hostages were finally returned on January 21, 1981, the very day of Reagan's inauguration, giving him a boost of popularity from the start. Weapons began to be shipped to Iran in February 1981.

Reagan's Presidency was the "golden age" of the military-industrial complex. William Casey, who moved from Reagan's Campaign Manager to Director of the CIA, turned the CIA back into the tool of imperialism that it was at its beginning. He relied on the CIA's competitor the DIA (Defense Intelligence Agency), to force the CIA into supporting his policy by publishing a document entitled "The Soviet Role in Revolutionary Violence," which convinced

---

[187] Parry, *America's Stolen Narrative, op. cit.,* pos. 3228-3493.

Reagan and shaped his militaristic foreign policy. Thanks to the Strategic Defense Initiative, a space defense plan better known as "Star Wars," the defense budget exploded.

On March 30, 1981, President Reagan was the victim of a failed attempt on his life. The next day, the *Houston Post* revealed on its front page that "Bush's Son Was to Dine with Suspect's Brother." Scott Hinckley, the would-be assassin's brother, was invited on the 31st by Neil Bush, elder son of the Vice-President. Moreover, in 1978, Neil Bush had stayed in the town of Lubbock, Texas, where John Hinckley was studying. Jack Hinckley, John and Scott's father, was working for World Vision, a front organization for the CIA. These coincidences were not investigated, and it was concluded that John Hinckley was simply mentally deranged. Hinckley is, to this day, confined in a psychiatric hospital. A note he once wrote about a conspiracy of which he believes he had been the instrument was regarded as further proof of his insanity.[188]

President Reagan was also the oldest President in the history of the United States. Subject to long naps but with a short attention span, he delegated most of his powers, leaving Bush to act on his own initiative in many areas. According to White House Press Secretary James Brady, "George [was] involved in all the national security stuff because of his special background as CIA director."[189] Through a series of directives, Bush was placed at the control center of all secret operations. He therefore played a key decision-making role in the so-called Iran-Contra scheme, which involved two distinct operations: firstly, the secret arms sales to Iran, which continued after the release of the hostages; and secondly, the shuffling of the profits from these sales to support the Contras, terrorists groups opposed to the Nicaraguan revolutions.

The sale of arms to Iran, which violated an official embargo, was conducted through Israel, who saw the benefit of having its two worst enemies, the Iraqis and Iranians, killing each other for eight years (1980-1988). The operations

---

[188] Webster Tarpley, *George Bush: The Unauthorized Biography,* Executive Intelligence Review, 1992 (reprint Progressive Press), p. 363-84.

[189] Tarpley, *George Bush, op. cit.,* p. 365.

would help forge deep links between American and Israeli military-industrial complexes, as well as between their intelligence services. In 1981, for example, photos obtained by the American KH-11 spy satellite made it possible for Israel to destroy the French-made Iraqi nuclear center in Osirak, on June 7, 1981. The profits generated by the sale of arms to Iran will be siphoned off to Latin America to support the Contras, militias opposed to the Sandinista revolutionaries in Nicaragua (named in memory of Augusto Sandino, the democratic President assassinated in 1934). The Contras had no support among the Nicaraguan people, and brought a reign of terror to the villages. Alerted by reports of cruelty, including murder, rape, torture, mutilation, kidnapping and racketeering, the Carter administration had discontinued U.S. support for the Contras. In 1982 Congress passed the Boland Amendment, completed in 1984, which prohibited any governmental entity to support, directly or indirectly, paramilitary operations in Nicaragua. But the National Security Council and the CIA circumvented the ban, secretly training, arming and funding the Contras in Honduras, thereby maintaining a Nicaraguan civil war that would claim 30,000 lives. Delivery of weapons to the Contras came in large part from Israel: some had been confiscated from the Palestine Liberation Organization during the invasion of Lebanon in 1982, others had been purchased in Poland and Czechoslovakia and smuggled through Yugoslavia. In Latin America, the shipments went through Honduras, Bolivia and Panama. On October 25, 1984, the *Associated Press* disclosed a manual written by the CIA for the Contras, entitled *Operaciones guerra de guerrillas en sicológicas (Psychological Operations in Guerrilla Warfare)*. The manual explains how "Armed Propaganda Teams" can build political support for the Contras through intimidation, violence and disinformation. It recommends "selective use of violence for propagandistic effects" and stresses that, in order to "neutralize" politicians, "if possible, professional criminals will be hired, to carry out specific selective jobs." To turn the people against the socialist government, it is recommended that they move "demonstrators into clashes with the authorities, to provoke riots or shootings, which lead to the killing of one or more persons, who will be seen as the martyrs; this situation should be taken advantage of immediately against the Government to create even bigger conflicts."[190]

---

[190] Joanne Omang et Aryeh Neier, *The CIA's Nicaragua Manual: Psychological Operations in Guerrilla Warfare,* Vintage Books, 1985.

The technique promoted in 1984 by the CIA in Nicaragua will be employed, but without success, in 2002 in Venezuela. On April 11th, generals bought by the National Endowment for Democracy (a CIA front) overthrew President Hugo Chavez by pretending that his supporters, the *Chavistas*, had shot and killed a dozen anti-Chavez demonstrators. But thanks to a popular uprising, the coup failed and Chavez, kidnapped by the generals, was finally liberated and reinstalled. It will be proven that the victims had in fact been shot by snipers for the purpose of justifying the coup, prepared already six months earlier with CIA's help.[191]

The press' unveiling of the "Iran-Contra" scandal would bring the ordeal to an end in 1986. A congressional committee will indict a "cabal of zealots," blamed for having nothing but a "disdain for the law," including Lieutenant Colonel Oliver North of the National Security Council. Bush, who had learned to tread softly and leave few fingerprints, claimed to have been kept "out of the loop," and narrowly escaped charges, despite evidence of his direct contact with the Cuban Felix Rodriguez, one of the key men in the Nicaragua operations. Rodriguez was, as documented above, a veteran officer of the Bay of Pigs, and as such, a suspect in the Kennedy assassination. Once elected President, Bush pardoned all those indicted in the investigation, and his Presidential pardon canceled the trial in which he would have been called to testify.

---

[191] See John Pilger's documentary *The War on Democracy,* 2007.

After Kennedy's assassination, Cuban exile Felix Rodriguez worked under the CIA in Nicaragua then in Bolivia, where he hunted down Che Guevara. He is here posing with Che on October 9, 1967, before having him shot (and keeping his Rolex watch as a trophy). In the 70s, Rodriguez worked in Vietnam for Operation Phoenix, responsible for the murder of about 200,000 civilians. In the 80s, he was involved in the illegal support of the Contras of Nicaragua, for which he had frequent contacts with Vice-President George H. W. Bush.[192]

The covert operations of the Reagan-Bush administration also had important repercussions in the Republic of Panama, a country officially liberated from the Columbians in 1903 by the Americans, who thereby took control of the future Suez Canal. In 1978, Jimmy Carter signed a treaty with President Omar Torrijos providing for the transfer of the Canal Zone to the Panama government and the evacuation of U.S. occupation troops by the end of the 20th century. But the CIA maintained close ties since 1968 with the right arm of Torrijos and Chief of Intelligence, Major Manuel Noriega, whose power relied heavily on narco-business. Eight months after the accession to power of the Reagan-Bush team, July 31, 1981, Torrijos' staff plane exploded in midair, and Noriega was placed as the supreme commander of the armed forces and the Chief Executive of the country. While the NSC and the CIA extended their actions against the Sandinistas in Nicaragua, Noriega aided the delivery of arms to the Contras. The aircraft being used to deliver weapons to Panama would depart from the airport in Mena, Arkansas, later to return under military protection with cocaine purchased from cartels in Colombia. One of the key figures involved in this double trafficking was an Israeli man named Michael Harari, former head of covert operations at Mossad. He had become essential to Noriega since 1982, ensuring his safety through a team of Israeli security personnel and enemy surveillance, as well as money laundering services through Swiss banks. Harari's main CIA contact was Felix Rodriguez.[193] In this way, the CIA became a major player in the explosion of cocaine trafficking and consumption in the 80s. Before that, it had facilitated the trafficking of

---

[192] Spartacus Educational : www.spartacus.schoolnet.co.uk/JFKroderiguez.htm
[193] Andrew and Leslie Cockburn, *Dangerous Liaison: The Inside Story of the U.S.-Israeli Covert Relationship,* HarperCollins, 1991, p. 244-61.

heroin from Asia in the 70s, during the wars in Vietnam and Afghanistan, as was revealed by journalist Gary Webb in 1997.[194]

In an attempt to defuse the Iran-Contra scandal, the Reagan-Bush administration decided to turn against Noriega. In 1987 he was formally charged with drug trafficking and racketeering in the United States. The Senate Subcommittee on Terrorism, Narcotics and International Operations concluded that, "the saga of Panama's General Manuel Antonio Noriega represents one of the most serious foreign policy failures for the United States. […] It is clear that each U.S. government agency which had a relationship with Noriega turned a blind eye to his corruption and drug dealing, even as he was emerging as a key player on behalf of the Medellin Cartel."[195] In December 1989, under pretext of the execution of an American soldier by Panamanian soldiers, President George H. W. Bush sent 26,000 troops to Panama as part of Operation Just Cause, causing thousands of deaths, mostly civilians, and the exodus of 20,000 or 30,000 refugees.

George H. W. Bush can't help laughing while mentioning the lone gunman theory of the Warren Commission, in his eulogy of Gerald Ford on the 2nd of January, 2007, as even the *New York Times* reporter mentioned in his transcript of the speech: "After a deluded gunman assassinated President Kennedy (Bush laughed!), our nation turned to Gerald Ford and a select handful of others to make sense of that madness. And the conspiracy theorists can say what they will, but the Warren Commission report will always have the final definitive say on this tragic matter."[196]

---

[194] Gary Webb, *Dark Alliance: the CIA, the Contras, and the Crack Cocaine Explosion,* Seven Stories Press, 1999.

[195] Mark Tran, "Manuel Noriega – from US friend to foe", *The Guardian,* April 27, 2010, www.guardian.co.uk/world/2010/apr/27/manuel-noriega-us-friend-foe.

[196] *New York Times*: www.nytimes.com/2007/01/02/washington/02cnd-ford-ghwb.html?_r=0. Watch on YouTube, "George Bush Sr. smiling at JFK Assassination": www.youtube.com/watch?v=jpRiQleaBkQ

BOOK TWO:
9/11

14. From Cold War to Clash of Civilizations

On July 25, 1990, the American ambassador to Iraq, April Glaspie, asked Saddam Hussein to explain his military movements along the Kuwait border. Saddam reminded her of the situation: Iraq, ruined by the war with Iran, found itself unable to repay the 80 billion dollars borrowed from Kuwait, a country which Saddam believes Iraq protected during the conflict. Furthermore, Saddam was accusing Kuwait of overproduction in the much-coveted oil industry, which was seen to weaken Iraq's market competitiveness, and to demonstrate a non-compliance of certain drilling agreements. Finally, Saddam considered Kuwait as *ipso facto* Iraq, given its artificial creation by the British Empire after the First World War. Glaspie indicated to Saddam that Washington took no position on the disagreements between Kuwait and Iraq, and that in general, her administration had "no opinion on the Arab-Arab conflicts." She assured him that regardless of Iraq-Kuwait relations, the United States had no intention "to start an economic war against Iraq." Saddam, who had secretly taped the discussion and later made it public, logically interpreted America's promise of non-interference as a sort of "yellow light." On August 2nd, he launched the invasion of Kuwait, taking military control of the country within two days. The Arab League sought to negotiate the withdrawal of Iraqi troops with a diplomatic compromise, and Saddam, a longtime supporter of the Palestinian cause, even pledged to withdraw if Israel withdrew from the territories it illegally occupied, but the administration of George H. W. Bush rejected all proposed plans.[197] Instead, through the use of fake information, they led the Saudis to believe that Saddam had plans to invade their country as well, and thereby convinced them to accept the stationing of U.S. troops on their soil. In January 1991, the U.S. launched Operation Desert Storm, dropping 940,000 bombs, including the experimental "combined effect munitions," or "cluster bombs," containing each 200 scattering sub-munitions.

---

[197] Jonathan Cook, *Israel and the Clash of Civilizations: Iraq, Iran and the Plan to Remake the Middle East,* Pluto Press, 2008, p. 19-21.

A young Kuwaiti named Nay-
irah al-Sabah spoke before
the Security Council of the
United Nations on October
10, 1990. In a sobbing voice
interrupted by tears, she told
having seen Saddam Hus-
sein's soldiers rush into a
hospital and pull babies out
of incubators to throw them
on the floor. It was later revealed that she was a member
of the royal family and had
taken drama courses—and,
of course, had never wit-
nessed the scenes she described (though she may have believed them to be true).

Emboldened by the success of the first Gulf War—on the battleground and in
public opinion— President George H. W. Bush postured himself as the
prophet of a "New World Order" in a famous speech to Congress on September 11, 1990, announcing "an era in which the nations of the world, East and
West, North and South, can prosper and live in harmony. [...] A world in
which nations recognize the shared responsibility of freedom and justice. A
world where the strong respect the rights of the weak."[198] So much for propaganda. In the Machiavellian deep state, the avowed goal was to take advantage
of the end of the Cold War for a shift towards an American global empire;
such would be the vision of Zbigniew Brzezinski, the former National Security
Advisor to President Carter, who saw quite frankly the world as *The Grand
Chessboard* (the title of his memoirs published in 1997). What interested him
was the expansion of American imperial power into Eurasia, employing if necessary "maneuver and manipulation in order to prevent the emergence of a
hostile coalition that could eventually seek to challenge America's primacy."
One perceived obstacle to such uncontested expansionism is democracy, for
"democracy is inimical to imperial mobilization"; and, "as America becomes
an increasingly multi-cultural society, it may find it more difficult to fashion a
consensus on foreign policy issues, except in the circumstance of a truly massive and widely perceived direct external threat." Such is the lesson of Pearl
Harbor, Brzezinski notes: "The public supported America's engagement in
World War II largely because of the shock effect of the Japanese attack on
Pearl Harbor."[199]

---

[198] Watch on YouTube, "Bush Before a Joint Session of Congress (September 11, 1990)",
www.youtube.com/watch?v=7iUX3yP9M8g
[199] Zbigniew Brzezinski, *The Grand Chessboard: American Primacy And Its Geostrategic
Imperative,* Basic Books, 2007, p. 198, 211, 24-5.

In 1996, at the beginning of Clinton's second term, a Republican think tank, the Project for a New American Century (PNAC) would develop along the same lines of Brzezinski's logic. Its founders, who adopted the label "neoconservatives," intended to use the defeat of communism as a means to consolidate American hegemony and in so doing, prevent the emergence of a rival power. Their stated goal is to "extend the current *Pax Americana*," which entails "a military that is strong and ready to meet both present and future challenges."[200] In its September 2000 report entitled *Rebuilding America's Defenses*, PNAC anticipates that U.S. forces must become "able to rapidly deploy and win multiple simultaneous large-scale wars." This requires a profound transformation, including a new military corps, the "U.S. Space Forces," to control both space and cyberspace, and the development of "a new family of nuclear weapons designed to address new sets of military requirements." Unfortunately, according to the authors of the report, "the process of transformation [...] is likely to be a long one, absent of some catastrophic and catalyzing event—like a new Pearl Harbor."[201] There is, again, the reference to Pearl Harbor as a politically strategic event. Neither the members of PNAC nor Brzezinski can ignore that the Japanese attack on December 7, 1941, which generated public support in favor of the war and led the Congress to grant President Roosevelt full military power, had been not only foreseen with precision, but deliberately provoked by Washington, while the command of the Hawaii military base had been kept in the dark. Twelve days before Pearl Harbor, the Defense Secretary Henry Stimson summarized a conversation with Roosevelt in his diary: "The question was 'how should we maneuver [the Japanese] into firing the first shot" (Robert Stinnett, *Day of Deceit,* 2000).[202] For all intended readers of PNAC's literature, "Pearl Harbor" is a codeword for "fabricated pretext."

The mobilization of public opinion in favor of an imperial policy can only be accomplished through an enemy attack: in the absence of a real attack, a threat can do, real or imaginary, as long as it is backed by a good propaganda machine. It is here that the slogan invented by Bernard Lewis and echoed by his assistant Samuel Huntington makes its entrance and, given sufficient echo in the mainstream media, becomes the defining myth of the 21st century: before the "New Order World" comes the "Clash of Civilizations."[203] Huntington, who was an advisor to the State Department under Reagan and Bush, considers the relationship between civilizations on the Darwinian mode of "the survival

---

[200] PNAC official website: www.newamericancentury.org/statementofprinciples.htm).

[201] PNAC official website: www.newamericancentury.org/RebuildingAmericasDefenses.pdf

[202] Robert Stinnett, *Day of Deceit: the Truth About FDR and Pearl Harbor*, Simon & Schuster, 2000.

[203] The phrase was first used by Lewis in an article in the September 1990 issue of *The Atlantic Monthly* entitled "The Roots of Muslim Rage."

of the fittest." With that perspective, he sought to provide America with a new enemy, given the decline of the Soviet threat: "The fundamental problem for the West is not Islamic fundamentalism. It is Islam, a different civilization whose people are convinced of the superiority of their culture and are obsessed with the inferiority of their power."[204] Soon the medieval term "crusade" will re-enter the official discourse.

In that struggle for survival between civilizations, only physical force matters, says Huntington: "The West won the world not by the superiority of its ideas or values or religion, but rather by its superiority in applying organized violence. Westerners often forget this fact, non-Westerners never do."[205] At the dawn of the 21st century, the means of such violence were ready for such a new global paradigm, as the Joint Chiefs of Staff acknowledged in their *Joint Vision 2020* booklet published May 30, 2000; there they state the necessity of "transforming the joint force for the 21st Century to achieve full spectrum dominance," this last phrase being defined as "the ability of U.S. forces [...] to defeat any adversary and control any situation across the full range of military operations."[206]

Between 1992 and 1994, a parody of intellectual debate was acted in the press, opposing, on one side, Francis Fukuyama and his prophecy of the "End of History"—meaning "the universalization of Western liberal democracy as the final form of human government"—and, on the other side, Samuel Huntington and his vision of the "Clash of Civilizations." The 9/11 attacks made Huntington look like a visionary, and allowed Bernard Lewis to hammer the message in his *What Went Wrong? The Clash between Islam and Modernity in the Middle East* (2003). Fukuyama and Huntington are both members of the Trilateral Commission (as is Brzezinski); Fukuyama is also a member of PNAC.

With the election in 2000 of George W. Bush, son of George H. W. Bush, two dozen PNAC neoconservatives were placed in key positions of foreign policy. The only thing still missing was a "new Pearl Harbor" to allow the full capacity of their power to be mobilized. The attacks of September 11, 2001, were

---

[204] Samuel Huntington, *The Clash of Civilizations and the Remaking of World Order,* Simon & Schuster, 1996, p. 217.
[205] Huntington, *The Clash of Civilizations, op. cit.,* p. 51.
[206] *Joint Vision 2000*:
www.fs.fed.us/fire/doctrine/genesis_and_evolution/source_materials/joint_vision_2020.pdf

exactly what the PNAC was waiting for. Before September 11th, the PNAC recommended an increase in the annual defense budget of 95 billion dollars. Actually, it has exceeded that. Since the start of the war in Afghanistan, the official Department of Defense base budget exceeds $400 billion, while the "real defense budget," is calculated by the Center for Defense Information at $986.1 billion for 2012.[207] Thus the U.S. spends far more than the rest of the world combined, while continuing to provide half the weapons for the world market. Thus, US policymakers' commitment to the militarization of the planet is reflected in the Federal Budget, and validated, de facto, by the September 11 attacks.

In 2003, Bremer would be promoted Administrator of the Coalition Provisional Authority (CPA), the body that would govern occupied Iraq. Under his leadership, 9 billion dollars disappeared in fraud, corruption and embezzlement, according to a report by the Special Inspector General for Iraq Reconstruction, Stuart Bowen, published January 30, 2005.[208]

Two hours after the towers collapsed, the Chairman of the National Commission on Terrorism, Lewis Paul Bremer, appeared on NBC, calm and assured, explaining: "Bin Laden was involved in the first attack on the WTC which had as its intention doing exactly what happened here, which is the collapse of those towers. He certainly has to be a prime suspect. But there are others in the Middle East, and there are at least two States, Iran and Iraq, which should at least remain on the list as essential suspects." In so many words, Bremer constructed a narrative encompassing the past—by recalling the 1993 attacks against the World Trade Center—and the future—by virtually telling the American people to now expect two wars against Iraq and Iran. When the reporter from NBC drew a predictable parallel between the day's attack and Pearl Harbor, Bremer confirmed: "It is the day that will change our lives. It is the day when the war that the terrorists declared on the US [...] has been brought home to the U.S."[209]

---

[207] Read on antiwar.com/blog/2012/02/20/the-real-us-military-budget-1-trillion/
[208] Read on CNN.com, "Audit: U.S. lost track of $9 billion in Iraq funds", January 31, 2005, edition.cnn.com/2005/WORLD/meast/01/30/iraq.audit/
[209] Watch on YouTube: "Paul Bremer interview, NBC, 12:46, 9/11": www.youtube.com/watch?v=j2pW6WZhZrQ

In the days that followed, the President's speeches (written by the neoconservative David Frum) would characterize the terrorist attack as the trigger for a world war of a new type, one fought against an invisible enemy scattered throughout the Middle East. First, vengeance must come not only against bin Laden, but also against the State harboring him: "We will make no distinction between those who committed these acts and those who harbor them" (September 11). Second, the war is extended to the world: "Our war on terror begins with Al Qaeda, but it does not end there. It will not end until every terrorist group of global reach has been found, stopped and defeated" (September 20).

Seven countries were declared "Rogue States" for their support to global terrorism: Iran, Iraq, Syria, Libya, Sudan, Cuba and North Korea (September 16). Third, any country that does not support Washington will be treated as an enemy: "Every nation, in every region, now has a decision to make. Either you are with us, or you are with the terrorists" (September 20).[210] These new rules would provide a pretext for an inexhaustible aggression against any Muslim country. In a few days, the American people were led into a war against terrorism, then to a war against global terrorism, then a global war against terrorism, finally finding themselves in a world war against Muslim civilization, since all Muslim countries house radical Islamists, and therefore potential terrorists. In this new war, the term "civilian" does not apply, just as "terrorists" will not be treated as soldiers. During October 2001, the Attorney General John Ashcroft put forward for vote his USA PATRIOT ACT [211] that created the status of "illegal combatant"—a category that denied prisoners of war the rights established under the Geneva Convention.

With the WTC rubble still burning, a second event reinforced the terror of the American people and led them to uncritically stand behind their government. On September 18th and October 9th, four letters contaminated with anthrax were mailed, first to Florida and then to New York and Washington, addressed to journalists and senators (curiously, two senators opposed to the USA PATRIOT Act, Tom Daschle and Patrick Leahy). The letters were written in such a way as to clearly identify the author as Muslim: "You cannot stop us. We have this anthrax. You die now. Are you afraid? Death to America. Death to Israel. Allah is great." Twenty-two people were infected and five died. Panic set in. The mail system was blocked with the inspection of billions of letters. For the first time in its history, the Congress closed down. America had its collective mind riveted to the nightmare of biological warfare, while politicians and journalists speculated on the guilt of bin Laden or Saddam Hussein.

---

[210] Bush's speeches can be found on: www.presidentialrhetoric.com/.
[211] USA PATRIOT stands for Uniting and Strengthening America by Providing Appropriate Tools Required to Intercept and Obstruct Terrorism.

Prior to the sending of the contaminated letters, the FBI received an anonymous letter accusing a professor Ayaad Assaad, an American of Egyptian origin, of being a bio-terrorist filled with hatred towards the United States. It was determined that the strains of anthrax were electrostatically treated for better dispersion, the product of sophisticated technology, and came from the military laboratory in Utah where Assaad worked. On October 3, 2001, the FBI arrested and interrogated Assad, but quickly found him innocent. The FBI did not, however, pursue its investigation when it was revealed by two articles in the *Hartford Courant* in 2001 and 2002, that in 1992 laboratory surveillance cameras had captured Lieutenant Colonel Philip Zack entering the storage location illegally, and that, in the same period, pathogens had disappeared from the center. Zack had been discharged from the laboratory after a complaint by Assad for receiving a racist letter co-signed by Zack.[212]

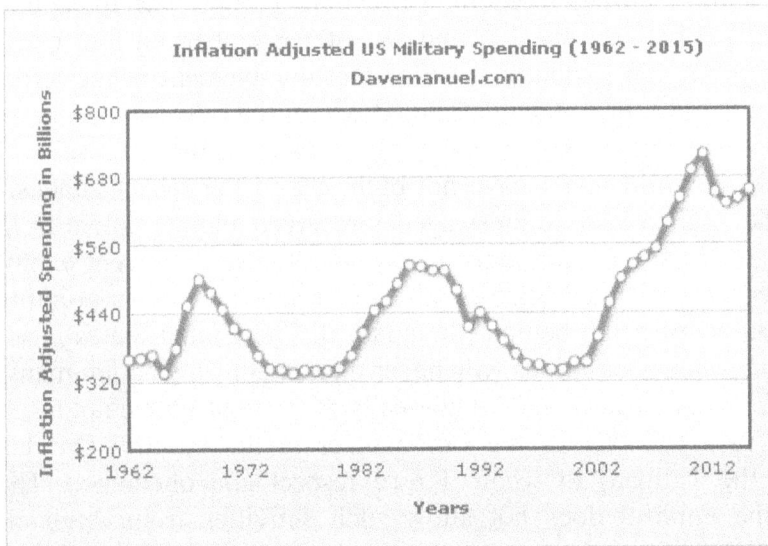

Inflation Adjusted US Military Spending (1962 - 2015)
Davemanuel.com

US military spending, i.e. the death industry's turnover, on the decline after the end of the Cold War, has reached unprecedented heights since 9/11.

[212] Lynne Tuohy and Jack Dolan, "Turmoil in a Perilous Place", December 19, 2001 (s3.amazonaws.com/911timeline/2001/hartfordcourant121901.html), and "Anthrax Missing From Army Lab," January 20, 2002 (www.ph.ucla.edu/EPI/bioter/anthraxmissingarmylab.html).

15. A for "Afghanistan"

On October 7, 2001 the military offensive in Afghanistan began, marketed to the world as Operation Enduring Freedom. The official purpose was to capture Osama bin Laden. Yet between the 12th and 28th of September, on four occasions in the Arab press, bin Laden had denied any involvement in the terror attack. On September 16th, in a statement broadcast on the international news channel Al Jazeera and relayed by several Western media outlets, he said: "I would like to tell the world that I have not orchestrated the recent attacks." That same day, the Afghan Islamic Press agency received another denial from bin Laden, translated in the French daily *Le Monde*: "After the recent explosions that occurred in the United States, some Americans have been pointing fingers and accused us of being behind [the attacks]. The United States is accustomed to making such accusations, whenever their enemies, who are many, deal them a blow. On this occasion, I categorically affirm that I have not taken this action [...] I'm a follower of the Commander of the Faithful [Mullah Omar, leader of the Taliban] to whom I owe respect and obedience. The Commander of the Faithful does not allow such activities from Afghanistan."[213] This denial will not discourage the Security Council of the United Nations, on September 18, 2001, from demanding the "immediate and unconditional" delivery of bin Laden by the Taliban.

The Taliban refused to hand over bin Laden without proof of his guilt, but were willing to make concessions to avoid the bombing and invasion of Afghanistan. They rushed an envoy to Washington, proposing to try bin Laden in an international court. All of their proposals were rejected with hardly a look. Two weeks after the attacks in a televised episode of *Meet the Press*, Secretary of State Colin Powell stated that he would present evidence of the guilt of bin Laden. Undoubtedly this well-disciplined soldier, nicknamed Forrest Gump by some detractors, rather naively believed that such evidence existed. The next

---

[213] Philippe Broussard, "En dépit des déclarations américaines, les indices menant à Ben Laden restent minces", *Le Monde,* September 25, 2001.

day, President Bush had to take him by the hand and oversee his retraction: all evidence was classified and therefore inaccessible to the public. On September 28th, in an interview with the Pakistani newspaper *Ummat*, Bin Laden said again: "I have already said that I am not involved in the September 11 attacks in the United States. As a Muslim, I try my best to avoid telling a lie. I had no knowledge of these attacks, nor do I consider the killing of innocent women, children, and other humans an appreciable act. Islam strictly forbids causing harm to innocent women, children, and other people. […] The United States should try to trace the perpetrators of these attacks within itself."[214]

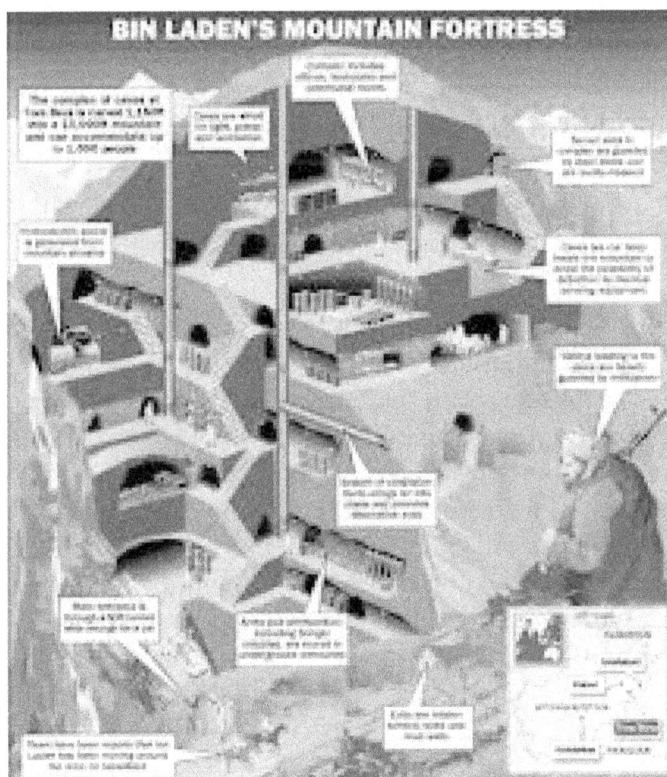

The underground fortress of Tora Bora where bin Laden was reported to hide, as drawn by the London *Times* and commented by Donald Rumsfeld on *Meet the Press* (NBC) on December 2, 2001: "This is serious business. And there is not one of those, there are many of those," Rumsfeld stressed.[215] These cartoon-like complexes, sold to a gullible public, had no more reality than Saddam Hussein's "Weapons of Mass Destruction."

The situation for Afghans is a very bitter déjà-vu. After the intervention in Afghanistan by the Soviet Army in December 1979, the United States gave their support to the mujahedeen resistance, or, such is the official story. The deep truth is the opposite: Zbigniew Brzezinski boasted in an interview with French weekly magazine *Le Nouvel Observateur* in January 1998, to have se-

---

[214] Translation by BBC World Monitoring Service, in Webster Griffin Tarpley, *9/11 Synthetic Terror Made in USA,* Progressive Press, 2008, p. 136-8. Also on www.globalresearch.ca/interview-with-osama-bin-laden-denies-his-involvement-in-9-11/24697.

[215] Watch on YouTube, "Bin Laden's Cave according to Rumsfeld": www.youtube.com/watch?v=FGhGHxw0mSo

cretly armed Afghan Islamists in July 1979 through Pakistani secret services (Inter-Services Intelligence, ISI), in an attempt to lure the USSR into "their Vietnam War."[216] The technique, already experimented successfully in Guatemala and Chile, is to destroy an enemy regime by financing and arming internal opposition and hired mercenaries, that is, use civil war as a proxy for direct intervention. In this case, it was the USSR that was meant to be destabilized, through Afghanistan. From the point of view of Brzezinski, Afghanistan, a backward country without oil, is nothing more than a sacrificial pawn on the "Grand Chessboard" of geostrategic play—despite causing the death and exile of a third of its population. As usual, drug trafficking came in with arms trafficking: the trucks delivering weapons to the Afghan rebels came back with heroin to Karachi, as the Pakistani weekly *The Herald* explained in January 1987. As a result, the poppy fields multiplied, and opium production in Afghanistan increased from 100 tons in 1971 to 800 tons in 1979, reaching 2,000 tons in 1991. After the Soviet withdrawal, the heavily armed warlords and drug traffickers plunged the country into a civil war that killed another half a million people. And legions of fanatic foreign jihadists were made permanently available for international terrorism.[217]

There is still a deeper truth under Brzezinski's story: by embezzling U.S. funds, the Pakistani ISI has turned into a sprawling structure, a state within the State, with a staff estimated at one hundred and fifty thousand. Its goal has always differed from that of its American sponsor: what the U.S. wanted in Afghanistan was to arm an anti-Soviet resistance, while ISI wanted to arm a pro-Pakistani force likely to install a friendly regime. The ISI thus channeled U.S. aid to the extremist movement of Gulbuddin Hekmatyar, who had no popular base and was therefore easily controlled, instead of the moderate Ahmad Shah Massoud and his Northern Alliance, hostile to Pakistan's influence and closer to Iran. From 1994 on, the Pakistani Taliban, armed by ISI with U.S. weapons and money, conquered most of Afghanistan, which then became a shelter for extremists of all kinds.

Until the late 1990s, despite their rhetoric vilifying the Taliban for their violations of human rights, Washington has looked upon the Taliban regime rather favorably, to the extent that the relative stability they brought to the country could afford the opportunity to pursue the construction of an oil and natural gas pipeline connecting Turkmenistan to the Indian Ocean, funded by UNOCAL (Union Oil of California). Even though the relationship was complicated in 1998 because of the attacks against U.S. embassies that some attributed to the Taliban, negotiations continued along with humanitarian aid to

---

[216] "Les révélations d'un ancien conseiller de Carter", *Le Nouvel Observateur*, 15 janvier 1998.
[217] Peter Dale Scott, *American War Machine: Deep Politics, The CIA Global Drug Connection, and the Road to Afghanistan*, Rowman & Littlefield, 2010, p. 40.

the tune of $113 million in 2000, and similar figures in 2001. From February to August 2001, the Bush administration intensified talks with Islamabad, as documented by French specialists Jean-Charles Brisard and Guillaume Dasquié in *Forbidden Truth* (2002). But in July, the United States lost confidence in the ability of the Taliban to stabilize the country, and their negotiators threatened: "either you accept our offer of a carpet of gold, or we bury you under a carpet of bombs."[218] The negotiations broke down, and overnight the Taliban became an obstacle to the project; a military option was then blueprinted. Operationalization only needed an acceptable excuse, which was given on September 11th. The fact that the operation is set in motion less than a month after the attacks serves as proof that it was planned in advance. On October 10th, three days after the start of the war, the U.S. State Department informed the Pakistani Minister of Petroleum that the pipeline project could now be reactivated; unsurprisingly, the U.S. ambassador to Afghanistan, Zalmay Khalilzad and the future new president, Hamid Karzai, had both been consultants to UNOCAL for years.[219]

The Taliban's responsibility for the September 11 attacks was rendered easier to sell to the American public by the fact that the Taliban had just been charged with another crime committed two days before: the assassination of their internal enemy, the commander Ahmad Shah Massoud. The assassins were two Tunisians with Belgian passports pretending to be journalists, but armed with a camera filled with explosives. According to the argument used by Western media, bin Laden and the Taliban sponsored the attack since they feared Massoud would ally with the U.S. as part of the inevitable American retaliation for September 11th. The argument is absurd: how could the Taliban, who had until then failed to defeat Massoud's Northern Alliance, hope to defeat the United States? What bears consideration is rather that Massoud was notoriously hostile to the Americans, who for their part had provided him no support in his fight against the Soviets or the Taliban. If Massoud had been alive after the Taliban's debacle in October 2001, he would have been a roadblock: under UN mandate the United States could not oppose a legitimate leader of the country, and he alone had the resources to unite the various Afghani factions. Massoud would have resisted American economic and political takeover. With Massoud gone the Bush administration was able to install Hamid Karzai, an opportunist that Massoud had jailed in 1994 on charges of being a Pakistani agent.

---

[218] Jean-Charles Brisard and Guillaume Dasquié, *Forbidden Truth: U.S.-Taliban Secret Oil Diplomacy, Saudi Arabia and the Failed Search for Bin Laden,* Nation Books, 2002.
[219] On this episode of deep history, read Stephen Sniegoski, *The Transparent Cabal: The Neoconservative Agenda, War in the Middle East, and the National Interest of Israel,* Enigma Edition, 2008, p. 128-36.

Ahmad Shah Massoud, the "Lion of Panshir," would sometimes name General Charles de Gaulle as his role model—the man who had resisted American domination after WWII. Massoud was supported by Europe and, in April 2001, was invited to speak at the European Parliament in Strasbourg, at the initiative of its French President Nicole Fontaine.

Was September 11 a new "Pearl Harbor"? In other words: Was Al-Qaeda allowed to destroy the World Trade Center (WTC) and kill thousands of innocent people, simply to justify a war? This is the "let-it-happen-on-purpose" (LIHOP) theory: overall relatively harmless because the willful ignorance of a threat can be easily disguised as negligence or incompetence, and doesn't lead to court marshaling—as the Pearl Harbor case shows. It is questionable to what extent this argument is not a safeguard, a damage-control strategy to counter the much more devastating "made-it-happen-on-purpose" (MIHOP) thesis. According to the latter, bin Laden and Al-Qaeda are innocent of the September 11 attacks, which are the biggest false flag operation ever conducted. If the argument seems outrageously implausible to some, it is because of their ignorance of deep state politics, and its well-established legacy of false flag terror. By itself, Operation Northwoods proves that the National Security State is capable of such turpitude, in the absence of a moral President determined to resist it.

Calling themselves the *9/11 Truth Movement*, hundreds of thousands of American citizens are now convinced that "9/11 was an inside job." Although treated with contempt by the mainstream media, the movement is now joined by elected officials like senators Cynthia McKinney and Mike Gravel, not to mention heads of states like late Hugo Chavez of Venezuela and Mahmoud Ahmadinejad of Iran. Their arguments are based on technical analyses provided by engineers and airline pilots who conclude the impossibility of the official explanation, on thousands of conflicting testimonies from survivors and firefighters, and on a multitude of contradictory facts evidenced by independent teams of investigators. Much of the work has been popularized by major video documentaries such as Dylan Avery's *Loose Change* series, now viewed more than 125 million times on Google Video. The following two chapters present a summary of their arguments.

President Hugo Chavez of Venezuela was an informed "9/11 truther," and shared his opinion on September 12, 2006: "The hypothesis is not absurd [...] that those towers could have been dynamited. A building never collapses like that, unless it's with an implosion. The hypothesis that is gaining strength [...] is that it was the same U.S. imperial power that planned and carried out this terrible terrorist attack or act against its own people and against citizens of all over the world. Why? To justify the aggressions that immediately were unleashed on Afghanistan, on Iraq."[220]

---

[220] Read the dispatch by *Associated Press* on September 12, 2006, "Chavez says U.S. may have orchestrated 9/11": www.nbcnews.com/id/13401534/ns/world_news-americas/t/chavez-says-us-may-have-orchestrated/

16. Skyscrapers and Pancakes

Let's begin with the World Trade Center. According to the official account, on the morning of September 11th, the 400-meter high twin skyscrapers were hit successively by two airplanes: first the North Tower (WTC1) at 8:46 am, and then the South Tower (WTC2) at 9:02 am. The planes were identified as two Boeing 767s flying out of Boston, chartered respectively by American Airlines (AA11) and United Airlines (UA175). The South Tower collapsed on itself vertically at 9:59 am, less than an hour after being struck. In an identical fashion, the North Tower collapsed two hours after the impact, at 10:28 am. In total, 2,751 people are reported to have died, including 157 passengers and the crew on both aircrafts.

How could these steel-framed skyscrapers collapse vertically and at the speed of free fall? Common sense infers a relationship of cause and effect between the aircraft impact and the towers' collapse. This is assumed by the Federal Emergency Management Agency (FEMA), the governmental institute that produced the *World Trade Center Building Performance Study* in May 2002.[221] To assuage the protests raised by flagrant inconsistencies in this report, further investigation was entrusted to the National Institute for Standards and Technology (NIST), which would publish its *Final Report on the Collapse of World Trade Center Towers* in September 2005.[222] Both reports are based on the assumption that the planes caused the towers to fall and make no mention of any other hypothesis. More specifically, they argue that the fire resulting from the impact of the planes severely weakened the steel structure, thereby causing the collapse of one floor, which then caused a chain reaction rather callously referred to as "pancake collapse."

However, a few months before the attacks, on January 25, 2001, the head of construction for the WTC, Frank DeMartini, said in a videotaped interview

---

[221] Downloadable on the FEMA website: www.fema.gov/library/viewRecord.do?id=1728
[222] NIST: www.nist.gov/customcf/get_pdf.cfm?pub_id=909236

that each twin tower "was designed to have a fully loaded 707 crash into it. [...] I believe that the building probably could sustain multiple impacts of jet liners." The building's structure, made of two tubes of steel columns and crossbars, was fashioned somewhat like a mosquito net; "this jet liner is like a pencil puncturing this screen netting. It really does nothing to this screen netting."[223] We will never know how DeMartini could explain the collapse of the towers eight months later, because he died that day in his WTC office. But the hundreds of academics gathered around Steven Jones in the association Scholars for 9/11 Truth, and the nearly two thousand architects and engineers who joined Richard Gage in Architects & Engineers for 9/11 Truth, declare that it is physically impossible that the planes and resulting fires would have been sufficient to cause the collapse of the towers. "No steel building has ever been destroyed by fire," noted Bill Manning, editor of *Fire Engineering* magazine in the January 2002 issue, calling the government investigation "a half-baked farce."[224] Steel begins to melt at a temperature close to 1,500°C; after the ball of fire resulting from the airplane fuel's immediate ignition on impact, the fire did not exceed 1,000°C, as the black smoke escaping from the towers indicates. NIST even admitted that "none of the recovered steel samples showed evidence of exposure to temperatures above 600°C for as long as 15 minutes."[225]

According to dissenting engineers, the only explanation for the collapse of the towers is the use of explosives. The theory relies on several observations. First, there are hundreds of testimonies from firefighters and other witnesses who heard and felt the rumblings of explosions before the collapse. In 2005, the New York Fire Department (FDNY) released 503 recorded oral testimonies given by firefighters shortly after the events: 118 of them describe sequences of synchronized explosions just before the collapse, well below the zone of impact. For example, Karin Deshore's testimony, who was in the South Tower: "Somewhere around the middle of the World Trade Center, there was this orange and red flash coming out. Initially it was just one flash. Then this flash just kept popping all the way around the building and that building had started to explode. The popping sound, and with each popping sound it was initially an orange and then red flash came out of the building and then it would just go all around the building on both sides as far as I could see. These popping sounds and the explosions were getting bigger, going both up and down and then all around the building."[226] Hundreds of firefighter survivors,

---

[223] Watch on YouTube, "WTC Towers Designed to Withstand Impact of Loaded Boeing 707": www.youtube.com/watch?v=9fQlC2AIWrY

[224] Bill Manning, "$elling out the investigation", *Fire Engineering,* January 1st, 2002, www.fireengineering.com/articles/print/volume-155/issue-1/departments/editors-opinion/elling-out-the-investigation.html

[225] NIST: www.nist.gov/el/disasterstudies/wtc/

[226] "Witnesses to the Towers' Explosion", on 911review.com/coverup/oralhistories.html

who believe that the towers collapsed due to explosions and not the planes, have formed the association Firefighters for 9/11 Truth. Their testimonies are consistent with those of many civilian survivors.

William Rodriguez, janitor at the WTC, witnessed several powerful explosions in the basement of the North Tower, before and after the impact of the plane. Although decorated for his heroic conduct that day (he saved fifteen persons with his own hands and opened the way for the firefighters), Rodriguez has not been able to make himself heard by the 9/11 Commission, and has become actively involved in the 9/11 Truth movement.[227]

The use of explosives is also the only possible explanation for the horizontal projection of huge sections of the outer frame, clearly visible in the films of the towers' collapse. Some of these chunks of steel weighing hundreds of tons were propelled over 150 meters and lodged in neighboring buildings. Furthermore, only powerful explosives could have caused the pulverization of all the non-metallic parts of the building, such as concrete, furniture and even human bodies—between 2005 and 2006, more than 700 small human fragments were found on the roof of the nearby Deutsche Bank building.[228]

The pyroclastic dust that flooded through the streets at high speed after the collapse, not unlike the dust from a volcano, indicates a high temperature mixture of hot gases and relatively dense solid particles, a phenomenon impossible from a simple collapse.[229]

---

[227] See his website : www.william911.com

[228] Jim Dwyer, "Pieces of Bone Are Found on Building at 9/11 Site", *New York Times,* 6 april 2006: www.nytimes.com/2006/04/06/nyregion/06remains.html?_r=0

[229] Prager, *911: America Nuked, op. cit.,* p. 90. See also the photos published by the online journal *9-11 Research,* "Twin Towers' Dust Clouds", 911research.wtc7.net/wtc/evidence/photos/dust.html

Finally, the presence of molten metal in the wreckage, observed by countless witnesses for more than three weeks after the attack, is inexplicable within the framework of the official theory, but is easily explained by the presence of incompletely burned explosives, their combustion slowed by lack of oxygen. Firefighter Philip Ruvolo testified before Étienne Sauret's camera for his film *Collateral Damages* (2011), "You'd get down below and you'd see molten steel — molten steel running down the channel-ways, like you were in a foundry — like lava."[230] The engineer Leslie Robertson, co-designer of the twin towers, testified at the National Conference of Structural Engineers on October 5, 2001: "As of 21 days after the attack, the fires were still burning and molten steel was still running."[231] In fact, firemen were fighting fires at Ground Zero for 99 days after September 11.

"Collapse" or "explosion"? Words matter. On this photo of the North Tower, we can see steel beams projected hundreds of meters away, explosion far below the breaking point, and the cloud of dust that will turn on the ground into a pyroclastic flow.

In the eyes of many researchers, the truly decisive proof of the use of explosives did not come from the Twin Towers (Towers 1 and 2 of the WTC), but from Tower 7, a neighboring 47-story skyscraper that collapsed at 5:20 pm, about seven hours after the Twin Towers. Its fall, visible on the Internet from multiple angles, occurred at the speed of free fall within seven seconds, both perfectly symmetrical and vertical, looking exactly like a standard "controlled demolition." The mass media remained so discreet about this third tower that few people have heard of its collapse. FEMA barely mentions it in its 2002 report, concluding that office fires had broken out and must have caused the collapse, but that: "The specifics of the fires in WTC 7 and how they caused the building to collapse remain unknown at this time. Although the total diesel fuel on the premises contained massive potential energy, the best hypothesis has only a low probability of occurrence."[232] How can we possibly understand that last sentence, but as the near admission of a lie? Under pressure from citi-

---

[230] Watch on YouTube, "Molten Metal Flows at Ground Zero":
www.youtube.com/watch?v=ZG_ePshHA8o
[231] Christopher Bollyn, *Solving 9-11: The Deception that Changed the World,* 2012, p. 260.
[232] "FEMA's Investigation", *9-11 Research,* 911research:
911research.wtc7.net/wtc/official/fema.html

zen groups dissatisfied with such weak explanations, NIST was tasked with confirming the fire thesis in a special report on Tower 7. The preparation of that report was dragged out until November 2008, after a preliminary report in June 2004.

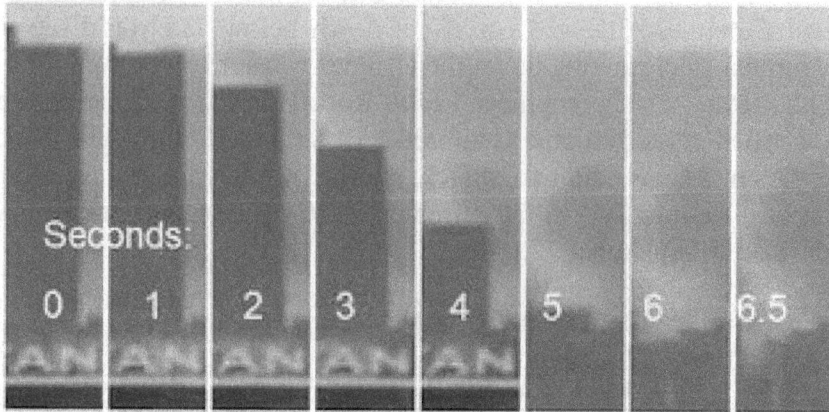

Without having been hit by any plane, and after only a few minor office fires, Building 7 suddenly collapsed vertically and symmetrically at 5:20 pm, at the speed of free fall. When shown the images without knowing their origin, Danish demolition expert Danny Jowenko declared without hesitation: "This is a controlled demolition. [...] This was a hired job, performed by a team of experts." Jowenko died in a frontal car collision with a tree on July 16, 2011.[233]

The collapse of Tower 7 may be the "smoking gun," but it still remains difficult to explain the motive for its demolition. If the collapse of the Twin Towers was done to shock public opinion and prepare for the war against terrorism, what was the purpose of demolishing Tower 7, which no plane had hit and was categorically ignored by the press? We do not know. But some 9/11 investigators conjecture that Tower 7 had to be destroyed because it had been home to the technical center of the plot: indeed, its offices housed the Emergency Command Center of New York Mayor Rudolph Giuliani, as well as government agencies such as the Department of Defense, the CIA and the Secret Service, not to mention the Internal Revenue Service and the Securities and Exchange Commission, which held all the records of the investigation of Enron, the biggest financial scandal in history.

As for the strange timing of the sudden collapse of WTC7, one can assume that it resulted from a flaw in the wiring: the collapse was probably scheduled for the morning, so as to be rendered invisible by the dust cloud from the Twin Towers. This assumption stems from the testimony of two New York City police officers, Michael Hess and Barry Jennings, who were in Tower 7 at 9:15 am when they felt a series of explosions. After having voiced his doubts about

---

[233] See on YouTube : www.youtube.com/watch?v=-zHHvo6U4lA

the official 9/11 story, Jennings died in 2008 of undisclosed causes, two days before the release of the NIST report on Tower 7.[234] Another piece of evidence that WTC7 fell later than scheduled is that television networks were informed of its collapse before it even took place. CNN correspondent Alan Dodds reported by telephone at 11:07 am that a firefighter had just told him that a third building of fifty floors had collapsed. Similarly, Aaron Brown announced on CNN at 4:15 pm: "We are getting information now that one of the other buildings, Building 7 in the World Trade Center complex, is on fire and has either collapsed or is collapsing."[235]

At 4:54 pm, Jane Standley, BBC World correspondent in New York, announced the collapse of WTC7, while it was still seen standing behind her. It didn't actually fall until 25 minutes later. Richard Porter, director of information at BBC World, attributed this "mistake" to "the chaos and confusion of the day."[236]

The man who could certainly give the reason for the collapse of Tower 7 is its owner Larry Silverstein, the real estate shark who also leased the Twin Towers from New York City in the spring of 2001. Interviewed for the PBS documentary *America Rebuilds* in September 2002, Silverstein said about Tower 7: "I remember getting a call from the fire department commander, telling me that they were not sure they were going to be able to contain the fire, and I said, 'We've had such terrible loss of life, maybe the smartest thing to do is pull it.' And they made that decision to pull and we watched the building collapse."[237] Because it is impossible to "pull," i.e. "implode" a skyscraper without weeks of preparation, Silverstein subsequently retracted, explaining that by "pull," he

---

[234] A blog is dedicated to him: barryjenningsmystery.blogspot.fr
[235] YouTube, "Aaron Brown CNN WTC7 not collapsed":
www.youtube.com/watch?v=VerKCCwORMM
[236] YouTube, "BBC Reports Collapse of WTC Building 7 Early":
www.youtube.com/watch?v=ltP2t9nq9fI. Porter's comments is on
www.bbc.co.uk/blogs/theeditors/2007/02/part_of_the_conspiracy.html
[237] David Ray Griffin, *9/11 Contradictions*, Arris Books, 2008, p. 263. YouTube, "Larry Silverstein admits WTC7 was pulled down on 9/11":
www.youtube.com/watch?v=p5DMjnbmhXo

meant "evacuate" the team of firefighters from it, as if that decision was his responsibility. It is important to know that just after acquiring the Twin Towers in the summer of 2001, Silverstein renegotiated the insurance contracts to cover them against terrorist attacks for the amount of $3.5 billion, and made sure that he would retain the right to rebuild after such an event. After the attacks, he took his insurers to court in order to receive double compensation, claiming that the two planes were two separate attacks. After a long legal battle, he pocketed $4.5 billion.[238] This was a good turn of fortune, given the additional fact that the Twin Towers had to be decontaminated for asbestos, a process which had been indefinitely postponed since the 1980s because of its cost estimated at nearly $1 billion in 1989; in 2001, the New York Port Authority had been all too happy to shift responsibility to Silverstein.[239]

---

[238] Tom Topousis, " WTC Insure War is Over," *New York Post,* 24 May, 2007, www.nypost.com/p/news/regional/item_AOAnGWwzd8lRjdDeV1NmOK
[239] "Towers' Destruction 'Solved' Asbestos Problem", *9-11 Research,* 911research.wtc7.net/wtc/evidence/asbestos.html

17. Ghost Planes

The government's narrative on 9/11 says that the Boeing 757 of Flight UA93 (from New Jersey to San Francisco) crashed at Shanksville, Pennsylvania, after the passengers fought the hijackers and prevented them from flying the aircraft into the White House or Camp David. But in the images of the impact site released on the same day, it is impossible to distinguish any wreckage of an airliner; even the reporters who had rushed to the scene were perplexed. The first to arrive there, Jon Meyer of WJAC-TV, an NBC affiliate in Pennsylvania, declared: "I was able to get right up to the edge of the crater. […] All I saw was a crater filled with small, charred plane parts. Nothing that would even tell you that it was the plane. […] There were no suitcases, no recognizable plane parts, no body parts."[240] The Mayor of Shanksville, Ernie Stull, early on the scene with his sister and a friend, declared in March 2003: "Everyone was puzzled, because the call had been that a plane had crashed. But there was no plane. […] Nothing. Only this hole."[241]

Photographer Scott Spangler recalls his surprise when looking at the crash scene of UA93: "I didn't think I was in the right place. I was looking for a wing or a tail. There was nothing, just this pit."[242]

---

[240] www.historycommons.org/entity.jsp?entity=jon_meyer
[241] 911review.com/errors/phantom/flight93.html
[242] www.historycommons.org/entity.jsp?entity=scott_spangler

The Boeing 757 of Flight AA77 (from Washington to Los Angeles) that alleg-edly crashed into the Pentagon also could not be found. French journalist Thierry Meyssan was the first to draw conclusions in *9/11: The Big Lie*, a dis-senting investigation published in March 2002 based on pictures from the De-partment of Defense and *Associated Press*.[243] The lawn before the crash site was immaculate, the two or three pieces of debris that could be seen were ri-diculously small, and could not be identified as belonging to a Boeing. The reporter Jamie McIntyre of CNN, who arrived at the Pentagon an hour after the crash, was perplexed: "From my close-up inspection, there is no evidence of a plane having crashed anywhere near the Pentagon... the only pieces left that you can see are small enough that you can pick up in your hand. There are no large tail sections, wing sections, fuselage, nothing like that anywhere around which would indicate that the entire plane crashed into the side of the Pentagon."[244]

Lt. Col. Karen Kwiatkowski of the U.S. Air Force, who was on the scene within min-utes after the explosion at the Pentagon, reported: "I saw nothing of significance at the point of impact—no airplane metal or cargo debris was blowing on the lawn in front of the damaged building as smoke billowed from within the Pentagon. [...] all of us staring at the Pentagon that morning were indeed looking for such debris, but what we expected to see was not evident."[245]

Was the plane buried deep into the building? No photo taken inside the crash site shows even the slightest credible scrap of a plane, and witnesses say that they did not see anything that would suggest an airplane. April Gallop was in her office with her son of two months, 10 or 15 meters from the impact zone. She felt an explosion, and then the ceiling fell in on her; in making her way towards the exit with her child, she saw nothing that made her think that a plane had crashed, "no wreckage, no airplane fragments, no engines, no seats, no luggage, no fuselage sections with rows of windows, and especially, no blazing quantities of burning jet fuel."[246]

---

[243] Thierry Meyssan, *9/11: The Big Lie,* Carnot, 2002.
[244] YouTube, "Live CNN Report of Jamie McIntyre at the Pentagon": www.youtube.com/watch?v=C02dE5VKeck
[245] Karen Kwiatkowski, "20 Months and 585 Pages Wasted — Your Government at Work for You!": www.lewrockwell.com/kwiatkowski/kwiatkowski88.html
[246] Listen to April Gallop on www.youtube.com/watch?v=EgExsz5q74Y

"**I look at the hole in the Pentagon, and I look at the size of an airplane that was supposed to have hit the Pentagon, and I say: the plane does not fit in that hole. So what did hit the Pentagon? What hit it? Where is it? What's going on?**" **(General Albert Stubblebine, head of the U.S. Army Intelligence and Security Command from 1981 to 1984).**[247]

Did Flight 77 just vanish? Did the fire, hardly noticeable in the photos, melt its hundred tons of metal, as was suggested by the government? If that were in fact the case, how did they manage to identify all the passengers through their fingerprints and DNA analysis, as has been claimed? (None of the dead bodies, by the way, has been identified by a relative: they were all transferred to a military base, where they were incinerated.)

We are asked to believe that the plastic nose of a Boeing 757 made this hole after going through five other reinforced concrete walls, as Rumsfeld himself announced on *Good Morning America* (ABC), September 13.[248] It resembles rather the damage done by a shell with a hollow charge, designed to perforate such walls.

The recordings of 85 video cameras, either placed at the Pentagon or in the general vicinity, were seized by government agents, but no recognizable image of the aircraft was made public. Only one sequence was released by court order in May 2006, and it includes four images that show an object exploding as it hits the Pentagon, but they do little to suggest that it is an airplane that caused the blast. Curiously, the film is dated

---

[247] In the documentary *One Nation Under Siege* by William Lewis, 2006. The sequence is on YouTube, "Maj. Gen. Albert Stubblebine Questions Flight 77": www.youtube.com/watch?v=QflySbvIZfA
[248] Griffin, *9/11 Contradictions, op. cit.,* p. 207.

September 12, not 11. According to some experts, the yellow light emitted by the explosion in the images could not have been caused by jet fuel, and neither can the odor of cordite (an explosive made from nitroglycerine, nitrocellulose and nitroguanidine) that some Pentagon employees have reported.[249]

Professional pilots united around Rob Balsamo as part of Pilots for 9/11 Truth have analyzed the trajectory of Flight AA77 provided by the National Transportation and Safety Board (NTSB) and demonstrated that it was physically impossible for a Boeing airliner. The aircraft descended in an extremely perilous spiral maneuver, finally hitting the second floor of the west façade horizontally, without hitting the turf in front of the building. It is impossible, since at such low altitude and high speed, such a plane loses all of its lift.[250] And even if it were possible, the feat would have been beyond the capacity of Hani Hanjour, the alleged pilot of the aircraft. A few months before September 11th, Hanjour was written up for incompetence by his Arizona flight school JetTech, who then called for the withdrawal of his license. An instructor at JetTech is quoted in the *New York Times*, April 5, 2002 saying: "I'm still to this day amazed that he could have flown into the Pentagon. He could not fly at all." The other supposed hijackers in the plane were no better: Nawaq al-Hazmi and Khaid al-Mihdhar's instructor in San Diego declared to the *Washington Post* (September 24, 2001): "Their English was horrible, and their mechanical skills were even worse. [...] It was like they had hardly even ever driven a car."[251]

In a CNN interview on September 15, 2001, then again on BBC on September 19th, Egyptian President Hosni Mubarak questioned the official U.S. explanation regarding 9/11. As a fighter pilot, he said in a later article, "I find it hard to believe that people who were learning to fly in Florida could, within a year and a half, fly large commercial airlines and hit with accuracy the towers of the World Trade Center which would appear, to the pilot from the air, the size of a pencil."[252] Mubarak would soon pay the price.

Air defense is the responsibility of NORAD (North American Aerospace Defense Command), and in particular its NEADS (Northeast Air Defense Sector)

[249] 9-11 Research, "Crash-Explosion at Pentagon - More than Jet Fuel Combustion?": 911research.wtc7.net/pentagon/analysis/conclusions/explosion.html
[250] pilotsfor911truth.org/pentagon.html
[251] Griffin, *9/11 Contradictions, op. cit.*, p. 201.
[252] "Historical memento: Hosni Mubarak's misgivings about official 9/11 account": www.voltairenet.org/article172031.html

department. NORAD had successfully intercepted 67 planes throughout the twelve months preceding September 11, 2001, each time in less than twenty minutes. Intercept tactics are triggered at the slightest alarm, as part of precautionary measures. Even if we assume that NORAD could not have intercepted Flights AA11 and UA175 before they crashed into the Twin Towers, it is incomprehensible that it could not intercept Flight AA77, which supposedly crashed 50 minutes later into the Pentagon, the most secure building in the world. Something or somebody must have deliberately prevented normal procedure, as Robert Bowman, Director of Advanced Space Programs Development for the U.S. Air Force, has assumed: "If our government had done nothing that day and let normal procedure be followed, those planes, wherever they were, would have been intercepted, the Twin Towers would still be standing and thousands of dead Americans would still be alive."[253]

Contradicting Condoleezza Rice and President Bush, who declared in 2002 that no one could have predicted this kind of attack, *USA Today* revealed on April 18, 2004 that NORAD was conducting, four times a year since 1999, military drills—or war games—that involved aircraft hijacked by terrorists and directed against the Pentagon and the World Trade Center.[254] With these new facts, the rather shallow excuses for American air defense ineffectiveness on September 11 were turned on their head: it was then explained that on that very day, NORAD was occupied with five military exercises, three of which, under the names of Vigilant Guardian, Global Guardian, and Vigilant Warrior, were simulated hijackings, both with real and virtual flights. Consequently, according to Colonel Robert Marr, head of NEADS, as many as twenty-nine "hijacked planes" were on the radar screens at NORAD on that day. According to Lieutenant Colonel Dwane Deskins, head of Vigilant Guardian quoted in an article in the *Syracuse Post-Standard* on January 20, 2002, everyone concerned at NEADS initially thought that the announcement of the hijacking of Flight AA11 was part of the ongoing military exercises.[255]

This aspect of the case is crucial to understanding the unfolding of the attacks on September 11th. As explains Captain Eric May, a former intelligence officer in the U.S. Army, "the easiest way to carry out a false flag attack is by setting up a military exercise that simulates the very attack you want to carry out."[256] Once the exercise is fully developed, it will require nothing more but to change a single parameter to turn the operation from simulated to real. Those who plan and oversee the drill are not necessarily those who hijack it to turn it into real.

---

[253] YouTube, "Dr. Bob Bowmn reviews 9/11": www.youtube.com/watch?v=lUOOnhbf-hA. Bowman also appears on documentaries by Architects & Engineers for 9/11 Truth.
[254] Steven Komarow and Tom Squitieri, "NORAD had drills of jets as weapons", *USA Today*, April 18, 2004: usatoday30.usatoday.com/news/washington/2004-04-18-norad_x.htm?csp=15
[255] Griffin, *9/11 Contradictions, op. cit.*, p. 41-5, 81-2.
[256] *Global Research*, February 23, 2008, quoted in Bollyn, *Solving 9-11, op. cit.*, p. 90.

Most participants in the 9/11 synthetic terror act, accustomed to obey military orders and the established "rules of the (war) game," perform their appointed mission without knowing that the attack will turn out to be "real." When they realize what they have been involved in, they simultaneously grasp the danger of raising objections; they themselves have been framed. As in the Kennedy assassination, military discipline is the key to ensuring the necessary silence of all unwilling, or unknowing participants.

Hours after the London bombings of July 6, 2005 (claimed by an improbable "Secret Al-Qaeda in Europe"), Peter Power, a former Scotland Yard officer turned manager of a private security company, revealed on BBC Radio 5, then again on ITV News, that he was conducting on that very morning, for a private company of the City, a simulation employing one thousand persons, "based on simulta-neous bombs going off precisely at the railway stations where it happened this morning." "So we had to suddenly switch an exercise from 'fictional' to 'real'." The web-site of his company Visor Consultants emphasizes that the crisis drills they de-sign aspire to be "Making the scenario come alive and be as realistic as possible." It would be foolish to think that Power has made a blunder by his revelation; he probably saved his life.[257]

All things considered, it is highly doubtful whether any of the airline flights reportedly hijacked on 9/11 were involved in the attacks. The Bureau of Transportation, which holds precise records of all flights, has no trace of Flight AA77 on September 11th; it was not planned at Dulles Airport that day, and its takeoff was not recorded. As for Flight UA93, it doesn't normally circulate Tuesdays, but as an exception, it had taken passengers initially planned for Flight UA91, which had been canceled due to a "crack in the windshield." This flight was recorded at takeoff, but then it is also recorded as having landed in San Francisco at noon, 45 minutes late. Finally, the mayor of Cleveland, Mi-chael White, was quoted at 11:50 am on *ABC News* saying that a Boeing 767 flying out of Boston was forced to make an emergency landing in Cleveland

---

[257] Nick Kollerstrom, *Terror on the Tube: Behind the Veil of 7/7,* Progressive Press, 2011, p. 294-6. See on YouTube, "Peter Power 7/7 Terror Rehearsal": www.youtube.com/watch?v=JKvkhe3rqtc

due to a bomb threat, and had been taken to a secure area of the airport to be evacuated. The plane was identified as Flight UA93—although a Boeing 767 out of Boston corresponded rather to the Flight UA175.[258]

The problem of the "transponders" is also perplexing. This device transmits the position of aircraft to control towers, and also allows the pilot to send alert and emergency messages. Incredibly, none of the four pilots or their professional copilots entered the four-digit code on the transponder which signals an assault on the cockpit—a maneuver that takes only three seconds. In fact, each aircraft actually cut their respective transponders, and then completely disappeared from secondary radars for nearly an hour while going through radar gaps. For example, AA77 left Washington for Los Angeles, disappeared from radars near Ohio and was spotted again an hour later near Washington DC.[259]

According to official reports, many passengers of Flights UA93, UA175 and AA77 had made calls to relatives or friends from their portable phones. Details of these calls (by passengers named Jeremy Glick, Peter Hanson, Brian Sweeney, Mark Bingham, Elizabeth Wainio, Marion Britton, Sandra Bradshaw, Tom Burnett, Edward Felt, CeeCee Lyles) were reported as early as September 13th on mainstream TV channels and newspapers (like *The Washington Post*). But they are highly problematic, because the technology required to make high-altitude phone calls was not developed until 2004. Moreover, some calls include oddities completely incongruent with the context, exemplified by Mark Bingham's call to his mother a few seconds before his death: "Hi, Mom. This is Mark Bingham."[260]

Two calls were allegedly made from AA77 by Barbara Olson to her husband Ted Olson. The Olsons are both public figures: Barbara was a well-known CNN reporter, and Ted has been Solicitor General during the first Bush term (after defending Bush in the disputed 2000 election, and then Dick Cheney when he refused to submit to Congress Enron-related documents during their investigation). Barbara Olson's calls, reported on CNN in the afternoon of September 11th, contributed to crystallizing some details of the official story, such as the "box cutters" used by the hijackers. Repeatedly invited on television shows, Ted Olson frequently contradicted himself when questioned regarding the calls from his wife. Sometimes he said she "called him twice on a cell phone " adding that the second call was cut because "the signals from cell phones coming from airplanes don't work that well." Sometimes he said that his wife called collect from the "air phone" because "she somehow didn't have

---

[258] YouTube, "9/11 Hijacked Flight Makes Emergency Landing in Cleveland": www.youtube.com/watch?v=3YPMNVA2y1M

[259] See the film *9/11 Intercepted* by Pilots for 9/11 Truth on YouTube: www.youtube.com/watch?v=TtRScsFPUbE

[260] Griffin, *9/11 Contradictions, op. cit.,* p. 170-82; Tarpley, *9/11 Synthetic Terror, op. cit.,* p. 321-4.

access to her credit cards." This second version is as impossible as the first, because a credit card is required to activate the phones in the seats, even for a collect call, though really the entire argument is moot, given that the seats on AA77 were not equipped with telephones (as confirmed by American Airlines). The most troubling contradiction appeared in 2006, during the trial of supposed terrorist Zacarias Moussaoui: in their report on Flight AA77, the FBI attributed only one call from Barbara Olson, and it was an unconnected call lasting 0 seconds.[261]

Given the many impossibilities woven throughout the official story, the alternative hypothesis that seems most likely is that none of the four airplanes were in fact the Boeing 767 or 757s the world was told about. Flights AA77 and UA93 probably never existed. As for Flights AA11 and UA175, which reportedly hit the Twin Towers, several hypotheses are in competition among 9/11 truthers. Many surmise that they had been replaced by drones—planes equipped with automatic remote control technology, and without passengers.[262] But numerous witnesses have declared having seen no planes, while others saw missiles. No consensus has been reached on these matters. Simon Shack, in a groundbreaking documentary (*September Clues,* 2007), has analyzed the images of the second crash (South Tower) broadcast on September 11th and later, and argued that they are fakes, fabricated with various video editing software.[263] This also applies to the only image of the first crash (North Tower), miraculously captured by the mysterious brothers Jules and Gédéon Naudet. The TV forgeries have been further explored by Ace Baker in his 2012 documentary *9/11 The Great American Psy-Opera,* where he gives credence to professor Morgan Reynolds who has long claimed that the aluminum planes shown to penetrate the steel towers without resistance defy physical laws, and therefore must be video artifacts.[264] Richard D. Hall of rich-planet.net, however, after having attempted to show that the virtual planes added to the images were masking a missile-type object, has pointed out shortcomings in the video-compositing theory, and proposed an alternative theory based on holographic projections.[265] Although there is yet no consensus on the method employed to create the illusion, it is today clearly established that the planes penetrating the towers like butter, without being shattered or even de-

---

[261] Griffin, *9/11 Contradictions, op. cit.,* p. 72-8. These inconsistencies are reported in *The Wall Street Journal,* May 16, 2013: online.wsj.com/article/PR-CO-20130516-909978.html

[262] Read for example Dean Hartwell, *Planes without Passengers: the Faked Hijackings of 9/11,* kindle, 2nd ed, 2012.

[263] Watch on YouTube: www.youtube.com/watch?v=aWl8mUSDIwU. Further discussions on the "September Clues Research Forum": cluesforum.info/

[264] See chapters 6 and 7 on: www.youtube.com/playlist?list=PLEA05F393EC843D80

[265] On YouTube, "New 9/11 Video and Radar Analysis", www.youtube.com/watch?v=GTSzHmHnR78. Also "Richard D. Hall debunks Simon Shack and recants his original 'Ball Theory'", www.abovetopsecret.com/forum/thread846419/pg1

celerated at impact, as seen on multiple TV footages, can in no way be real. The initial explosions seen at that precise moment must have another explanation.

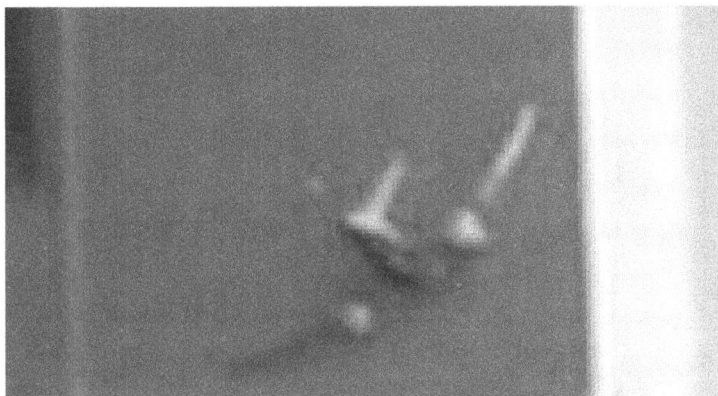

In this pic from the CNN footage of the second crash, the aluminum plane has half disappeared into the steel tower: a material impossibility.

If no planes hit the Twin Towers any more than the Pentagon or the field outside Shanksville—all 9/11 Flights having been probably created virtual in the context of a drill— then all discussions regarding the failures of U.S. defenses must be counted as diversions from the main issue. Of course, if the planes did not fly on that day, neither did the passengers. False identities were created, and it would seem that the Intel agencies involved suffered severe shortages in this regard. For Flight AA77, for example, only 53 passengers are listed, while the plane's capacity is 239. Among the 53 passengers plus 9 crew members, only 14 persons are listed in the Social Security Death Index. And only 5 of these have relatives who received the 9-11 Compensation Fund offered by the State. Moreover, the passenger list comprises an abnormal percentage of Navy officers and aeronautic engineers (13 out of 53). The other three "flights" show similar percentages of capacity and recorded deaths (no family of the victims of Flight UA93 requested compensation, for example).[266]

---

[266] Read "Flight 77 Passengers" on *9-11 Review,* 911review.org/Wiki/Flight77Passengers. shtml, and "The 9/11 Passenger List Oddity" by Vincent Sammartino (2004), on *9/11 Scholars Forum,* 911scholars.ning.com/profiles/blogs/the-911-passenger-list-oddity

18. The Art of the Patsy

Peter Dale Scott was one of the first scholars to point out some parallels between the Kennedy assassination and the September 11th attacks. Each of these events was specifically designed to justify the illegitimate invasion of a foreign country and the overthrow of its hostile regime: Cuba in the first case, Afghanistan in the second, with the difference that the invasion of Cuba was eventually called off. Each of the two false flag crimes also preceded a second lie that justified war, conducted unilaterally by the United States against a far away country: the mock incident in the Gulf of Tonkin justified the aggression against North Vietnam, just as the lies surrounding Saddam Hussein's "weapons of mass destruction" justified the war against Iraq. Unlike the first two crimes, the two secondary lies are today publicly recognized as such by politicians and historians alike. In both cases, the plot originated in the upper echelons of the National Security State, and directly served the interests of the military-industrial complex and all its parasites. In both cases, the goal was to traumatize the American nation with a crime so heinous as to transform the public's fear into hatred and build a national consensus for war against some stereotypical enemy who poses a mortal threat: Communism in the former case, Islamism in the second.

It is also interesting to look at the preparation and eventual execution of the two "deep events"; doing so reveals a characteristic pattern and thereby allows for the development of a "theory of false flag operations," and an increased ability to expose them. In both cases, for example, we note that the pseudo-culprit is identified almost instantaneously, along with the murder weapon. Oswald was arrested and accused in the hour that followed his alleged crime. Bin Laden was not arrested, but his name was plastered across TV screens everywhere by a slew of so-called terrorism experts in the hours following the collapse of the towers.[267] The aim is to quickly and efficiently cut off any al-

---

[267] See his conference on November 18, 2006, "JFK & 9/11: Insights Gained From Studying Both": www.youtube.com/watch?v=hBozfOm9ngY

ternative theory and inspire confidence in the veracity of the official narrative, marginalizing in advance all the skeptics. Official information, in this kind of event, circumvents public discussion and debate, preventing the people from collectively building hypothesis, interpretations, and meaning. Less than a week after September 11th, the Pakistani General Hamid Gul, a former ISI Director, keenly analyzed the technique: "Within 10 minutes of the second twin tower being hit in the World Trade Center, CNN said Osama bin Laden had done it. That was a planned piece of disinformation by the real perpetrators. It created an instant mindset and put public opinion into a trance, which prevented even intelligent people from thinking for themselves."[268] Studies show that information received from an authority during a period of emotional shock—and thus rational vulnerability—is embedded into the memory of the trauma, in such a way that the distinction between facts and interpretation becomes impossible.

Mark Walsh was interviewed by Fox News (for which he works as a freelancer) in the hour following the disintegration of the towers, providing the ideal eyewitness testimony. "I saw this plane come out of nowhere and just ream right into the side of the Twin Tower exploding through to the other side, and then I witnessed both towers collapse, the first, and then the second, mostly due to structural failure because the fire was just too intense."[269] Conflating the observation and the technical explanation, in the very terms destined to become official, serves to cover the explanation which naturally comes to the mind of a neutral witness, such as journalist Don Dahler commenting on ABC News: "The entire building has just collapsed, as if a demolition team set off..."[270]

Once the authorities assuredly designate a patsy, it becomes almost unnecessary to provide evidence of his guilt. It is remarkable that the FBI never formally charged bin Laden for the attacks of September 11th; he appears on the list of the ten most wanted criminals on their official website, but only as a suspect in the attacks against the U.S. embassies in Tanzania and Kenya. When questioned by journalist Ed Hass of the *Muckraker Report* in June 2006, FBI

---

[268] Watch CNN Gul's interview of December 8, 2008 on YouTube, "Pakistani ISI General Hamid Gul '9/11 Inside Job'": www.youtube.com/watch?v=mSLgC4cTKcs

[269] YouTube, "Fox News – Rick Leventhal interviews 9/11 WTC witness, Mark Walsh": www.youtube.com/watch?v=07hJhmiWZSY

[270] YouTube, "NIST FOIA - ABC News GMA2 Clip4.avi – Don Dahler": www.youtube.com/watch?v=yD_GCJbsLdU

spokesman Rex Tomb said: "The reason why 9/11 is not mentioned on Osama bin Laden's 'Most Wanted' page is because the FBI has no hard evidence connecting bin Laden to 9/11."[271] Even the identification of the hijackers was presented to the public without any evidence; instead, conflicting information abounds, casting serious doubt about those identified: the flight manifests first provided by United Airlines and American Airlines did not include the name of any of the 19 hijackers, and there are no video images showing them boarding. The little evidence of their identity that has been made public is so convenient it's rendered hardly credible, for example two passports and one identity card of the hijackers recovered miraculously from the crash sites of Flights AA11, AA77 and UA93, or a Qur'an and flight manual in Arabic left by Mohamed Atta in a rental car.

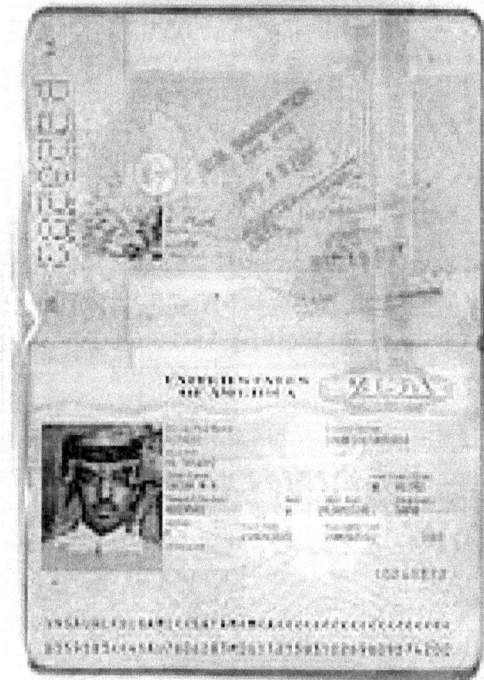

The "magic passport" of Satam Al Suqami, supposed to have escaped Flight AA11 at the moment of the impact, to be then picked up in a street of Manhattan by an anonymous passerby and handed to the FBI. Likewise, the passport of Ziad Jarrah, pilot of Flight UA93, was found at Shanksville near the crash site, and the ID of Majed Moqed, one of the hijackers of Flight AA77, came out unburnt in front of the Pentagon, while the plane had vaporized.

A further parallel between the immediate identifications of the pseudo-culprits Oswald and bin Laden deserves to be mentioned: in both cases, they were charged with a second crime which strengthened the suspicion of their guilt in the public mind. An hour after Oswald was pinpointed, he was reported to have shot a police officer, J. D. Tippit, who had recognized him and approached him in the street. Similarly, the responsibility of the Taliban in the attacks of September 11th was made easier to believe by the report, one day before, of Commandant Massoud's assassination, readily attributed to the same Al-Qaeda-Taliban alliance.

A good patsy is a dead patsy; that is another fundamental rule of false flag operations that we can see applied in both Kennedy's assassination and September 11th. Once designated, the falsely accused culprit must be eliminated as

---

[271] Griffin, *9/11 Contradictions, op. cit.,* p. 191.

soon as possible, because he will have nothing to lose in speaking out, and he knows enough to realize that he is the subject of something malicious. Lee Harvey Oswald was shot by Jack Ruby two days after his alleged crime. That was already a bit late; the plan was probably to shoot him dead while trying to arrest him in the Texas Theater, where Jack Ruby was present according to manager George Applin. The news of Tippit's murder would have been used to present Oswald as armed and dangerous and justify the shooting that led to his killing. It is unfortunate for the conspirators that Oswald had time to realize what was happening and say to the press: "I'm just a patsy." This might be one of the mistakes that prompted them to abandon their Communist conspiracy theory, which would have incurred too many inconsistencies—including FBI agents interrogating him and thereafter not recognizing his voice on the Mexico tapes produced by the CIA.

In any case, a patsy's claims to innocence are barely a speed bump when up against the steamroller of an aligned media; bin Laden's denial meant nothing. As for the suicide hijackers, they were dead by definition. Again, however, problems arose: a few days after the FBI identified the culprits (September 14th), seven of the nineteen hijackers came forward through various channels, proving that they were alive—in Morocco, Saudi Arabia and elsewhere—and consequently innocent.[272] The father of the supposed ringleader Mohamed Atta, a respected lawyer from Cairo, told the German magazine *Bild am Sonntag* in late 2002 that "[his] son called [him] the day after the attacks, September 12," and that he was hiding out of fear for his life.

As for bin Laden, it's not until April 30, 2011, in the operation known as "Neptune's Spear," that he is supposed to have been eliminated by a SEAL commando, shot fatally in the head in his home in Abbottabad, Pakistan. His body, we were told, was dumped in the sea after identification. The only picture presented to the public was a vulgar photomontage, as the media quickly acknowledged. The farce would be funny if not for the tragic epilogue: Friday, August 5th, 2011 around 11 pm, a Chinook helicopter of the U.S. Army crashed in a province in central Afghanistan after being hit by two rocket-propelled grenades (RPG-7s) shot, we are told, by the Afghan resistance. The attack killed 38, including 30 members of Navy SEAL Team 6, the elite unit who had led Neptune's Spear. And thus there will be less chance of contradiction to the official story of bin Laden's death. Family members of the dead SEALs are now raising questions, however.[273]

---

[272] See whatreallyhappened.com/WRHARTICLES/hijackers.html and news.bbc.co.uk/2/hi/1559151.stm

[273] Todd Venezia, "22 Osama-unit Navy SEALs killed as Taliban rocket shoots down helicopter over Afghanistan", *New York Post,* August 7, 2011:
www.nypost.com/p/news/international/seals_struck_down_YzZb5FNZ7jZjHlB9fmY1bP

The cheap Photoshop fake of bin Laden's corpse, sold to the public before being denounced as a fraud days later.

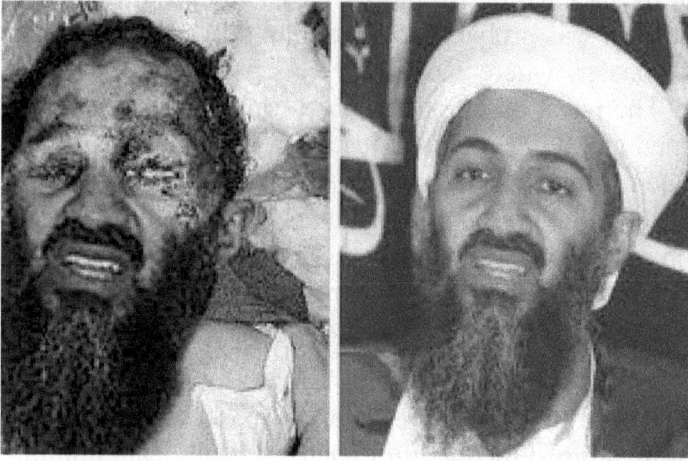

It's likely that bin Laden actually died in late 2001, as was announced by the Pakistani President Musharraf (CNN, January 18, 2002), the Afghan President Hamid Karzai (CNN, October 7, 2002), and the leader of the anti-terrorism division of the FBI, Dale Watson (BBC, July 18, 2002). On January 28, 2002, CBS reported that on the eve of September 11th bin Laden had been treated in a military hospital in Pakistan for kidney dialysis, and was escorted by the Pakistani army. How could he have survived until 2011, holed up in the caves of Afghanistan, when he had to undergo dialysis every three days? More troubling still: two months earlier, bin Laden stayed at the American Hospital in Dubai, where he was visited by the local CIA station chief Larry Mitchell. This information comes from credible sources (administrative management of the hospital, members of the Saudi royal family, and French Intelligence) and was covered by French newspaper *Le Figaro* in October 2001.[274]

There were two advantages in holding back the announcement of bin Laden's death until 2011. First, it allowed the continued invasion of Afghanistan under the auspices of a manhunt. Second, it allowed bin Laden to "speak" when needed, and thus clear the doubts raised by his denials; better than a dead patsy, the architects of the September 11 deception created for themselves a virtual patsy. The guilt of bin Laden is based mainly upon three video confessions "accredited by the CIA." The first was mysteriously found in December 2001 in Jellalabad, translated and released two months later. Despite the poor image quality, it is easy to see that the character presented as bin Laden is hardly a credible semblance.[275]

---

[274] Alexandra Richard, "La CIA aurait rencontré Ben Laden en juillet", *Le Figaro,* October 31, 2001:www.globalresearch.ca/articles/RIC111A.html
[275] 911research.wtc7.net/disinfo/deceptions/binladinvideo.html

On the left, the Bin Laden of the December 2001 video. On the right, the real Bin Laden.

The second video appeared in October 2004, a week before the elections that reappointed George W. Bush. An independent analysis by the Swiss institute IDIAP specialized in perceptual intelligence, basing their study on comparisons with twenty previous recordings of bin Laden, concluded with 95% probability that the voice on the October tape is not that of bin Laden.[276] A third video reached the public on September 8, 2007, in which bin Laden announced an intensification of Al-Qaeda activities in Iraq; this just before the debate in Congress regarding the need for new troops in Iraq. The image is frozen for most the message, and even when it is not, the quality is so bad that it is impossible to verify whether the movement of the lips corresponds to the soundtrack. Additionally, the videos of 2004 and 2007 were filmed in the same studio with the same frame and the same posture, but bin Laden looks younger on the second (he had dyed his beard black, it was explained).

Bin Laden videos from 2004 and 2007. The later video was provided to the government by the Search for International Terrorist Entities Institute (SITE), founded by Israeli-American Rita Katz, daughter of an Iraqi Jew executed by Saddam Hussein on the charge of spying for Israel.[277]

---

[276] Greg Felton, *The Host and the Parasite: How Israel's Fifth Column Consumed America,* Bad Bear Press, 2012, p. 292.

[277] Joby Warrick, "Bin Laden, Brought to You by...", *Washington Post,* September 12, 2007, www.washingtonpost.com/wp-dyn/content/article/2007/09/11/AR2007091102465.html

After September 11th just like after Kennedy's assassination, it was necessary to appease doubts with a Presidential Commission of inquiry. The 9/11 Commission was created in November 2002, and was led by Thomas Kean and Lee Hamilton, but its executive director was Philip Zelikow, who also happened to be the senior editor of the *NSS* 2002 document defining Bush's preemptive war doctrine. In 2006, Kean and Hamilton revealed in their book *Without Precedent: The Inside Story of the 9/11 Commission*, that the Commission "was set up to fail" from the beginning, Zelikow having already written a synopsis and a conclusion for the final report before the first meeting. He controlled all the working groups, prevented them from communicating with each other, and gave them the singular mission to prove the official story; Team 1A, for example, was tasked to "tell the story of Al-Qaeda's most successful operation—the 9/11 attacks." All information, and any request for information, had to pass through him. On top of that, most of the information obtained by the commissioners from the CIA and NORAD was "far from the truth," according to Kean and Hamilton. The Commission had no access to any direct evidence or even the recordings of the interrogations of the suspected Al-Qaeda members, which came to them third hand "in the form of reports, not even transcripts." Commission members had to be content, for example, with CIA affirmations that the confessions of Khalid Sheikh Mohammed (described as the operational manager of the attacks), obtained between 183 waterboarding sessions, were certifiable evidence that bin Laden had authorized and supported the operation.[278] Before the Commission published its final report in July 2004, several members expressed their frustration and resigned. One of them, Max Cleland, called the Commission a "national scandal": "One of these days we will have to get the full story because the 9-11 issue is so important to America. But the White House wants to cover it up."[279] John Farmer, the Senior Counsel, said for his part in *The Washington Post*: "what government and military officials had told Congress, the Commission, the media, and the public about who knew what when—was almost entirely, and inexplicably, untrue."[280]

The Commission also threw a veil over one of the most disturbing facts around 9/11, which happened on the stock exchange: between the 6th and the 10th of September 2001, there were massive purchases of "put options," twenty-five times higher than average, on American Airlines and United Airlines, whose shares fell 40% after the attacks, but also on companies housed in the WTC such as Morgan Stanley Dean Witter & Co. and Merrill Lynch & Company. The International Organization of Securities Commissions (IOSCO) concluded

---

[278] Griffin, *9/11 Contradictions, op. cit.*, p. 195-6.

[279] "The White House Has Played Cover-Up", *Democracy Now*:
www.democracynow.org/2004/3/23/the_white_house_has_played_cover

[280] Dan Eggen, "9/11 Panel Suspected Deception by Pentagon", *Washington Post*, August 2, 2006: www.washingtonpost.com/wp-dyn/content/article/2006/08/01/AR2006080101300.html

on October 15th that the gains had been in the hundreds of millions of dollars and could be the "largest insider trade ever committed." The Commission rejected the hypothesis in a few lines: "further investigation has revealed that the trading had no connection with 9/11. A single US-based institutional investor with no conceivable ties to Al-Qaeda purchased 95 percent of the UAL puts on September 6 as part of a trading strategy that also included buying 115,000 shares of American [Airline] on September 10." In other words: postulating that the culprit was Al-Qaeda, and noting that the investors in question did not have the Al-Qaeda profile, enabled the Commission to conclude implicitly that these suspicious transactions were just an unfortunate coincidence. The "institutional investor" in question was Alex Brown Inc., a subsidiary of Deutsche Bank whose former CEO and Chairman A.B. "Buzzy" Krongard (until 1998) had just become Executive Director of the CIA in March 2001.[281]

---

[281] 9/11 Consensus Panel: www.consensus911.org/point-g-2/; Tarpley, *9/11 Synthetic Terror, op. cit.,* p. 319-23.

19. Al-Qaeda, the All-Purpose Enemy

The plotters against Kennedy in 1963 chose their patsy Oswald, not only to distance themselves from suspicion, but also to redirect attention toward a false conspiracy by a foreign government, as a means to justify a war of retaliation, in that case against the Republic of Cuba. The same goes for the patsies of September 11th, except that they were supposed to belong to a transnational organization, a diffuse and networked enemy that could be singled out in almost any country. Al-Qaeda is the Swiss Army knife of war propaganda, and if it didn't exist, it would have to be invented to make sense of the War on Terror. In fact, that is the case, according to many secret service insiders. Alain Chouet, director of French secret services (DGSE) from 2000 to 2002, denounced before the French Senate on January 29th, 2010 the "obsessive insistence of Westerners to invoke this mythical organization," with the dual perverse effect of encouraging unrelated terrorists or merely two-bit criminals to claim allegiance to Al-Qaeda in an effort to be taken seriously, and encouraging Muslim regimes to describe their opponents as members of Al-Qaeda as a justification for repressing them, normally with the assistance of Westerners.[282]

As Jason Burke explains in *Al-Qaeda: The True Story of Radical Islam* (2007), the myth of Al-Qaeda was first created in January 2001 during the trial of four men suspected in the bombings against the U.S. embassies in Kenya and Tanzania in 1998. It was then that the FBI adopted, for the legal requirements of the charge, the idea of an organization structured under the orders of bin Laden, which was arbitrarily given the name "al Qaeda" (an Arabic word meaning "the list" or "the database," and referring to a list of all the would-be jihadists who had passed through bin Laden's training camps in Afghanistan, first set up with CIA support during the Soviet War). The idea that such a "list" constituted an organization was drawn solely from the testimony of Jamal al-Fadl, a former associate of bin Laden who had robbed him and who received 100,000 dollars from the U.S. government in exchange for his testi-

---

[282] Reopen911: www.reopen911.info/video/dgse.html

mony. Created as a legitimatization for anti-terrorist actions, both at home and abroad, the concept evoked by the term "Al-Qaeda" has now become so broad and misconstrued that it ceases to designate any actually existing terrorist organization.[283]

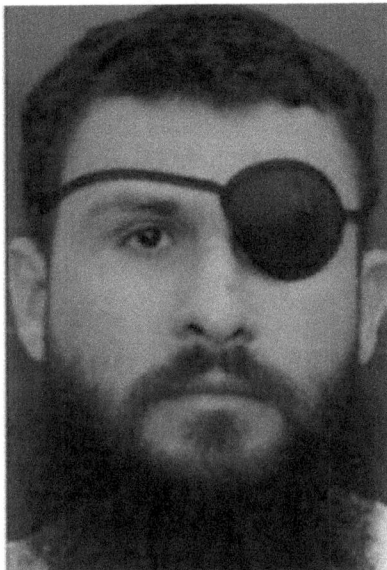

The 9/11 Commission report builds its accusation of bin Laden largely on the "confession" of Abu Zubaydah, a Saudi presented as "a longtime ally of bin Laden." Imprisoned since 2002 and still not formally prosecuted, Zoubaydah is said to have yielded decisive information under torture by waterboarding (at least 83 times). But in September 2009, the government was forced to admit that Zubaydah had never been a member of Al-Qaeda, and had no advanced knowledge of the 9/11 attacks. The error was blamed on Zubaydah's mythomania.[284]

In the aftermath of September 11th, Afghanistan was first to be singled out, since it is there that Osama bin Laden was supposed to be found. From 1996, bin Laden was close to Mullah Omar, supreme chief of the Taliban, and in 1997 demonstrated his allegiance in marrying one of Omar's daughters. It was therefore logical for the U.S. to take vengeance for 9/11 on Afghanistan's Taliban regime. Behind bin Laden were the Taliban; but behind the Taliban was Pakistan, from where they came and got their support—with U.S. funds. Pakistan is thus indirectly charged during the aftermath of September 11th. Though no formal charges were made, the press delivered their own indictment on ISI complicity. General Ahmed Mahmud, head of the ISI, was fingered by information first reported by *The Times of India* on October 9, 2001: "U.S. authorities sought his removal after confirming the fact that $100,000 were wired to WTC hijacker Mohamed Atta from Pakistan by [ISI agent] Ahmed Omar Said Sheikh at the instance of General Mahmud."[285] If Mohamed Atta was in fact just a patsy, this information can only be interpreted as blackmail against the ISI and Pakistan, in an effort to force their cooperation with the United States in the destruction of the Taliban regime. Perhaps the ISI had truly paid money to Atta, and then Atta was chosen as the fictive terrorist leader for precisely this rea-

---

[283] Jason Burke, *Al-Qaeda: The True Story of Radical Islam,* Penguin, 2007, p. 20-4.

[284] Kevin Ryan, "Abu Zubaydah Poses a Real Threat to Al Qaeda", www.voltairenet.org/article177178.html

[285] "General Mahmud Ahmad", *9-11 Review:* 911review.org/Sept11Wiki/Ahmad,GeneralMahmud.shtml

son—just like Oswald had been chosen for his fabricated connection to pro-Castro groups.

General Mahmud, who had regularly visited Washington since 1999, happened to be there between the 4th and the 11th of September 2001. There he met with George Tenet, Director of the CIA, and Marc Grossman, Under Secretary of State for Political Affairs. At the time of the attacks, he was attending a breakfast meeting that included Bob Graham, Chairman of the Senate Intelligence Committee, and Porter Goss, Chairman of the House Intelligence Committee; "we were talking about terrorism, specifically terrorism generated from Afghanistan," reported Graham, who would be appointed with Goss to the 9/11 Commission.[286] It's not known what Mahmud was told when news of the attacks reached them, but he would retire the following month and leave politics, joining the religious movement Tablighi Jamaat.

On September 24, 2010, President Mahmoud Ahmadinejad of Iran declared before the General Assembly of the United Nations that: "The majority of the American people, as well as most nations and politicians around the world agree with this view [...] that some segments within the U.S. government orchestrated the attack to reverse the declining American economy and its grips on the Middle East in order to save the Zionist regime." By an ironic twist, we were told in December 2012 that Al-Qaeda has issued a statement from Yemen asking that Iranian President Mahmoud Ahmadinejad cease contesting them the merit of the 9/11 attacks.[287]

One can easily imagine that those who orchestrated the September 11th attacks would have wanted to pressure the Pakistani government into aligning themselves with their version of the attacks. But the rumors about the links between Al-Qaeda and the ISI may also have been conceived to damage the U.S.-Pakistan relationship, rather than improve it. The staging of bin Laden's cap-

---

[286] Tom Flocco, "Secret Hearings Hide 911 Terrorist Links to Congress/White House": www.bibliotecapleyades.net/sociopolitica/esp_sociopol_911_3.htm

[287] Read David Gardner, "'Hateful and offensive': Obama slams Iranian president after he blames America for 9/11 attacks", in *The Daily Mail,* September 24, 2010: www.dailymail.co.uk/news/article-1314667/Ahmadinejad-tells-UN-Some-believe-9-11-work-Americans-save-Israel.html

ture fits that interpretation, for it allowed the U.S. to accuse Pakistan, after Afghanistan, of having given asylum to bin Laden for 10 years, which is tantamount to treason on the part of an allied country. Among several authors defending this line is CIA veteran Bruce Riedel in *Deadly Embrace: Pakistan, America, and the Future of Global Jihad* (2011). According to Riedel, the quiet life of bin Laden in the suburbs of Abbohabad suggests "an astonishing degree of duplicity" by Pakistan, which could be "the secret patron of global jihad on a scale almost too dangerous to conceive. We would need to rethink our entire relationship with Pakistan and our understanding of its strategic motives."[288]

It is not clear whether there was a plot intended to destabilize or undermine relations between the United States and Pakistan; but it is certain that such a plot existed in regard to Saudi Arabia. Bin Laden is Saudi, and 15 of the 19 alleged hijackers of September 11th were Saudis. Whoever crafted that list must have wanted to damage Saudi Arabia's image in America, and possibly to blackmail its rulers. But why? Have not the Saudis remained loyal suppliers of oil since 1975? Just like for Pakistan, the public was provided with "leaked" information that the 9/11 Commission had received "evidence" linking Al-Qaeda to members of the Saudi royal family. The final report said nothing to that effect, but commissioner Bob Graham disclosed it in an interview with PBS in December 2002, and again in a book entitled *Intelligence Matters: The CIA, the FBI, Saudi Arabia, and the Failure of America's War on Terror* (2004), where he denounced the government censorship of 28 pages of the Commission's report dealing with Saudi support to terrorists.[289] "Why would the Saudis have given substantial assistance to at least two of the hijackers, and possibly all 19?" asked Graham rhetorically, "The answer I have come to is survival—survival of the state and survival of the House of Saud." Graham wants us to believe that the Saudi princes helped bin Laden strike the United States for fear he would otherwise stir social unrest at home. As for Bush, if we are to believe Graham, he covered up the 9/11-Saudi connection because of "the special personal friendship between the [Saudi] royal family and the highest levels of our national government [meaning the President]."[290]

To understand the absurdity of such an accusation, it is enough to know that the Saudis stripped Osama bin Laden of his citizenship in April 1994, exasperated by his nagging accusations for their acceptance of U.S. military presence

---

[288] Bruce Riedel, *Deadly Embrace: Pakistan, America, and the Future of Global Jihad,* Brookings Institution, 2011, p. 5.

[289] Bob Graham, *Intelligence Matters: The CIA, the FBI, Saudi Arabia, and the Failure of America's War on Terror,* Random House, 2004.

[290] "Saudi Arabia: Friend or Foe?" *The Daily Beast,* July 11, 2011: www.thedailybeast.com/articles/2011/07/11/saudi-arabia-fried-or-foe-asks-senator-bob-graham.html

on the holy ground of Islam since the first Gulf War. In his *Declaration of War Against the Americans Occupying the Land of the Two Holy Places*, released in 1996, bin Laden called for the overthrow of the Saudi monarchy, and in 1998, he admitted his role in the November 13, 1995 attack against the headquarters of the National Guard in Riyadh. Osama bin Laden is the sworn enemy of the Saudis. It is unimaginable that the Saudis conspired with Osama bin Laden against the United States; however, it is plausible that the Saudis conspired *against* bin Laden *with* the Bushes, by pegging him in a false attack to get the U.S. Army on his heels, while liquidating the Taliban regime for UNOCAL's Afghanistan interests.

The commercial partnership forged by the Bushes with Saudi Arabia is notorious. It started when CIA Director George H. W. Bush first traded with the bin Mahfouzs and the bin Ladens, through a company of aircraft brokerage entrusted to Jim Bath.[291] Commercial exchanges were broadened during the Gulf War, which allowed the elder President Bush to pose as protector of Saudi Arabia. The Carlyle Group, of which George Bush is a shareholder, played a central role, and is notoriously linked with a nephew of King Fahd. A scandal broke out in March 2001, during one of Bush's visits to Saudi Arabia, as acting head of the Carlyle Group. The nature of his meeting with King Fahd raised questions: was this a diplomatic meeting, private business travel, or both? On the same occasion, the former President also met the bin Laden family, in business with Carlyle since 1990. On September 11, 2001, George Bush and Shafig bin Laden (Osama's half-brother) were holding a meeting of the Carlyle Group in Washington, with several hundred investors in attendance. The news caused considerable embarrassment for the Bush family in the aftermath of 9/11. In the following week, at the request of the Saudi ambassador to Washington Bandar bin Sultan (nicknamed Sultan Bush because of his close ties to the President's family), and in violation of the flight ban maintained by the FAA (Federal Aviation Administration), a Boeing 747 from Saudi Arabian Airlines was allowed to leave the United States, carrying 140 Saudis, including Shafig bin Laden and twenty members of his family.[292]

The idea of a conspiracy emanating from inside the Bush administration, which is the common wisdom of the 9/11 Truth movement, faces a major contradiction: if the responsibility of Osama bin Laden is a prefabricated lie, so are the elements that are potentially embarrassing for the Saudi state, and indirectly for the Bush family. The involvement of the Bush clan in the planning of the September 11th scheme (and not only in its cover-up) is plausible, but the choice of bin Laden as a patsy does not seem very wise, especially if the objective was to divert suspicion away from the Bush family. This paradox can

---

[291] Baker, *Family of Secrets, op. cit.,* p. 280-98.
[292] Éric Laurent, *La Face cachée du 11 Septembre,* Plon, 2004, p. 119-22.

be resolved if we consider that a complex operation like 9/11, designed to change dramatically the course of world history, necessarily involves several powerful networks, whose long-range interests do not necessarily coincide, and who hold each other hostage after the operation.

It is impossible, at this stage, to know exactly who knew what and who did what on 9/11, but it is conceivable that the Bush clan was outsmarted by the real masterminds, the President believing he had allowed a limited and harmless false flag attack (involving for example only two virtual planes and an explosion in the Pentagon) for the limited purpose of invading Afghanistan and get the UNOCAL project going, while the master plotters raised the stakes by adding two fake planes into the WTC, and then forced Bush into the Iraq invasion that his father had refused them in 1991, bullying even Colin Powell to support it by who knows what blackmail. To test this hypothesis, it is necessary to carefully scrutinize the various layers in the Bush administration.

On the 4th of March, 2001, Fox TV broadcast the first episode of the series *The Lone Gunmen*, watched by 13 million Americans. Computer hackers working for a secret cabal within the government hijack a jet by remote control with the intent to crash it into one of the Twin Towers, while making it appear to have been hijacked by Islamic terrorists. At the last seconds, the pilots manage to regain control of the plane. The purpose of the failed operation was to trigger a world war under the pretense of fighting terrorism.[293] Could this be another kind of psychological "vaccine," meant to denigrate in advance conspiracy theories as inspired by fiction? At the same time, it conditioned in advance the 9/11 Truth movement toward the hypothesis of the remote controlled planes.

---

[293] YouTube, "The Lone Gunmen Pilot – 9/11 Predictive Programming": www.youtube.com/watch?v=z3WW6eoLcLI

20. Bush and the "Crazies"

The fact that George W. Bush was the man placed in 2001 at the "surface" of the American State (as opposed to its "depth") is highly significant. "If you had said to me: 'name 25 million people who would maybe be president of the United States', he would probably not be in that category," once said of him David Rubinstein, founder of the Carlyle Group, after having accepted him into the board of directors as a favor to his father.[294] How had a man so notoriously shallow as George W. Bush been elected head of the most powerful country in the world? One obvious answer is that he was the son of George H. W. Bush, who left the misleading impression of a rather reasonable Republican president. The son of a President is not unlike a Vice-President: he is granted more confidence through connections than any other candidate in the running. Voters could even assume that Bush II would have been guided by Bush I, which proved to be far from the truth. To the journalist Bob Woodward, who wanted to know if he ever asked his father for advice, Bush Jr. said in 2004: "Well, no... He is the wrong father to appeal to for advice. [...] There's a higher Father that I appeal to."[295] Is this born-again profile genuine, or just an act taught by his communication advisor Karl Rove (called *Bush's Brain* by his biographers James Moore and Wayne Slater)?[296] Opinions are divided, but the evangelist Billy Graham, to whom Bush Jr. credits his conversion in his 1999 memoirs, has claimed to have no memory of any serious conversation with him.[297] In any case, Bush Jr.'s most significant conversion took place on September 11th 2001: "He became President, but he didn't know why, and on September 11, he discovered why," has famously said neoconservative Mi-

---

[294] *Democracy Now,* July 3, 2003:
www.democracynow.org/2003/7/3/democracy_now_exclusive_why_the_carlyle)
[295] Sniegoski, *Transparent Cabal, op. cit.,* p. 324.
[296] James Moore, *Bush's Brain: How Karl Rove Made George W. Bush Presidential,* John Wiley & Sons, 2003.
[297] *A Charge to Keep: My Journey to the White House,* William Morrow, 1999.

chael Ledeen.[298] It was then that Bush Jr., who had so far spent about 40% of his presidential life on vacation, found his true calling: "My administration has a job to do and we're going to do it. We will rid the world of the evil-doers" (September 16); "I want justice. And there's an old poster out West, I recall, that says, 'Wanted: Dead or Alive'" (September 17).

Close behind President Bush stood Vice-President Dick Cheney, who had chosen himself for that position after leading the victorious Bush campaign. He made the vice-presidency into a Presidency in disguise. According to his biographers Lou Dubose and Jake Bernstein (*Vice: Dick Cheney and the Hijacking of the American Presidency*, 2006), "Dick Cheney has become the most powerful Vice-President ever to occupy the office, exercising authority that often subsumes the President's."[299] Cheney was not only the most powerful but also the most secretive: he has successfully resisted against all requests for transparency on the pretext that the vice-presidency is not implicated under the Freedom of Information Act because it is not really a branch of the executive.

Empowered by Bush Jr. to compose the transition team, Cheney began by placing his mentor Donald Rumsfeld as head of the Department of Defense. Rumsfeld and Cheney had been inseparable since the 1970s. They belong to the most hawkish wing of the Republican Party: systematically demanding a stronger army, a unilateralist approach and a disregard for international law. It was Gerald Ford who had first introduced them into the White House, naming Rumsfeld as his Chief of Staff, who then made Cheney his Deputy. Having inspired Ford in the cabinet reshuffle which became known journalistically as the "Halloween Massacre," Rumsfeld then seized the position of Secretary of Defense, while Cheney replaced him as Chief of Staff. Thus there appeared for the first time the explosive combination of Rumsfeld at Defense, Cheney in the White House. Then, with the help of one of the most powerful lobbies ever created, the Committee on the Present Danger, funded by arms industrialists such as David Packard, Rumsfeld and Cheney persuaded President Ford and his new CIA director George H. W. Bush to appoint an independent committee, known as Team B, to revise upward the CIA estimates on the Soviet threat. Team B was composed of twelve experts chosen from among the most fanatical cold warriors, such as General Lyman Lemnitzer (the Chairman of the Joint Chiefs fired by Kennedy) and Paul Nitze (the principal author of the NSC-68 document in 1950). The committee would produce a terrifying report that claimed Moscow to be in possession of not only a large and sophisticated arsenal of weapons of mass destruction, but also the will to dominate all of Europe and the Middle East, and the readiness to start a nuclear confrontation.

---

[298] From the film *Le Monde selon Bush,* by William Karel, 2004:
www.imdb.com/title/tt0416043/quotes
[299] Dubose and Bernstein, *Vice, op. cit.,* p. x.

Pointing to a "window of vulnerability" in the U.S. defense system, Team B's report advocated a broad and urgent increase in the defense budget, which began under Carter and then accelerated under Reagan. Today, historians agree that the assessments of Team B were maliciously alarming: in reality, the USSR was already lagging behind militarily, and had no intent to expand its sphere of influence.

On their comeback under Bush Jr.'s presidency, Cheney and Rumsfeld took on powers that would prove decisive for their control of the September 11th operation. May 8, 2001, President Bush announced the creation of the Office of National Preparedness (ONP), subject to FEMA but placed directly under the control of the Vice-President, who thereby became responsible for coordinating the government's response to terrorist attacks on U.S. soil. Then by an order issued on June 1, 2001 by the Joint Chiefs of Staff (CJCSI 3610.01A), the responsibility for ordering the destruction of a hijacked and/or menacing airplane was given solely to the Secretary of Defense. As a result, on September 11, 2001, the Rumsfeld-Cheney tandem alone had the power to hinder any intervention against the attacks, real of fictitious.

Norman Mineta, Secretary of Transportation from 2001 to 2006, was with Dick Cheney and his deputy at the PEOC (White House bunker) at 9:20 am. He gave this testimony before the 9/11 Commission, on the 23rd of May, 2003: "During the time that the airplane was coming in to the Pentagon, there was a young man who would come in and say to the Vice-President, 'The plane is 50 miles out.' 'The plane is 30 miles out.' And when it got down to 'the plane is 10 miles out,' the young man also said to the Vice-President, 'Do the orders still stand?' And the Vice-President turned and whipped his neck around and said, 'Of course the orders still stand. Have you heard anything to the contrary?'"[300] Could Cheney's order be anything else than a stand-down order?

The Pentagon is not only the nerve center of the deep state; it is also the marketplace of the military-industrial complex. September 10, 2001, Donald Rumsfeld publicly announced that $2.3 trillion were missing from the accounts of the Department of Defense, and later an additional $1.1 trillion was declared unaccounted for: just for comparison, this is more than one thousand times the

---

[300] Griffin, *9/11 Contradictions, op. cit.,* p. 22-30, filmed on YouTube, "Cheney gave Stand Down Order": www.youtube.com/watch?v=QlM8Sui6-X0

colossal losses of Enron, which triggered a chain of bankruptcies that same year. The mystery of these trillions that just evaporated into thin air is an issue that had to be resolved by financial analysts at Resource Services Washington (RSW). Unfortunately, their offices were destroyed by "Al-Qaeda" the morning following Rumsfeld's public announcement, which then became quickly buried under more pressing news. If we are to believe the *National Transportation and Safety Board* (NTSB), the hijackers or Flight AA77, rather than hitting the Command Center on the eastern side of the Pentagon (where the Defense Secretary and the Joint Chiefs had their offices), accomplished an impossible downward spiral at 180° which lasted three minutes, in order to hit the west side of the building precisely at the location of the accounting offices. The 34 experts at RSW perished in their offices, together with 12 other financial analysts, as is noted in the biography of the team leader Robert Russell for the National 9/11 Pentagon Memorial: "The weekend before his death, his entire office attended a crab feast at the Russell home. They were celebrating the end of the fiscal-year budget completion. Tragically, every person that attended that party was involved in the Pentagon explosion, and are currently missing."[301]

By an incredible coincidence, one of the financial experts trying to make sense of the Pentagon financial loss, Bryan Jack, was reported to have died at the precise location of his office, not because he was working there that day, but because he was on a business trip on Flight AA77. In the words of the *Washington Post*: "Bryan C. Jack was responsible for crunching America's defense budget. He was a passenger on American Airlines Flight 77, bound for official business in California when his plane struck the Pentagon, where, on any other day, Jack would have been at work at his computer."[302]

Behind Rumsfeld and Cheney—or below, in accordance with the "Deep Politics" depth metaphor—is the group of so-called neoconservatives. Rumsfeld and Cheney maintained symbiotic relationship with many of these individuals since the 70s: the neoconservatives pumped their ideology through their many think tanks such as the American Enterprise Institute for Public Policy Research (AEI) or the Hudson Institute, while Rumsfeld and Cheney put the concepts into action through the political machinery. It was to the prominent neoconservatives Richard Pipes and Paul Wolfowitz, protégés of Richard Perle,

---

[301] The National 9/11 Pentagon Memorial: pentagonmemorial.org/explore/biographies/sgm-robert-e-russell-usa-retired.
[302] "Remembering: The Pentagon Victims": www.washingtonpost.com/wp-srv/metro/specials/attacked/victims/v_235.html

that Rumsfeld and Cheney had entrusted the management of Team B. After the Carter period, neoconservatives played a major role in the election of Ronald Reagan, who reciprocally named a dozen of them into positions involving national security and foreign policy: Richard Perle and Douglas Feith to the Department of Defense, Richard Pipes to the National Security Council, and Paul Wolfowitz, Lewis "Scooter" Libby, and Michael Ledeen to the State Department. Once ascended to Presidency, Bush Sr. would try to limit the influence of those he called "the crazies," but he would be forced to give the post of Defense Secretary to Dick Cheney, who naturally brought along Paul Wolfowitz and Scooter Libby. The latter two are the authors of a secret report, *Defense Planning Guidance*, leaked by the *New York Times* March 7, 1992, which advocated imperialism, unilateralism and, if necessary, preemptive war "for deterring potential competitors from even aspiring to a larger regional or global role."[303] With the help of a new Committee for Peace and Security in the Gulf, co-chaired by Richard Perle, neoconservatives would argue—without success for this time—for the overthrow of Saddam Hussein after Operation Desert Storm in Kuwait. During the Clinton Presidency, the neocons consolidated their alliance with Rumsfeld and Cheney by creating the think tank Project for the New American Century (PNAC), under William Kristol and Robert Kagan in 1997.

The American Enterprise Institute (AEI), founded in 1943 by businessmen opposed to the New Deal, was overtaken in the 70s by the neocons, who tripled its budget. Some weeks before launching the war against Iraq, President George W. Bush congratulated them: "At the American Enterprise Institute some of the finest minds in our nation are at work in some of the greatest challenges to our nation. You do such good work that my administration has borrowed twenty such minds."[304]

In 2000, Cheney and Rumsfeld brought a new wave of powerful neoconservatives into the U.S. government: Cheney made Scooter Libby Chief of Staff; David Frum, a friend to Richard Perle, became the President's principal speechwriter; and Ari Fleischer became White House Press Secretary. Cheney could not oppose the appointment of Colin Powell as Secretary of State, but put him in tandem with John Bolton, a right-leaning Republican, assisted by

---

[303] "Excerpts From Pentagon's Plan: 'Prevent the Re-Emergence of Rival", *The New York Times,* March 8, 1992: www.nytimes.com/1992/03/08/world/excerpts-from-pentagon-s-plan-prevent-the-re-emergence-of-a-new-rival.html?pagewanted=all&src=pm
[304] "Full text: George Bush's speech to the American Enterprise Institute", *The Guardian,* February 27, 2003: www.guardian.co.uk/world/2003/feb/27/usa.iraq2

the neoconservative David Wurmser. Cheney appointed Condoleezza Rice as National Security Advisor; Rice was not, strictly speaking, a neoconservative, but had been for years under the spell of one of the most aggressive neoconservatives, Philip Zelikow, an expert in "catastrophic terrorism" who became her consultant for the Middle East (Rice's field of expertise being limited to the Soviet Union); as advisors to Rice were also recruited William Luti and Elliot Abrams (both simultaneously assistants to the President), while Eliot Cohen would be brought in to assist when Rice would replace Powell in the State Department in 2007. It is, however, in the Department of Defense under Donald Rumsfeld, that the three most influential neoconservatives would be in the position to shape foreign policy: Paul Wolfowitz, Richard Perle and Douglas Feith, the latter occupying the crucial position of Director of the Defense Policy Board, responsible for defining military strategy. Not to forget Dov Zakheim, Undersecretary of Defense (Comptroller), tasked to help track down the Pentagon's 2.3 trillion dollars worth of unaccounted transactions. So it was that these neoconservatives found themselves in the positions they had coveted, as councilors and brokers for the President and his ministers.

John Bolton is a unilateralist who declared in 1994: "There is no such thing as the United Nations. There is only the international community, which can only be led by the only remaining superpower, which is the United States."[305] In 2005, to punish the United Nations for its reluctance to make war on Iraq, President Bush named Bolton U.S. ambassador to the U.N.

The indictment of Saudi Arabia, which seems written into the script of September 11th, bears the signature of the neoconservatives. After the attacks of September 11th, David Wurmser opened the hostilities in the *Weekly Standard* with an article entitled "The Saudi Connection" claiming that the royal family was behind the attack.[306] The Hudson Institute, a bas-

---

[305] Kurt Nimmo, "John Bolton to the UN", *Counterpunch,* March 8, 2005: www.counterpunch.org/2005/03/08/john-bolton-to-the-un/

[306] "The Saudi Connection : Osama bin Laden's a lot closer to the Saudi royal family than you think,"
The Weekly Standard, October 29, 2001:
www.weeklystandard.com/Content/Public/Articles/000/000/000/393rwyib.asp

tion for neoconservative doctrine, has long led a virulent campaign demonizing the Saudi dynasty, under the leadership of its co-founder Max Singer (now director of research at the Institute for Zionist Strategies in Jerusalem). In June 2002, the Institute sponsored a seminar entitled "Discourses on Democracy: Saudi Arabia, Friend or Foe?" where all the presentations suggest that "foe" is the correct answer. A special event was held to launch the book *Hatred's Kingdom: How Saudi Arabia Supports the New Global Terrorism*, written by Dore Gold, an Israeli who has served as advisor to Netanyahu and Sharon and as ambassador to the United Nations. On July 10, 2002, the Franco-American neoconservative Laurent Murawiec, a member of the Hudson Institute and the Committee on the Present Danger, appeared before Richard Perle's Defense Policy Board to explain that Saudi Arabia is "the kernel of evil, the prime mover, the most dangerous opponent" and recommend that the United States invade, occupy and fragment the state. He summarized his "Grand Strategy for the Middle East" with these words: "Iraq is the tactical pivot, Saudi Arabia the strategic pivot, Egypt the prize."[307] Murawiec is the author of several books demonizing Saud, such as *Princes of Darkness: the Saudi Assault on the West* (2005).

Although virtually omnipresent in the Bush administration, the neoconservatives are, in fact, the main instigators of the soft "conspiracy theory" on 9/11, which admits responsibility of Al-Qaeda but focuses its accusations on the connections between Bush, the Saudis and bin Laden. In their book published in 2003, *An End to Evil: How to Win the War on Terror*, Richard Perle and David Frum argue that "the Saudis qualify for their own membership in the axis of evil," and implore President Bush to "tell the truth about Saudi Arabia," namely that the Saudi princes finance Al-Qaeda.[308] These fabricated rumors of Saudi involvement in 9/11 are, in fact, indicative of a power struggle between several players within the deep state, not unlike the suppression of the pseudo Oswald-Castro connection. The situation in which the President found himself at the time of the attacks—reading *The Pet Goat* with primary school-children in Florida—dramatically illustrates how he was removed from direct control of ongoing operations. His ensuing arraignment alongside the Saudis indicates that he was held hostage by his co-conspirators. And what did they get from him? The invasion of Iraq.[309]

---

[307] Thomas E. Ricks, "Briefing Depicted Saudis as Enemies Ultimatum Urged To Pentagon Board", *The Washington Post,* August 6, 2002.

[308] Sniegoski, *Transparent Cabal, op. cit.,* p. 204.

[309] On the plotters' control of president Bush, read Tarpley, *9/11 Synthetic Terror, op. cit.,* p. 272-301.

President Bush is still listening to schoolchildren at 9:12 am, while the second tower has been hit at 9:01. We can only conjecture about his thoughts during these ten minutes made memorable by Michael Moore's *Fahrenheit 9/11*. This could be the equivalent to the Zapruder film for Kennedy: the moment when Bush was turned into a dummy—the next thing to a corpse—while Cheney was taking over real government.

21. Weapons of Mass Deception

According to notes obtained by David Martin, correspondent on the National Security Council for CBS News, only five hours after the explosion at the Pentagon, Donald Rumsfeld gathered his team in the National Military Command Center and asked them to provide "all and any information" to target Iraq: "Best info fast. Judge whether good enough hit Saddam Hussein at same time. Not only UBL [Osama bin Laden]. Go massive. Sweep it all up. Things related and not."[310] Richard Clarke, head of counter-terrorism within the National Security Council, revealed in his book *Against All Enemies* (2004) that on September 12th, President Bush personally asked him to provide evidence of a link between Saddam Hussein and the attacks. When he submitted a report concluding that there was no connection, the report was returned by a deputy with a note saying "Please update and resubmit," apparently unshown to the President.[311]

In 1983, Rumsfeld had been President Reagan's special envoy in Bagdad to discuss with Saddam the renewal of diplomatic and economic relations.

On September 19th and 20th, Richard Perle's Defense Policy Board met in the company of Paul Wolfowitz and Bernard Lewis (inventor of the self-fulfilling

---

[310] Julian Borger, "Blogger bares Rumsfeld's post 9/11 orders", *The Guardian,* February 24, 2006: www.guardian.co.uk/world/2006/feb/24/freedomofinformation.september11
[311] Richard Clarke, *Against all Enemies: Inside America's War on Terror,* Simon & Schuster, 2004.

prophecy of the "clash of civilizations"),[312] but in the absence of Colin Powell and Condoleezza Rice. Those assembled agreed on the need to overthrow Saddam Hussein at the end of the initial phase of the war in Afghanistan. They prepared a letter to Bush, written in PNAC letterhead, to remind him of his historic mission: "even if evidence does not link Iraq directly to the attack, any strategy aiming at the eradication of terrorism and its sponsors must include a determined effort to remove Saddam Hussein from power in Iraq. Failure to undertake such an effort will constitute an early and perhaps decisive surrender in the war on international terrorism."[313] The argument of a link between Saddam and Al-Qaeda is here toned down, and in the summer of 2002, President Bush and British Prime Minister Tony Blair would merely allude to "broad linkages" between Saddam and Al-Qaeda. Perle, on the other hand, would continue to claim against all evidence that Mohamed Atta, the alleged ringleader of the 9/11 terrorists, had met with Iraqi diplomat Ahmed Khalil Ibrahim Samir in Prague in 1999. On September 8, 2002, in Milan, Perle even dished the "scoop" to the Italian daily *Il Sole,* that "Mohammed Atta met Saddam Hussein in Baghdad prior to September 11. We have proof of that," but would refrain from repeating such a ridiculous claim in the United States.[314]

The rumors of a link between Saddam and Al-Qaeda were finally abandoned in favor of a more elaborate *casus belli*: the worldwide threat posed by Saddam's "weapons of mass destruction." To concoct this next lie, Cheney and Rumsfeld had to circumvent CIA director George Tenet, who knew well (thanks in part to Saddam's son-in-law Kamel Hussein, who had fled Iraq in 1995 after being in charge of its military industry) that Saddam was no longer in possession of such weapons. At the end of the summer of 2002, Cheney and Rumsfeld renewed their winning Team B strategy, essentially overtaking the CIA with a parallel structure set up to produce the alarmist report they needed: it will be the Office of Special Plans (OSP), a special unit within the Near East and South Asia (NESA) offices at the Pentagon. Nicknamed "the Cabal," the OSP was controlled by neoconservatives William Luti, Abram Shulsky, Douglas Feith and Paul Wolfowitz. It based its estimates on information provided by Ahmed Chalabi, an Iraqi con artist sentenced to 22 years in prison in Jordan for bank fraud and having not set foot in Iraq since 1956; he was bribed with the promise of a seat at the top of the Iraqi state after the overthrow of Saddam. Lieutenant Colonel Karen Kwiatkowski, who worked for the NESA at this time, testified in 2004 to the incompetence of members of the OSP, whom she saw "usurp measured and carefully considered assessments, and through sup-

---

[312] Bernard Lewis, *What Went Wrong? The Clash between Islam and Modernity in the Middle East,* Harper Perennial, 2003.

[313] Sniegoski, *Transparent Cabal, op. cit.,* p. 144.

[314] Gary Leupp, "Richard Perle's Bombshell in Milan", *Conterpunch,* September 10, 2002: www.counterpunch.org/2002/09/10/richard-perle-s-bombshell-in-milan/

pression and distortion of intelligence analysis promulgate what were in fact falsehoods to both Congress and the executive office of the president [...]. This was creatively produced propaganda."[315]

In September 2002, in preparation for the war, Bush signed the *National Security Strategy report* (*NSS* 2002), which defined what would be called the "Bush doctrine"—despite being nothing other than an update to the 1992 "Wolfowitz doctrine." In order to "deny, contain, and curtail our enemies' efforts to acquire dangerous technologies," the document states, "America will act against such emerging threats before they are fully formed." Assuming that "our best defense is a good offense" and that "the events of September 11, 2001 [...] open vast, new opportunities," the authors recommend "taking anticipatory action to defend ourselves, even if uncertainty remains as to the time and place of the enemy's attack. To forestall or prevent such hostile acts by our adversaries, the United States will, if necessary, act preemptively." Thus was prepared the justification for a "preemptive" attack against Iraq.[316]

What remained to do was to convince the American public and Congress, with a tough speech by the President, on October 7, 2002: "Saddam Hussein," Bush said, "is a homicidal dictator who is addicted to weapons of mass destruction,"[317] and who could at any time "provide a biological or chemical weapon to a terrorist group or individual terrorists." Bush further claimed that Saddam also possessed the aircrafts and drones necessary to "disperse chemical or biological weapons across broad areas [...], targeting the United States"; even worse, "the evidence indicates that Iraq is reconstituting its nuclear weapons program." He asks rhetorically, "if we know Saddam Hussein has dangerous weapons today, and we do, does it make any sense for the world to wait to confront him as he grows even stronger and develops even more dangerous weapons?" Time is running out, for Saddam "could have a nuclear weapon in less than a year. And if we allow that to happen, a terrible line would be crossed. [...] Facing clear evidence of peril, we cannot wait for the final proof, the smoking gun that could come in the form of a mushroom cloud."[318]

No one doubts that Bush's anti-Iraq rhetoric was crafted by his neoconservative advisors. The neocons had been vilifying Saddam Hussein and calling for his overthrow since the first Gulf War. David Wurmser, for example, published *Tyranny's Ally: America's Failure to Defeat Saddam Hussein* (1999), among other virulent books against Muslim countries. In 2000, the American Enterprise Institute published *Study of Revenge: Saddam Hussein's Unfinished War Against America*, whose author, Laurie Mylroie, acknowledged her debt to Scooter Libby, David Wurmser, John Bolton, Michael Ledeen, and above

---

[315] Sniegoski, *Transparent Cabal, op. cit.,* p. 162.

[316] www.state.gov/documents/organization/63562.pdf

[317] www.presidentialrhetoric.com/speeches/10.7.02.html

[318] Sniegoski, *Transparent Cabal, op. cit.,* p. 155.

all Paul Wolfowitz and his wife Clare Wolfowitz (also a member of the AEI). Mylroie does not hesitate to call Saddam Hussein the brain behind worldwide anti-American terrorism, attributing to him without evidence the 1993 attack against the World Trade Center, the Oklahoma City bombing in 1995, and the attack against the *USS Cole* in Yemen in 2000. According to her, what most threatens the U.S. is "an undercover war of terrorism, waged by Saddam Hussein," which is nothing more than "a phase in a conflict that began in August 1990, when Iraq invaded Kuwait, and that has not ended." Richard Perle has described this book as "splendid and wholly convincing."[319]

Paul Wolfowitz was called "the godfather of the Iraq war" by *Time Magazine*, and "the most hawkishly pro-Israel voice in the Administration" by *The Jewish Daily Forward*. He conceptualized "preemptive war" in 1992, and sold it as "the Bush doctrine" to the American media in 2001.[320]

Support for a preemptive strike against Iraq, however, was not unanimous. Some prominent men who had supported the war in Afghanistan, in the emotion of Sept. 11th, without worrying about the lack of evidence against bin Laden, were now opposing the invasion of Iraq. Even Brzezinski, who had implicitly called for some new "Pearl Harbor," refused to support the war in Iraq and criticized the effort with increasing severity. Bush Sr. objected, of course, but remained discreet. Hope of avoiding the oncoming catastrophe rested on Secretary of State Colin Powell. He had made it clear on February 24, 2001 that the sanctions against Iraq had been sufficient to prevent it from developing weapons of mass destruction. Yet, for reasons that remain largely unexplained, Powell played along the neocon tune; on February 5, 2003, he declared to the General Assembly of the United Nations, "there can be no doubt that Saddam Hussein has biological weapons and the capability to rapidly produce more, many more. And he has the ability to dispense these lethal poisons and diseases in ways that can cause massive death and destruction."[321] As former National Security Advisor under Reagan and Chairman of the Joint Chiefs of Staff under Bush Sr., Powell's stance carried considerable weight in American public opinion, but failed to win approval from the UN Security Council, thanks in part to French Foreign Minister Philippe de Villepin.

---

[319] Sniegoski, *Transparent Cabal, op. cit.,* p. 98.
[320] Sniegoski, *Transparent Cabal, op. cit.,* p. 118.
[321] Sniegoski, *Transparent Cabal, op. cit.,* p. 183.

On February 5, 2003, Secretary of State Colin Powell placed his reputation on the line, trying to convince the UN General Assembly of the that Saddam Hus- sein's WMD pose a threat to the world. Brandishing a tube of fake anthrax in his televised speech, he reactivated the trauma of the October 2001 anthrax letters: **"Less than a teaspoon of dry anthrax in an envelope shut down the United States Senate in the fall of 2001. Iraq declared 8,500 liters."[322]**

Bush and Blair had in fact already agreed to go to war against Iraq regardless of the UN Security Council final vote, during a meeting in Washington on January 31, 2003. According to a memo brought to public light by Phillipe Sands in his book *Lawless World,* 2005, and now known as "the White House Memo," Bush shared with Blair his "plans to lure Saddam Hussein into war by flying an aircraft over Iraq painted in UN colors in the hope he would shoot it down."[323] The stratagem was finally deemed unnecessary. The assault against Iraq was launched in March 2003, using the "Shock and Awe" method intended for "Rapid Dominance," a state of the art strategy dear to Rumsfeld, developed in 1996 by the National Defense University; the idea is to quickly crush the opponents and break their will through the use of heavy firepower intended to "paralyze or so overload an adversary's perceptions and understanding of events that the enemy would be incapable of resistance at the tactical and strategic levels."[324] In May 2003, Bush rather hastily declared: "Mission accomplished" in Iraq. In reality, what was supposed to be a blitzkrieg would prove worse than the Vietnam quagmire. As no trace could be found of Saddam's alleged "weapons of mass destruction," criticisms of the OSP's rigged data started to emerge. In 2004, George Tenet was forced to resign from the leadership of the CIA for his acceptance (however reluctant) of that faulty OSP intelligence; he was replaced by Porter Goss. Colin Powell also left his post in 2004, giving way to

---

[322] Powell's speech can be heard on YouTube, e.g. "Archive: Colin Powell's UN presentation on Iraq" (5 parts): www.youtube.com/watch?v=Nt5RZ6ukbNc

[323] Phillipe Sands, *Lawless World: America and the Making and Breaking of Global Rules,* Allen Lane, 2005. Roseway Bennet and Michael Evans, "Bush tried to lure Saddam into war using UN aircraft", *Times,* February 3, 2006:
www.thetimes.co.uk/tto/news/world/middleeast/iraq/article1994319.ece

[324] National Defense University, *Shock & Awe: Achieving Rapid Dominance:*
www.dodccrp.org/files/Ullman_Shock.pdf

Condoleezza Rice. He would regret publicly his speech to the UN, calling it "a blot on my record" and claiming to have been deceived.[325] His Chief of Staff, Colonel Lawrence Wilkerson, likewise would confess in 2006, soon after resigning: "My participation in that presentation at the UN constitutes the lowest point in my professional life. I participated in a hoax on the American people, the international community and the United Nations Security Council."[326]

It is in this context that in March 2006 Congress formed the Iraq Study Group, a bi-partisan commission that was critical of government decisions and pessimistic in regards to the evolution of the conflict. It was chaired by James Baker, who had been the campaign manager for George Bush Sr. and later his Chief of Staff and Secretary of State (at that time he had successfully opposed the neoconservatives' push for the invasion of Iraq). Robert Gates, CIA Director under Bush Sr., was also involved. The Iraq Study Group was rightly seen as an attempt by the Bush clan to save their now badly wounded legacy. In November of the same year, the parliamentary midterm elections brought severe popular sanctions against the war and forced Bush to demission Donald Rumsfeld and appoint Robert Gates in his place. The neocons, however, counter-attacked with an *ad hoc* pro-Surge group named Freedom's Watch, which financed a campaign of 15 million dollars attacking anti-Surge congressmen[327]. The President trusted his neocon advisors and remained deaf to popular opposition and the advice of his original political family: he announced in January 2007 the deployment of 20,000 additional troops, and then in April 2008 named General David Petraeus the new commander of coalition forces in Iraq, with a mission to lead a new assault called "the Surge."

Given the undisputed fact that the intelligence suggesting Saddam had weapons of mass destruction was nothing but a lie manufactured by the neoconservatives and sold to the American people by Bush, Cheney and Rumsfeld, what was the real reason for the invasion of Iraq? The consensual answer seems to be: Big Oil. Noam Chomsky dismisses even the need to argue: "Of course it was Iraq's energy resources. It's not even a question."[328] As a sign of the times, he has been joined by Alan Greenspan, director of the Federal Reserve, who likewise concedes "what everyone knows: the Iraq war is largely about oil" (*The Age of Turbulence,* 2007). Chomsky and Greenspan are, of course, believers in the official bin Laden explanation of 9/11, and detractors of the 9/11 Truth movement. Yet most 9/11 truthers agree with them on that crucial question of motive. Strangely, they also claim it to be self-evident, rather than demonstrated through serious investigation: "I personally believe that there is a

[325] Steven Weisman, "Powell Calls His U.N. Speech a Lasting Blot on His Record", *New York Times,* September 9, 2005: www.nytimes.com/2005/09/09/politics/09powell.html
[326] Transcript of the interview on: www.pbs.org/now/politics/wilkerson.html
[327] Paul Findley, in Sniegoski, *Transparent Cabal, op. cit.,* p. vii-x.
[328] Sniegoski, *Transparent Cabal, op. cit.,* p. 333.

deep relationship between the events of 9/11 and peak oil, but it's not some-thing I can prove," admits Richard Heinberg, a specialist in energy depletion, in the documentary *Oil, Smoke and Mirrors*.[329]

The problem is that there is no indication whatsoever that the oil lobby had encouraged the military intervention in Iraq. What oil companies had asked, rather, was the lifting of sanctions that prohibited them from dealing with Sad-dam's Iraq—the same as they are now asking for Iran. As James Petras has shown in *Zionism, Militarism and the Decline of US Power* (2008), "'Big Oil' not only did not promote the invasion, but has failed to secure a single oil field, despite the presence of 160,000 US troops, 127,000 Pentagon/State Department paid mer-cenaries and a corrupt puppet régime."[330] When in 2009 the licenses for ex-ploitation were auctioned, it was Russia and China who grabbed the lion's share, with even France's company Total coming ahead of U.S. companies.[331]

Proponents of the oil thesis like to foreground Halliburton, which has doubled its income in becoming the largest private contractor working for U.S. forces in Iraq. They rightly accuse Dick Cheney of having personally gained $50 mil-lion in promoting Halliburton, after having served as its CEO from 1995 to 2000. However, Halliburton and Cheney's personal gains in Iraq have little to do with a national strategy for control of natural resources. Furthermore, Halli-burton is not a petroleum company, but rather a civil engineering company that provides services to oil companies, as well as to armies. Besides, in the 1990s, even Halliburton (then under Cheney's leadership) had called for the lifting of sanctions on Iraq, Iran and Libya, and had even been charged a $3.8 million fine for having bypassed said sanctions. Yes, Dick Cheney has blood on his bank account—and he is not alone—but the United States of America as a whole won nothing in the war in Iraq, which cost the American people a whopping $3 trillion, according to lowest estimates (Joseph Stieglitz, *The Three Trillion Dollar War*, 2008).[332] As for the Bushes, renowned oil sharks, there is no indication that they stood to make personal financial gain, not to mention the fact that the aggressiveness of neoconservative rhetoric against Saudi Arabia has hurt their interests. No, the oil does not explain the war in Iraq, nor does it explain the war in Afghanistan, nor does it explain the planned war against Iran. And it certainly does not explain the extraordinary discipline of corporate medias in their support of the government 9/11 myth.

---

[329] In *Oil, Smoke and Mirrors,* documentary by Ronan Doyle, 2007.
[330] James Petras, *Zionism, Militarism and the Decline of US Power,* Clarity Press, 2008, p. 18.
[331] Sniegoski, *Transparent Cabal, op. cit.,* p. 335-8.
[332] Joseph Stieglitz, *The Three Trillion Dollar War: The True Cost of the Iraq Conflict,* WW Norton & CO, 2008.

22. Twenty-five Machiavellian crypto-Zionists

The neoconservative movement, which is a radical (rather than "conservative") Republican right, is, in reality, an intellectual movement born in the late 1960s in the pages of the monthly magazine *Commentary*, a media arm of the *American Jewish Committee*, which had replaced the *Contemporary Jewish Record* in 1945. *The Jewish Daily Forward* wrote in a January 6, 2006 article signed Gal Beckerman: "If there is an intellectual movement in America to whose invention Jews can lay sole claim, neo-conservatism is it. It's a thought one imagines most American Jews, overwhelmingly liberal, will find horrifying. And yet it is a fact that as a political philosophy, neo-conservatism was born among the children of Jewish immigrants and is now largely the intellectual domain of those immigrants' grandchildren." The neoconservative apologist Murray Friedman explains the Jewish dominance within his movement by the inherent benevolence of Judaism, "the idea that Jews have been put on earth to make it a better, perhaps even a holy, place" (*The Neoconservative Revolution: Jewish Intellectuals and the Shaping of Public Policy,* 2006).[333]

Just as we speak of the "Christian Right" as a political force in the United States, we could also therefore speak of the neoconservatives as representing the "Jewish Right." However, this characterization is problematic for three reasons. First, the neoconservatives are a relatively small group, although they have acquired considerable authority in Jewish representative organizations— which are so numerous that their activities need to be coordinated by a Conference of Presidents of Major American Jewish Organizations, with a current list of 51 members. The neoconservatives compensate for their small number by multiplying their Committees, Projects, and other think tanks, which gives them a kind of ubiquity; in 2003, *New York Times* journalist Thomas Friedman

---

[333] Sniegoski, *Transparent Cabal, op. cit.,* p. 26, 42.

could say of only twenty-five influential neocons: "if you had exiled them to a desert island a year and half ago, the Iraq war would not have happened."[334]

Second, the neoconservatives of the first generation mostly came from the left, even the extreme Trotskyist left for some luminaries like Irving Kristol, one of the main editors of *Commentary*. During the late 1960s the *Commentary* editorial staff began to break with the liberal, pacifist left, which they suddenly deemed decadent. Norman Podhoretz, editor of *Commentary* from 1960 until his retirement in 1995, was an anti-Vietnam War activist until 1967, but then in the 70s became a fervent advocate of an increased defense budget, bringing the journal along in his wake. In the 1980s, he opposed the policy of détente in his book *The Present Danger*. In the 1990s, he calls for the invasion of Iraq, and then again in the early 2000s. In 2007, while his son John Podhoretz was taking over as editor of *Commentary*, he asserted once again the urgency of a U.S. military attack, this time against Iran.

Third, unlike evangelical Christians who openly proclaim their unifying religious principles, neoconservatives do not display their Judaism. Whether they'd been Marxists or not, they appear mostly non-religious (although quite a few are sons or grandsons of rabbis, and at least one, Pentagon Comptroller Dov Zakheim, is an ordained rabbi). Their unifying ideology is mostly borrowed from Leo Strauss, so much so that they are sometimes referred to as "the Straussians"; Norman Podhoretz and his son John, Irving Kristol and his son William, Donald Kagan and his son Robert, Paul Wolfowitz, Adam Shulsky, all expressed their debt to Strauss. Leo Strauss, born to a family of German Orthodox Jews, was both pupil and collaborator of political theorist Carl Schmitt, himself a specialist of Thomas Hobbes and advocate of a "political theology" by which the State must appropriate the attributes of God. Schmitt was an admirer of Mussolini, and the legal counsel of the Third Reich. After the Reichstag fire in February 1933, it was Schmitt who provided the legal framework that justified the suspension of citizen rights and the establishment of the dictatorship. It was also Schmitt who, in 1934, personally obtained from the Rockefeller Foundation a grant for Leo Strauss to study Thomas Hobbes in London and Paris, to then finally end up teaching in Chicago.[335]

The thinking of Leo Strauss is difficult to capture, and certainly beyond the purview of this work. Strauss is often elliptic because he believes that truth is harmful to the common man and the social order and should be reserved for superior minds (religion is for the rest). For this reason, Strauss rarely speaks in his own name, but rather expressed himself as a commentator on classical

---

[334] Quoted in Ari Shavit, "White man's burden", *Haaretz,* April 3, 2003: www.haaretz.com/news/features/white-man-s-burden-1.14110

[335] Heinrich Meier, *Carl Schmitt and Leo Strauss: the Hidden Dialogue,* University of Chicago Press, 2006.

authors, such as Plato or Thomas Hobbes. Moreover, much like his disciple Allan Bloom (*The Closing of the American Mind*, 1988), he is careful to adorn his most radical ideas with humanist catchphrases, which often seem to contradict the core message. Despite the apparent difficulty, three basic ideas can easily be extracted from his political philosophy, which parallel those of Schmitt. First, nations derive their strength from their myths, which are necessary for government and governance. Second, national myths have no necessary relationship with historical reality: they are socio-cultural constructions that the State has a duty to disseminate. Third, to be effective, any national myth must be marked by a clear distinction between good and evil, for it derives its cohesive strength from the hatred of an enemy nation. As Abram Shulsky and Gary Schmitt write in an article "Leo Strauss and the World of Intelligence" (1999), for Strauss, "deception is the norm in political life"[336]—a rule neocons applied in the Office of Special Plans to fabricate the lie of Saddam's weapons of mass destruction.

Leo Strauss considered "Western" movies as a successful example of national mythic construction. In 1980, the neoconservatives bet all their chips on Hollywood actor Ronald Reagan and, twenty years later, on a born-again Christian invested with the mission of "ridding the world of evil-doers."

In his maturity, Strauss was an admirer of Machiavelli, whom he believes he understood better than anyone. In his *Thoughts on Machiavelli*, he parts from the intellectual trend of trying to rehabilitate the author of *The Prince* against the "simple opinion" which regards his work as immoral; such relativization of Machiavelli's immorality "prevents one from doing justice to what is truly admirable in Machiavelli; the intrepidity of his thought, the grandeur of his vision, and the graceful subtlety of his speech." Machiavelli's thought is so revolutionary, Strauss believes, that its ultimate implications could not be spelled out: "Machiavelli does not go to the end of the road; the last part of the road must be travelled by the reader

---

[336] "Leo Strauss and the World of Intelligence (By Which We Do Not Mean Nous)", in Kenneth L. Deutsch and John Albert Murley, ed., *Leo Strauss, the Straussians, and the American Régime,* Rowman & Littlefield, 1999.

who understands what is omitted by the writer." For this, Strauss is the guide, for "to discover from [Machiavelli'] writings what he regarded as the truth is hard; it is not impossible." Machiavelli's truth is not a blinding light, but rather a bottomless abyss that only the accomplished philosopher can contemplate without turning into a beast: there is no afterlife, and neither good nor evil, and therefore the ruling elite shaping the destiny of their nation need not worry about the salvation of their own souls. Hence Machiavelli, according to Strauss, is a patriot of a superior kind.[337]

For Machiavelli, nations, not men, can aspire to immortality. But for the neo-cons, one nation only is truly eternal: Israel. Neo-conservatism can best be understood as a modern Jewish development of Machiavelli's political thought. What characterizes the neoconservative movement is therefore not Judaism as a religious tradition, but rather Judaism as a political project—i.e. Zionism—by Machiavellian means. Some neocons, in fact, believe Machiavellism to be akin to Judaism. In the *Jewish World Review* of June 7, 1999, Michael Ledeen, who calls himself a "student of Machiavelli," argues that Machiavelli may have been a "secret Jew," as were in his time thousands of families nominally converted to Catholicism under threat of expulsion or death. "Listen to his political philosophy, and you will hear the Jewish music," wrote Ledeen, citing in support of this claim Machiavelli's contempt for the nonviolent ethics of Jesus and his admiration for the pragmatism of Moses, who was able to kill thousands from his own tribe in order to establish his authority.[338] If Machiavellians, almost by definition, normally move in disguise, some Zionists today do not hesitate to advertise Machiavellism, like Obadiah Shoher in *Samson Blinded: A Machiavellian Perspective on the Middle East Conflict* (2006).[339]

Obviously, if Zionism is synonymous with patriotism in Israel, it cannot be an acceptable label in American politics, where it means loyalty to a foreign power. This is why the neoconservatives do not represent themselves as Zionists on the American scene. Yet they do not hide it all together either. Elliott Abrams, Deputy National Security Advisor in the Bush II administration, wrote in his book *Faith or Fear* (1997): "Outside the land of Israel, there can be no doubt that Jews, faithful to the covenant between God and Abraham, are to stand apart from the nation in which they live. It is the very nature of being Jewish to be apart—except in Israel—from the rest of the population."[340] A better definition of Zionism would be hard to get.

---

[337] Leo Strauss, *Thoughts on Machiavelli,* University of Chicago Press, 1995.
[338] "What Machiavelli (A Secret Jew?) Learned from Moses", *Jewish World Review,* June 7, 1999, www.jewishworldreview.com/0699/machiavelli1.asp
[339] www.amazon.fr/Samson-Blinded-Machiavellian-Perspective-Conflict/dp/1847282180/ref=sr_1_1?s=english-books&ie=UTF8&qid=1371560857&sr=1-1
[340] *Faith or Fear: How Jews can Survive in a Christian America,* Simon & Schuster, 1997.

Breaking away from the classical political theory (inherited from Cicero) that sought to make virtue the condition of power, Machiavelli (1469-1527) asserted that only the appearance of virtue counts, and that the successful prince must be a "great simulator" who "manipulates and cons people's mind." The tyrant he most admired was Cesar Borgia, who after having appointed the cruel Ramiro d'Orco to subdue the province of Romania, had him executed with utter cruelty, thus reaping the people's gratitude after having diverted their hatred on another.

The corollary of such an idea is the right of Israel to be an "ethnic nation," that is, the apartheid practiced against Palestinian non-Jews: "there is a place in the world for non-ethnic nations and there is a place for ethnic nations," declared Douglas Feith in Jerusalem that same year 1997 (the year PNAC was founded) in his "Reflections on Liberalism, Democracy and Zionism." Israel is an ethnic nation since its conception by Zionist founder Theodor Herzl (*der Jundenstaat*, 1896). In American and European non-ethnic nations, by contrast, unrestricted immigration and multiculturalism should be encouraged.[341]

If one is entitled to consider the neoconservatives as Zionists, it is especially in noting that their foreign policy has always coincided perfectly with the interests of Israel (as they see them). For the last seventy years, Israel's interest has been understood as dependent on two things: the immigration of Eastern Jews, and the financial support of the Jews of the West (American and, to a lesser extent, European). Until 1967, the national interest pushed Israel toward the Soviet Union, while the support of American Jews remained quiet. The socialist and collectivist orientation of the Labor Party in power naturally inclined them in this direction, but Israel's good relations with the USSR were primarily due to the fact that the mass immigration of Jews was only possible through the good will of the Kremlin. During the three years following the end of the

---

[341] Sniegoski, *Transparent Cabal, op. cit.,* p. 119.

British mandate on Palestine (1948), which had hitherto limited Jewish immigration out of consideration for the Arab population, two hundred thousand Polish Jewish refugees in the USSR were allowed to settle in Palestine, with more coming from Romania, Hungary and Bulgaria.

The Six Day War was a decisive turning point: in 1967, Moscow protested against Israel's annexation of new territories, broke diplomatic relations with Tel Aviv and stopped the emigration of its Jewish citizens, which had accelerated in the previous month. It is from this date that *Commentary* became, in the words of Benjamin Balint, *"The Contentious Magazine that Transformed the Jewish Left into the Neoconservative Right"* (subtitle of his 2010 book *Running "Commentary"*).[342] The neoconservatives realized that, from that point, Israel's survival—and its territorial expansion—depended on the support and protection of another super-power, the U.S. military, and concomitantly that Israel's need for Jewish immigrants could only be fulfilled by the fall of communism. These two objectives converged in the deepening of the military power of the United States. This is why Irving Kristol commits members of the American Jewish Congress in 1973 to fight George McGovern's proposal to reduce the military budget by 30 percent: "this is to drive a knife into the heart of Israel. [...] Jews don't like a big military budget, but it is now an interest of the Jews to have a large and powerful military establishment in the United States. [...] American Jews who care about the survival of the state of Israel have to say, no, we don't want to cut the military budget, it is important to keep that military budget big, so that we can defend Israel."[343] This enlightens us on what reality Kristol was referring to, when he famously defined a neoconservative as "a liberal who has been mugged by reality" (*Neoconservatism: the Autobiography of an Idea, 1995*).[344] Like Kristol, Podhoretz warns his readers in 1979 that: "an American withdrawal into the kind of isolationist mood [...] that now looked as though it might soon prevail again, represented a direct threat to the security of Israel."[345]

In the late 60s, the neoconservatives joined the militarist fringe of the Democratic Party, headed by Senator Henry Scoop Jackson, a supporter of the Vietnam War who would challenge McGovern in the 1972 primaries. Richard Perle, parliamentary assistant to Jackson, wrote the Jackson-Vanik amendment, which made food aid to the Soviet Union conditional upon the free emigration of Jews. It was also within the office of Scoop Jackson that an alliance

---

[342] Benjamin Balint, *Running Commentary: the Contentious Magazine That Transformed the Jewish Left into the Neoconservative Right,* Public Affairs, 2010.

[343] *Congress Bi-Weekly,* quoted by Philip Weiss on *Mondoweiss.net,* May 23, 2007: mondoweiss.net/2007/05/30_years_ago_ne.html

[344] *Neoconservatism: the Autobiography of an Idea,* Ivan R. Dee, 1995.

[345] *Breaking Ranks,* 1979, quoted by Philip Weiss on *Mondoweiss.net,* April 24, 2007: mondoweiss.net/2007/04/norman_podhoret.html

between the neoconservatives and the Rumsfeld-Cheney tandem would be forged, an alliance which proved its toxicity when Rumsfeld and Cheney, once in the White House, allowed Perle to place his protégés Paul Wolfowitz and Richard Pipes in Team B—whose report would be published in *Commentary*. During the Carter period, neoconservatives allied with evangelical Christians, viscerally anti-communist and generally well disposed towards Israel, which they see as a divine miracle foreshadowing the return of Christ. The contribution of the neoconservatives to the Reagan victory allowed them to work within the government to strengthen the alliance between the United States and Israel; in 1981, the two countries signed their first military pact, then embarked on several shared operations, some legal and others not so, as evidenced by the network of arms trafficking and paramilitary operations embedded within the Iran-Contra affair. Militarism and Zionism had become so linked in their common cause, that in his 1982 book *The Real Anti-Semitism in America*, the director of the Anti-Defamation League Nathan Perlmutter could portray the pacifism of the "peacemakers of Vietnam vintage, transmuters of swords into plowshares," as a new form of anti-Semitism.[346]

With the end of the Cold War, the national interest of Israel changed once again. Their primary objective became not the fall of communism, but rather the weakening of Israel's enemies. Thus the neoconservatives underwent their second conversion, from anti-communism to islamophobia. To foster their new agenda, they created new think tanks such as the Washington Institute for Near East Policy (WINEP) led by Richard Perle, the Middle East Forum led by Daniel Pipes (son of Richard), the Center for Security Policy (CSP) founded by Frank Gaffney, and the Middle East Media Research Institute (MEMRI).

President George H. W. Bush, however, cultivated friendships with Saudi Arabia and was not exactly a friend of Israel; he resisted in 1991 an unprecedented pro-Israel lobbying campaign that called for $10 billion to help Jews immigrate from the former Soviet Union to Israel, complaining in a televised press conference on September 12th that "one thousand Jewish lobbyists are on Capitol Hill against little old me"—causing Tom Dine, the Executive Director of AIPAC, to exclaim, "September 12, 1991, is a day that will live in infamy."[347] Bush senior also resisted the neoconservatives' advice to invade Iraq after Operation Desert Storm. Finally, Bush's Secretary of State James Baker was deemed too receptive to Arab proposals at the Madrid Conference in November 1991. The Israel lobby, as a result, sabotaged Bush's chances for a second term and supported the Democrat candidate Bill Clinton. On September 2, 1994, the Israeli newspaper *Maariv* ran a story by Avinoam Bar-Yosef

---

[346] Andrew and Leslie Cockburn, *Dangerous Liaison: the Inside Story of the U.S.-Israeli Covert Relationship,* HarperCollins, 1991, p. 189.
[347] Alexander Cockburn, ed., *The Politics of Anti-Semitism,* AK Press, 2003, p. 104.

about "The Jews Who Run Clinton's Court," quoting a prominent Washington rabbi to the effect that "the term 'government of goyim'" has become "an outdated term in the U.S.," since the Clinton administration is "full of warm Jews" (i.e. dedicated Zionists). In the National Security Council, for example, "7 out of 11 top staffers are Jews. Clinton had especially placed them in the most sensitive junctions in the U.S. security and foreign administrations."[348]

Andrew Cockburn reports in his book on *Rumsfeld* (2007) the following conversation between the two George Bushes:
"What's a neocon?" Junior asked.
"Do you want names, or a description?"
"Description."
"Well, I'll give it to you in one word: Israel."[349]

During the Clinton years, the Madrid agreements were buried by the Oslo Accords (negotiated directly with an overwhelmed Yasser Arafat), thanks to the influence of an unprecedented number of pro-Israel government officials, notably in the State Department under Madeleine Albright and in the Defense Department under William Cohen. The neoconservatives, for their part, prepared their return with Rumsfeld and Cheney, and threw all their weight behind their ultimate think tank, the Project for the New American Century (PNAC). William Kristol, son of Irving, also founded in 1995 a new magazine, *The Weekly Standard*, which immediately became the dominant voice of the neoconservatives thanks to funding from the pro-Israeli Rupert Murdoch. In 1997, it would be the first publication to call for a new war against Saddam Hussein. It is also during the Clinton years that the FBI investigated an Israeli mole in the White House, who was enjoying privileged access to the National Security Council. According to British investigator Gordon Thomas (*Gideon's Spies*, 1999), the FBI investigation was called off when "Israel blackmailed President Clinton with phone-tapes of his steamy sex talks with Monica Lewinsky."[350] Others see a broader scheme. Noting that White House aide

---

[348] Avinoam Bar-Yosef, "The Jews Who Run Clinton's Court", *Maariv,* September 2, 1994, translated by Israel Shahak in *Open Secrets: Israeli nuclear and foreign policies*, Pluto Press, 1997.
[349] Andrew Cockburn, *Rumsfeld: His Rise, Fall, and Catastrophic Legacy,* Scribner, 2011, p. 219.
[350] With some exaggeration, *The New York Post* summarized in these words Gordon Thomas's findings in its cover story on March 5, 1998, although Thomas calls it a "complete distortion"

Lewinsky was the daughter of Zionist East European immigrants, and that she had kept her incriminating blue dress unwashed for two years as evidence of having had sex with the President, the Syrian newspaper *Tishrin Al-Usbu'a* concluded, in its August 24, 1998 issue: "Her goal was to embarrass President Clinton, to blackmail him and weaken his status before Netanyahu's government." But, of course, such reasoning is attacked by the Anti-Defamation League as anti-Semitic.[351]

After eight years of Clinton, the neocons finally had their revenge by having a second George Bush, son of the first, cornered into a second Iraq war in 2003. In 2008 their hold on him was such that they could convince him of launching a new "Surge" of 20,000 men despite strong public opposition, but with the support of their pro-Surge group Freedom's Watch, whose membership was, as the *Jewish Telegraph Agency* remarked, "almost all Jewish."[352] Thomas Neumann, Executive Director of the JINSA, could then describe Bush junior's administration as "the best administration for Israel since Harry Truman."[353]

To spread their war agenda, neoconservatives could rely of Rupert Murdoch's powerful News Corporation, which owned 175 written publications selling more than 40 millions newspapers each week, and 35 TV channels reaching 110 million viewers on four continents. In 2003, all of them were in favor of attacking Iraq. Murdoch is a friend of Ariel Sharon and a loyal supporter of the Likud party. He is also close to Tony Blair, who is the godfather of one of his children.

in his second edition (Gordon Thomas, *Gideon's Spies: The Secret History of the Mossad,* St. Martin's Press, 1999, p. 153).

[351] Anti-Defamation League : archive.adl.org/syria_media/syria_monica.asp

[352] Paul Findley, in Sniegoski, *Transparent Cabal, op. cit.,* p. vii-x.

[353] Quoted by Cook, *Israel and the Clash, op. cit.,* p. 33.

23. Double-talk

John Mearsheimer and Stephen Walt's book *The Israel Lobby and U.S. Foreign Policy* shocked the American public in 2007 by exposing the considerable influence of pro-Israel groups, the oldest of which being the Zionist Organization of America, and the most influential since the 1970s, the American Israel Public Affairs Committee (AIPAC). The authors demonstrate that "the Lobby" has been the major force driving the United States into the Iraq war and, more generally, into a foreign policy that lacks coherence and morality in the Middle East.[354] Yet the authors' thesis is incomplete because they underestimate the role played from within the government itself by the neoconservatives, who form the other arm of the pliers now gripping American foreign policy.

Based on the financial rewarding of those who support Israel, the influence of the pro-Israel lobby tends to promote to the top the most corrupt and lawless politicians. Rudolf Giuliani, the former mayor of New York, certainly fits in that category, together with the city's Police Chief Bernard Kerik, who went to prison for tax fraud after receiving a free "loan" of $250,000 from Israeli businessman Eitan Wertheimer during a trip to Israel in August 2001.

These two forces—the crypto-Zionists inside the government and the pro-Israel lobby outside—sometimes act in criminal complicity, as illustrated by the charge against Larry Franklin in 2005; as a member of the Office of Special Plans working under Douglas Feith, he passed classified defense documents to two AIPAC officials, Steven Rosen and Keith Weissman, who in turn

---

[354] John Mearsheimer and Stephen Walt, *The Israel Lobby and U.S. Foreign Policy,* Farrar Straus Giroux, 2008.

transmitted them to a senior official in Israel. Franklin was sentenced to thirteen years in prison (later reduced to ten years of house-arrest), while Rosen and Weissman were acquitted.[355] Most neoconservatives are active members of the second most powerful pro-Israel lobby, the Jewish Institute for National Security Affairs (JINSA), of which Dick Cheney and Ahmed Chalibi are also members, among others responsible for instigating the Iraq invasion. JINSA was founded in 1976 by American army officers, intellectuals, and politicians, with one of its stated aims "to inform the American defense and foreign affairs community about the important role Israel can and does play in bolstering democratic interests in the Mediterranean and the Middle East."[356] Colin Powell, according to his biographer Karen DeYoung, privately rallied against this "separate little government" composed of "Wolfowitz, Libby, Feith, and Feith's 'Gestapo Office'," which he also called "the JINSA crowd."[357]

In 2011, Powell's former Chief of Staff Lawrence Wilkerson openly denounced the duplicity of neoconservatives such as David Wurmser and Douglas Feith, whom he considered "card-carrying members of the Likud party. [...] I often wondered if their primary allegiance was to their own country or to Israel. That was the thing that troubled me, because there was so much that they said and did that looked like it was more reflective of Israel's interest than our own."[358] In fact, a significant number of neoconservatives are Israeli citizens, have family in Israel or have resided there themselves. Some are openly close to Likud, the nationalist party in power in Israel, and several have even been official advisors to Netanyahu; many are regularly praised for their work on behalf of Israel by the Israeli press. Paul Wolfowitz, for example, was nominated "Man of the Year" by the pro-Likud *Jerusalem Post* in 2003.

The duplicity of the neoconservatives becomes fully apparent from a document brought to public knowledge in 2008 by authors such as James Petras, Stephen Sniegoski and Jonathan Cook (see bibliography); it is a 1996 report by the Israeli think tank Institute for Advanced Strategic and Political Studies (IASPS), entitled *A Clean Break: A New Strategy for Securing the Realm*, written specifically for the new Israeli Prime Minister, Benjamin Netanyahu.[359] The team responsible for the report was led by Richard Perle, and included Douglas Feith, David Wurmser and his wife Meyrav Wurmser. Perle personally handed the report to Netanyahu on July 8, 1996. The same year, the same authors signed the founding manifesto of PNAC in the U.S., and four years later, they would be positioned in key posts of the U.S. military and U.S. foreign policy.

---

[355] Sniegoski, *Transparent Cabal, op. cit.,* p. 168-9.

[356] JINSA: www.jinsa.org/about

[357] Sniegoski, *Transparent Cabal, op. cit.,* p. 156.

[358] Sniegoski, *Transparent Cabal, op. cit.,* p. 120.

[359] The full text is on the IASPS website: www.iasps.org/strat1.htm

Questioned on September the 11th about the event of the day by James Bennet for the *New York Times*, Netanyahu let go: "It's very good [...] it will generate immediate sympathy [...], strengthen the bond between our two peoples."[360] He repeated it eight years later, at Bar-Ilan University: "We are benefiting from one thing, and that is the attack on the Twin Towers and Pentagon, and the American struggle in Iraq," adding that these events "swung American public opinion in our favor" (*Maariv*, April 17, 2008).[361]

HAARETZ.com

Back to Homepage   ● web

Jewish World | Haaretz Toolbar | Diplomacy | Defense | Opinion | National |
Focus U.S.A. | Stronger than Fiction | Business | Real Estate | Magazine | Week's End

↺ Talkback

Read   Respond

Likud chairman and opposition leader Benjamin Netanyahu. (Limor Edrey / Archives)

Last update - 00:00 16/04/2008

Report: Netanyahu says 9/11 terror attacks good for Israel

As its title suggests, the report *Clean Break* invites Netanyahu to break with the Oslo Accords of 1993, which officially committed Israel to the return of the territories it occupied illegally since 1967. The new Prime Minister should instead "engage every possible energy on rebuilding Zionism" and reaffirm Israel's right over the West Bank and the Gaza Strip: "Our claim to the land—to which we have clung for hope for 2,000 years—is legitimate and noble. [...] Only the unconditional acceptance by Arabs of our rights, especially in their territorial dimension, 'peace for peace,' [as opposed to the Oslo formula *peace for land*] is a solid basis for the future."[362] The authors of *Clean Break* therefore encourage Netanyahu to adopt a policy of territorial annexation, contrary not only to the official position of the United States and the United Nations, but also to the public commitments made by Israel. Even though he signed the "roadmap" intended to lead to an independent Palestinian State in September 1999, and maintained his position at the Camp David summit in July 2000, Netanyahu followed the advice of *Clean Break* and secretly worked to undercut the peace process, as he would actually brag during a private interview filmed without his knowledge in 2001: "I'm going to interpret the accords in such a way that would allow me to put an end to this galloping forward to the '67 borders." He also said: "I know what America is. America is a thing you can move very easily, move it in the right direction. They won't get in our way."[363]

---

[360] James Bennet, "Day of Terror: the Israelis; Spilt Blood is Seen as Bond that Draws 2 Nations Closer", *New York Times,* September 12, 2001: www.nytimes.com/2001/09/12/us/day-terror-israelis-spilled-blood-seen-bond-that-draws-2-nations-closer.html

[361] *Haaretz*: www.haaretz.com/news/report-netanyahu-says-9-11-terror-attacks-good-for-israel-1.244044

[362] Sniegoski, *Transparent Cabal, op. cit.,* p. 91.

[363] YouTube, "Netanyahu Admits Breaking Oslo Accords With Palestinians": hwww.youtube.com/watch?v=E7dw89jICTU.

"Richard Perle is a traitor. There's no other way to put it," wrote journalist Seymour Hersh in *The New Yorker* (March 17, 2003), referring to Perle's lies on Iraq.[364] Perle responded on CNN by calling Hersh "the closest thing American journalism has to a terrorist." In 1970 already, the FBI had suspected Perle's office of transmitting to the Israeli Embassy classified information obtained from Hal Sonnenfeldt, member of the National Security Council. Perle worked for the Israeli arms firm Soltam before advising the Israeli Prime Minister.

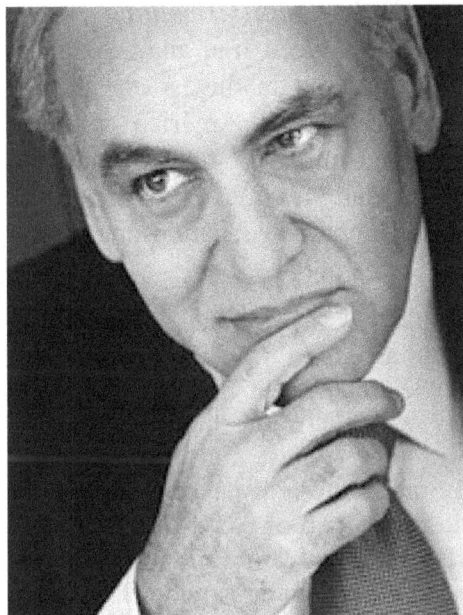

The recommendations to the Israeli government to sabotage the peace process in Palestine are presented by the authors of *Clean Break* as part of a larger plan to allow Israel to "shape its strategic environment," by "removing Saddam Hussein from power in Iraq," weakening Syria and Lebanon, and finally Iran. When Perle, Feith and Wurmser moved to key positions in the U.S. government, they arranged for the United States to implement the program, without Israel having to shed a single drop of blood. If there are differences between the *Clean Break* report written for the Israeli government in 1996 and the report *Rebuilding America's Defenses* written by the same authors for the U.S. government in 2000, it is not in the program itself, but rather the argued reasoning. First, *Clean Break* does not have Iraq as a threat, but as the weakest of the enemies of Israel, the least dangerous and the easiest to break. In a follow-up to *Clean Break*, entitled *Coping with Crumbling States: A Western and Israeli Balance of Power Strategy for the Levant*, Wurmser emphasizes the fragility of Middle East States, particularly Iraq: "the residual unity of the nation is an illusion projected by extreme repression of the state."[365] Thus the same initial action of overthrowing Saddam is recommended to both Israel and the United States, but for opposite and contradictory reasons. The weakness of Iraq, stressed in the Israeli documents, could never be a legitimate reason for the United States to invade Iraq; and so it was necessary to present Iraq to the Americans as a mortal threat to their country. Netanyahu himself authored an article in the *Wall Street Journal* in September 2002, under the title "The Case for Toppling Saddam," describing Saddam as "a dictator who is rapidly expanding his arsenal of biological and chemical weapons, who has used these

---

[364] Kurt Nimmo, "Expatriate Richard Perle", March 10, 2003: rense.com/general35/eax.htm
[365] Full text on www.iasps.org/strat2.htm. Quoted in Sniegoski, *Transparent Cabal, op. cit.*, p. 94-6.

weapons of mass destruction against his subjects and his neighbors, and who is feverishly trying to acquire nuclear weapons."[366] Nothing of such a threat, however, is mentioned in *Clean Break* or *Coping with Crumbling States*, which also make no mention of any connection between Iraq and Al-Qaeda, nor even of Al-Qaeda at all. The perspective on Iraq in the Israeli internal documents was the realistic one, while the motives given America was pure propaganda: by the time American troops moved into Iraq, that country had been ruined by a decade of economic sanctions that had not only rendered its army powerless, but also destroyed its once exemplary education and health care systems.

Madeleine Albright, born Marie Jana Korbelova in Prague, was U.S. ambassador to the UN during Clinton's first term (1993-1997), then Secretary of State during the second (1997-2000). She shaped U.S. post-Cold War interventionist policy, and justified it by calling the United States "the indispensible nation."[367] Asked on CBS to comment on a UNICEF report claiming that half a million Iraqi children had died because of UN enforced economic sanctions on Iraq, she replied: "We think the price is worth it."[368]

There is a second fundamental difference between the strategy recommended for Israelis and the propaganda sold to the Americans: while the second highlights both the security interest of the United States, and the noble ideal of spreading democracy in the Middle East, the first ignores these two themes. The changes proposed by the *Clean Break* authors are not expected to bring any benefit to the Arab world. Instead, the goal is clearly to weaken Israel's enemies by sharpening ethnic, religious and territorial disputes between countries and within each country. After the fall of Saddam, foresees the author of *Coping with Crumbling States*, Iraq will be "ripped apart by the politics of warlords, tribes, clans, sects, and key families," for the benefit of Israel. Furthermore, it is not democracy that *Clean Break* recommended for Iraq, but rather restoring a pro-Western monarchy. Such an outcome would obviously be unacceptable to the Americans, but when Lewis Paul Bremer, as head of the Coalition Provisional Authority (CPA) in 2003, brought about the destruction of the military and civilian infrastructure in the name of "de-Baathification," it was viewed as a success from the eyes of the Likud. Better still, by dissolving the army, Bremer indirectly created a disorganized pool of resistance of some 400,000 angry soldiers, en-

---

[366] Sniegoski, *Transparent Cabal, op. cit.,* p. 171. Full article on www.potomac-airfield.com/netanyahu.htm

[367] David Rothkoft, *Running the World: The Inside Story of the National Security Council and the Architects of American Power,* Public Affairs, 2004, p. 26.

[368] YouTube, "Madeleine Albright - 60 minutes": www.youtube.com/watch?v=FbIX1CP9qr4

suring chaos for a few years.[369] Daniel Pipes had the gall to write, three years after the invasion of Iraq: "the benefits of eliminating Saddam's rule must not be forgotten in the distress of not creating a successful new Iraq. Fixing Iraq is neither the coalition's responsibility nor its burden." And besides, he adds, "when Sunni terrorists target Shiites and vice-versa, non-Muslims are less likely to be hurt. Civil war in Iraq, in short, would be a humanitarian tragedy but not a strategic one." (*New York Sun*, February 28, 2006).[370]

The *New York Times* and other news outlets reported that, on the 19th of September 2005, the British SAS (part of the Special Forces) used a dozen tanks assisted by helicopters to tear down the prison of Basra in order to liberate two British agents who had just been arrested after forcing a checkpoint, dressed as Arabs in a car full of arms, munitions, explosives and detonators. It is believed they were part of a false flag terror unit planning to explode bombs during a religious event in the center of Basra, in order to exacerbate religious conflicts between Shiites and Sunnites. Captain Ken Masters, in charge of the investigation, was found hung in his military accommodation in Basra on the 15th of October.[371]

The difference between the neocons' Israeli and American discourses finds its explanation in the Israeli document *Clean Break* itself, which recommends Netanyahu present Israeli strategy "in language familiar to the Americans by tapping into themes of American administrations during the cold war which apply well to Israel." The Israeli State propaganda should "promote Western values and traditions. Such an approach […] will be well received in the United States." The references to moral values are thus nothing more than tactics to mobilize the United States. Finally, while the authors of the Israeli report stressed the importance of winning the sympathy and support of the United States, they also declared that their strategy would ultimately free Israel from American pressure and influence: "such self-reliance will grant Israel greater freedom of action and remove a significant lever of [United States] pressure used against it in the past."[372]

Passing off a threat against Israel as though it were a threat against the United States is a trick to which Netanyahu had no need to be converted; he has been employing it since the 1980s to rally Americans alongside Israel in the "inter-

---

[369] Cook, *Israel and the Clash, op. cit.*, p. 81.
[370] Cook, *Israel and the Clash, op. cit.*, p. 136.
[371] Sabrina Tavernise, "British Army Storms Basra Jail to Free 2 Soldiers From Arrest", *New York Times,* 20 September 2005:
www.nytimes.com/2005/09/20/international/middleeast/20iraq.html?_r=0
[372] Sniegoski, *Transparent Cabal, op. cit.*, p. 93.

national war on terrorism," a concept which he can claim to have invented in his books *International Terrorism: Challenge and Response* (1982) and *Terrorism: How the West can Win* (1986). In *An End to Evil* (2003), Richard Perle and David Frum likewise work the semantics to embed the fears of the Israelis into the minds of Americans, when for example they urge Americans to "end this evil before it kills again and on a genocidal scale. There is no middle way for Americans: It is victory or holocaust."[373]

It is, however, impossible for anyone to be consistently hypocritical, and it happens eventually that some neoconservative recklessly opens his thoughts to the public. Philip Zelikow, Counselor to Condoleezza Rice and Executive Director of the 9/11 Commission, said about the Iraqi threat during a conference at the University of Virginia September 10, 2002: "Why would Iraq attack America or use nuclear weapons against us? I'll tell you what I think the real threat is and actually has been since 1990: it's the threat against Israel. And this is the threat that dare not speak its name, because the Europeans don't care deeply about that threat, I will tell you frankly. And the American government doesn't want to lean too hard on it rhetorically, because it is not a popular sell."[374] That's really it in a nutshell: the United States must be led to make war with the enemies of Israel, and in order to that, Americans must be convinced that Israel's enemies are America's enemies.

In addition, it is necessary that the Americans believe that these enemies hate America for what it claims to represent (i.e. democracy, freedom, etc.), not because of its support for Israel. The signatories of the PNAC letter to President Bush on April 3, 2002 (including William Kristol, Richard Perle, Daniel Pipes, Norman Podhoretz, Robert Kagan, and James Woolsey) go as far as claiming that the Arab world hates Israel because it is a friend of the United States, rather than the reverse: "No one should doubt that the United States and Israel share a common enemy. We are both targets of what you have correctly called an 'Axis of Evil.' Israel is targeted in part because it is our friend, and in part because it is an island of liberal, democratic principles—American principles—in a sea of tyranny, intolerance, and hatred."[375] It is well known that America had no enemies in the Middle East before its covenant with Israel in the late 60s. On September 21, 2001, the *New York Post* published an opinion by Netanyahu propagating the same historical falsification, under the headline "Today we are all Americans": "For the bin Laden's of the world, Israel is

---

[373] Sniegoski, *Transparent Cabal, op. cit.,* p. 189.

[374] This remark was reported by the *Inter-Press Service* on March 29, 2004 under the headline "U.S.: Iraq war is to protect Israel, says 9/11 panel chief", then by *United Press International* the next day: www.upi.com/Business_News/Security-Industry/2004/03/30/UPI-Hears/UPI-16271080668142/

[375] PNAC: www.newamericancentury.org/Bushletter-040302.htm

merely a sideshow. America is the target."[376] Three days later *The New Republic* responded with a headline on behalf of the Americans: "We are all Israelis now."[377] The post-9/11 propaganda has created an artificially fusional relationship. Wrongly, Americans have understood September 11th as an expression of hatred towards them from the Arab world and have thus experienced immediate sympathy for Israel, an emotional link neoconservatives exploit without limit; Paul Wolfowitz declared April 11, 2002: "Since September 11th, we Americans have one thing more in common with Israelis. On that day America was attacked by suicide bombers. At that moment every American understood what it was like to live in Jerusalem, or Netanya or Haifa. And since September 11th, Americans now know why we must fight and win the war on terrorism."[378]

One of the goals is to encourage Americans to view Israel's oppression of the Palestinians as part of the global fight against Islamic terrorism. As Robert Jensen sums it up in the documentary *Peace, Propaganda and the Promised Land* directed by Sut Jhally and Bathsheba Ratzkoff (2004): "Since the Sept 11th attack on the US, Israel's PR strategy has been to frame all Palestinian action, violent or not, as terrorism. To the extent that they can do that, they've repackaged an illegal military occupation as part of America's war on terror."[379] On December 4, 2004, Prime Minister Ariel Sharon justified his brutality against the population of Gaza by claiming that Al-Qaeda had established a base there; but then in a press conference on December 6th, Nabil Shaath and Rashid Abu Shbak, respectively Planning and International Cooperation Minister and head of the Preventive Security Apparatus, provided evidence, in the form of telephone records, e-mails originating from Israel, and bank statements, that the Israeli secret services had themselves tried to create fake Al-Qaeda cells in the Gaza Strip, and recruited Palestinians under the name of bin Laden. The recruits had received money as well as (defective) weapons and, after five months of indoctrination, were instructed to claim a future attack in Israel on behalf of "the Al-Qaeda group of Gaza." Israeli services had intended, it seems, to mount an attack (whether real or false) against their own people and do so under the name of Al-Qaeda, as a new pretext for aggression against the inhabitants of the Gaza Strip.[380]

---

[376] Read on www.netanyahu.org/todwearealla.html
[377] Justin Raimondo, *The Terror Enigma: 9/11 and the Israeli Connection*, iUniversal, 2003, p. xiii.
[378] Raimondo, *The Terror Enigma, op. cit.*, p. 19.
[379] Documentary *Peace, Propaganda and the Promised Land* by Sut Jhally and Bathsheba Ratzkoff, 2004.
[380] Tarpley, *9/11 Synthetic Terror, op. cit.*, p. 100-1; "Israel 'faked al-Qaeda' presence", *BBC News World Edition*, December 8, 2002: news.bbc.co.uk/2/hi/middle_east/2550513.stm

Such Machiavellian strategy is not directed at Palestine only. In 2006, the Lebanese army discovered several networks of Arab mercenaries sponsored by the Mossad to plan assassinations and bomb attacks in Syria. The Lebanese Minister of Foreign Affairs Fawzi Salloukh prepared for the National Security Council of the UN a file on these black operations, which documented for example the case of Mahmoud Rafeh, a former Lebanese army officer who was caught laying a bomb in the city of Sidon and confessed having been hired by the Mossad (*Haaretz,* June 17, 2006).[381] We are left with little doubt that Israel has become the center of modern "synthetic terror," to use Webster Tarpley's expression.

Not that Israel has the monopoly of such stratagem. Articles in *The New York Times* and other outlets have revealed that the FBI hatches their own terrorist plots only to heroically prevent them at the last minute. The method goes like this: FBI agents infiltrate Muslim communities in order to find potential terrorists, encourage them, provide them with a target and the weapons or explosives, only to bust them on the verge of committing their misdeed, thus saving a grateful nation from a plot they had manufactured. The method allows the possibility to alternate successful and thwarted acts of terrorism, thus maintaining the citizens in a state of fear while strengthening their trust in their National Security State.[382]

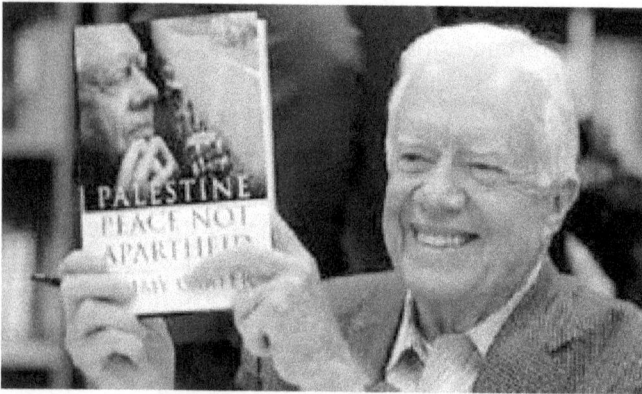

Double speech is an unchanging characteristic of Israel leadership, according to former President Carter's bitter experience, as he recalls in *Palestine: Peace not Apartheid* (2006): "The overriding problem is that, for more than a quarter century, the actions of some Israeli leaders have been in direct conflict with the official policies of the United States, the international community, and their own negotiated agreements."[383]

---

[381] Cook, *Israel and the Clash, op. cit.,* p. 141-2.

[382] David Shipler, "Terrorist Plots, Hatched by the F.B.I.", *New York Times, Sunday Review,* April 28, 2012: www.nytimes.com/2012/04/29/opinion/sunday/terrorist-plots-helped-along-by-the-fbi.html?_r=2&. See also Abby Goodnough, "Man is Held in a Plan to Bomb Washington", *New York Times,* September 28, 2001: www.nytimes.com/2011/09/29/us/massachusetts-man-accused-of-plotting-to-bomb-washington.html?_r=1&pagewanted=all

[383] Jimmy Carter, *Palestine: Peace Not Apartheid,* Scribner, 2007, p. 208.

24. *"Inside Job" or "Mossad Job"?*

The neoconservatives were prepared to exploit the 9/11 events politically and militarily, but they could not pull off the operation all by themselves. It required the technical participation of powerful people outside of government, super-*sayanim* so to speak. *Sayanim* ("collaborators" in Hebrew) are Zionist Jews living outside Israel and known to the Mossad as potentially ready to give a hand, in the form of an unlawful action, without asking embarrassing questions. According to the renegade Mossad agent Victor Ostrovsky (*By Way of Deception*, 1990), there are thousands of *sayanim* in the United States, and more in New York than anywhere else. Larry Silverstein, the WTC leaseholder, comes out as the archetype *sayan* of September 11th. He is a leading member of the United Jewish Appeal Federation of Jewish Philanthropies of New York, the largest American fundraiser for Israel (after the U.S. government). He is also an intimate friend of Benjamin Netanyahu, with whom he discusses on telephone every Sunday, according to the Israeli newspaper *Haaretz*. Silverstein's partner in the WTC lease, for the underground shopping center, was Frank Lowy, another Zionist "philanthropist" close to Ehud Barak and Ehud Olmert, and former member of the Haganah. The head of the New York Port Authority, who granted Silverstein and Lowy the lease, is none other than Lewis Eisenberg, another member of the United Jewish Appeal Federation and former Vice-President of AIPAC.

Other members of the 9/11 New York gang would have to be tracked down if an unbiased investigation was ever conducted. Zionist Michael Bloomberg, who succeeded Rudolph Giuliani as the mayor of New York in January 2002, would be called to explain the destruction of evidence accomplished by quickly selling the WTC steel rubble (approximately 70,000 tons) to Metals Management (run by another Zionist, Alan Ratner), to be shipped to China and India for recycling. According to the NIST report, the Boeing 767 that embedded itself into the North Tower "cut a gash that was over half the width of the building and extended from the 93rd floor to the 99th floor. All but the lowest of these floors were occupied by Marsh & McLennan, a worldwide insurance company, which also occupied the 100th floor."[384] The CEO of Marsh & McLennan is then Jeffrey Greenberg, son of Maurice Greenberg, a wealthy Zionist who contributed heavily to George W. Bush's 2000 campaign. Maurice Greenberg also happens to co-own Kroll Associates (renamed Kroll Inc. in August 2001), a security consultant firm which was in charge of security for the entire World Trade Center complex on 9/11. The Greenbergs were also the insurers of the Twin Towers and, on the 24th of July 2001, they took the precaution of having the contract reinsured by competitors, who had to indemnify Silverstein and Lowy after 9/11, and yet were not entitled to investigate themselves. And since this is a small world, in November 2000, Lewis Paul Bremer joined the Board of Directors of Marsh & McLennan. On September 11, 2001, Bremer, we recall, would be the Chairman of the National Commission on Terrorism appearing on NBC to name bin Laden as prime suspect and, in 2003, he would be appointed Administrator of the Coalition Provisional Authority in Iraq to level the Iraqi State to the ground and oversee the theft of almost a trillion dollars intended for its reconstruction.

There might have been accomplices in the airports and airline companies supposedly involved in the attacks. Both airports from which flights AA11, UA175 and UA93 reportedly took off (Logan Airport in Boston and Newark Airport near New York) subcontracted their security to International Consultants on Targeted Security (ICTS), a firm based in Israel and headed by Menachem Atzmon, a treasurer of the Likud. Also disturbing is the behavior of the American branch of Zim Israel Navigational, a maritime shipping giant half-owned by the Jewish state (and occasionally used as a cover for Israeli secret services): it moved its offices from the WTC, along with its 200 employees, September 4, 2001, one week before the attacks—"like an act of God, we moved," marveled the CEO Shaul Cohen-Mintz when interviewed by *USA Today*, November 17, 2001.[385] And, of course, the 9/11 mass deception would not have been possible without a strong hold on the mainstream media by loyal Zionist *sayanim,* who have long proven their efficiency at censoring critics of Israel.

The massive forewarning of Israelis is one of the most embarrassing aspects of 9/11. On September 27, 2001, the *Washington Post* reported that, "officials at instant-messaging firm Odigo confirmed today that two employees received text messages warning of an attack on the World Trade Center two hours before terrorists crashed planes into the New York landmarks." The first plane hit

---

[384] www.nist.gov/customcf/get_pdf.cfm?pub_id=909236, p. 20.
[385] Stephanie Armour, "Firms realize workplaces will never be the same", *USA Today*, September 17, 2001: usatoday30.usatoday.com/money/general/2001-09-17-workplace-changes.htm

the WTC "almost to the minute," confirmed Alex Diamandis, Vice-President of Odigo.[386] Odigo, headquartered in Israel, became part of Converse, an Israeli company which, according to investigator Carl Cameron, not only manages "just about every aspect of the US telephone system [together with Amdocs, also Israeli]," but also "provides the wiretapping equipment and software for US law enforcement agencies," and, to add suspicion, "works closely with the Israeli government."[387] The Odigo anomaly must be put in perspective with another puzzling but little known aspect of 9/11. The day after the attacks, a *Jerusalem Post* headline read "Thousands of Israelis missing near WTC, Pentagon" and the accompanying story stated that, according to Israel's Foreign Ministry figures, 4,000 Israelis working at the WTC were missing. The Israeli death toll was expected to be in the hundreds at least, and when George Bush announced before Congress on September 20th, that 130 Israelis had died in the WTC, that seemed proportionally a low number. And yet, it turned out to be grossly inflated: in the final reckoning, only one Israeli had actually died in the World Trade Center, the *New York Times* revealed on September 22.[388]

Jonathan Jay Pollard, analyst in the Navy, was arrested in 1985 and sentenced to life imprisonment for spying for Israel. Among thousands of top-secret documents that he passed to Israel were the worldwide code systems of the NSA, which Israel probably sold to the USSR in exchange for letting a million Jews emigrate for Palestine. In 1998, Netanyahu officially admitted that Pollard had been recruited by LEKEM, the Israeli spy project tasked with building a nuclear bomb, and simultaneously granted him Israeli citizenship.

On the ground, a large team of highly trained Mossad agents and other Israeli intelligence would have been necessary for the technical implementation of September 11th. Francesco Cossiga, President of Italy between 1985 and 1992,

---

[386] Brian McWilliams, "Instant Messages to Israel Warned of WTC Attack", *Newbytes (Washington Post Co.),* September 27, 2001:
911review.org/companies/Odigo/Isreal_warned_attack_9-11.html. Also Yuval Dror, "Odigo says workers were warned of attack", *Haaretz.* September 26, 2001.
[387] Carl Cameron, Fox News Series on Israeli Spying on US Telecommunications, quoted in Kollerstrom, *Terror on the Tube, op. cit.,* p. 41-2.
[388] Eric Lipton, "Estimates of toll may be too high", *New York Times*, September 22, 2001.

claimed in 2007 to the newspaper *Corriere della Sera*, that it was well known in informed circles in America and Europe that the September 11th attack "was planned and executed by the American CIA and Mossad with the help of the Zionist world in order to blame the Arab countries, and to persuade the Western powers to intervene in both Iraq and Afghanistan."[389] Alan Sabrosky, a professor at the U.S. Army War College and the U.S. Military Academy, voiced in June 2012 his conviction that 9/11 was "a classic Mossad-orchestrated operation" carried out with the complicity of the U.S. government, in order to lead the United States into a "war of civilizations" against the enemies of Israel—which is to say, against the Arab-Muslim world as a whole.[390]

Suspicion of Mossad guilt does not stem only from the reputation of the world's most powerful secret service, which a report of the U.S. Army School for Advanced Military Studies (SAMS), quoted by the *Washington Times*, September 10, 2001, described as "Wildcard. Ruthless and cunning. Has capability to target U.S. forces and make it look like a Palestinian/Arab act."[391] The involvement of the Mossad, together with other Israeli elite units, can be demonstrated by several little known facts. These facts have been compiled by Justin Raimondo, editorial director of Antiwar.com, in *The Terror Enigma: 9/11 and the Israeli Connection* (2003), and by Christopher Bollyn in more than a hundred articles written from 2001, and synthesized in his book *Solving 9-11: The Deception that Changed the World* (2012), but they have received little publicity in most 9/11 Truth investigative books and websites.[392]

Few people know, for example, that at the time of the attacks, the American federal police were busy dismantling the largest Israeli spy network ever caught on U.S. soil. In March 2001, the National Counterintelligence Center (NCIC) posted this message on its website: "In the past six weeks, employees in federal office buildings located throughout the United States have reported suspicious activities connected with individuals representing themselves as foreign [Israeli] students selling or delivering artwork." The NCIC states that, "these individuals have also gone to the private residences of senior federal officials under the guise of selling art."

---

[389] *Corriere della Sera*:
www.corriere.it/politica/07_novembre_30/osama_berlusconi_cossiga_27f4ccee-9f55-11dc-8807-0003ba99c53b.shtml
[390] Alan Sabrosky, "Demystifying 9/11: Israel and the Tactics of Mistake":
mycatbirdseat.com/2011/06/demystifying-911-israel-and-the-tactics-of-mistake/
[391] Rowan Scarborough, "U.S. troops would enforce peace Under Army study", *The Washington Times*, 10 September 2001: www.washingtontimes.com/news/2001/sep/10/20010910-025319-6906r/
[392] See also Christopher Ketcham, "What Did Israel Know in Advance of the 9/11 Attacks?" *CounterPunch*, 2007, vol. 14, p. 1-10: www.counterpunch.org/2007/03/07/what-did-israel-know-in-advance-of-the-9-11-attacks/)

Then in the summer, after a number of incidents of this type in its premises, the Drug Enforcement Agency (DEA) compiled a report which would be revealed to the public by the *Washington Post* on November 23, 2001, followed by a Carl Cameron's four-part documentary broadcast on Fox News from December 11, 2001. On March 14, 2002, an article in the French daily *Le Monde* signed by Sylvain Cypel also referred to the report, shortly before the France-based *Intelligence Online* made it fully accessible on the Internet.[393] The DEA report listed 140 Israelis, aged between 20 and 30, arrested since March 2001. Organized in twenty teams of four to eight members, they visited at least "36 sensitive sites of the Department of Defense." Many of them were identified as members of the Mossad, and six were in possession of phones paid for by a former Israeli Vice Consul. Sixty arrests occurred after September 11th, bringing the total number of Israeli spies arrested to 200. Those who were subjected to a lie detector test failed. However, thanks to a decision that would come from the Attorney General John Ashcroft, all were eventually released.

The report concluded, "the nature of the individuals' conducts [...] leads us to believe the incidents may well be an organized intelligence gathering activity."[394] However, the nature of the intelligence gathered remains mysterious. It could well be that espionage was not their primary mission, when one considers the training received by some in the Israeli army, according to the DEA report: "A majority of those questioned has stated they served in military intelligence, electronic signal intercept, or explosive ordnance units. Some have been linked to high-ranking officials in the Israeli military. One was the son of a two-star general, one served as the bodyguard to the head of the Israeli Army, one served in a Patriot mission unit." Another, Peer Segalovitz, officer in the 605 Battalion of the Golan Heights "acknowledged he could blow up buildings, bridges, cars, and anything else that he needed to."[395] It may be that this espionage activity—as ostentatious as it was unproductive—was really a secondary cover behind their primary cover as "art students"; the hypothesis is that their ostensible cover as art students was intended less to deceive than to draw attention to their more discreet, yet equally fake, cover as spies.

But why would these Israeli agents need to hang out as spies? One possible answer is suggested by a crucial detail mentioned in the DEA report: "The Hollywood, Florida, area seems to be a central point for these individuals."[396] Precisely, out of the 140 fake Israeli students identified before the attacks, more than thirty lived in or near the city of Hollywood, Florida (140,000 inhabitants), exactly where fifteen of the nineteen alleged Islamist hijackers had

---

[393] The full report is on: antiwar.com/rep/DEA_Report_redactedxx.pdf. It is quoted here from Raimondo and Bollyn's books.
[394] Raimondo, *The Terror Enigma, op. cit.*, p. x.
[395] Bollyn, *Solving 9/11, op. cit.*, p. 159.
[396] Raimondo, *The Terror Enigma, op. cit.*, p. 3.

regrouped (nine in Hollywood, six in the vicinity). One of the "art students" arrested, Hanan Serfaty, was renting two Hollywood apartments, respectively close to the apartment and to the P.O. Box of Mohamed Atta. What was the nature of the relation between the Israeli spies and the Islamist terrorists? Simple: the former were monitoring the latter. Such is, at least, the explanation relayed by the mainstream media. Listen, for example, to the March 5, 2002 newscast on national channel France 2, introducing the revelations of *Intelligence Online*: "... this espionage affair, which sows confusion: an Israeli network has been dismantled in the United States, particularly in Florida: one of its missions may have been to track the men of Al-Qaeda (this was before September 11th). Some sources go even further: they indicate that the Mossad would not have made available all the information in its possession."[397] From such presentation, Israel comes out only slightly tainted, since a spy agency cannot be blamed for not sharing information with the country it is spying in. At most Israel can be accused of "letting it happen"—a guarantee of impunity. Such damage control trick may be the real purpose served by the Israelis' spying activity; it was an alibi forged in advance. They were really Israeli false flag terror experts posturing as Israeli spies (and pretending to be Israeli art students, since a spy, by definition, must have a cover).

In reality, these two hundred or more Israeli agents were not spying on the alleged terrorists, but manipulating them, funding them, and ultimately disappearing them—while laying around a few of their passports and other belongings in the rubble of 9/11. The connection between these patsy terrorists and Israeli secret services is thus very similar to the connection between Oswald and the CIA. The hypothesis that the Mossad was manipulating nineteen Arabs, leading them to believe they were hired as agents while they were being prepared for sacrifice, is supported by the lavish lifestyle of these pseudo-terrorists, unexplainable without secret funding. Israeli Hanan Serfaty, who rented two flats near Mohamed Atta, had handled at least $100,000 in three months. Recall that the Florida "Mohamed Atta" was a fake. The real Mohamed Atta, who called his father after the attacks, was described by his family as reserved, pious, not solicitous of women and having a fear of flying. He had had his passport stolen in 1999 while studying architecture in Hamburg. The false Mohamed Atta in Florida was living with a stripper, ate pork, loved fast cars, casinos and cocaine.[398] As has been reported by the *South Florida Sun-Sentinel* on September 16, under the headline "Suspects' Actions Don't Add Up," "Atta" got drunk and intoxicated and paid for the services of several prostitutes in the weeks and days prior to September 11th, along with four other

---

[397] Watch on YouTube, "9/11, Israël et le mossad":
www.youtube.com/watch?v=Kq_Y9r1LEgk
[398] On Atta's girlfriend, see: www.youtube.com/watch?v=VAZkRq8m1xo

unlikely suicide bombers who had similar behavior—incompatible with the Islamic preparation for death.[399]

The hypothesis that the terrorists were not monitored, but manipulated and prepared as scapegoat by the Mossad, becomes even more credible when we read in the *New York Times* on February 19th, 2009, that Ali al-Jarrah, cousin of the alleged hijacker of Flight UA93 Ziad al-Jarrah, had spent 25 years spying for the Mossad as an undercover agent infiltrating the Palestinian resistance and Hezbollah since 1983. He is currently in prison in Lebanon.[400]

Michael Chertoff, son of a rabbi and of a Mossad pioneer, was heading the Criminal Division of the Department of Justice in 2001. As such, he was responsible for the retention and destruction of all the material evidence regarding the 9/11 attacks, from the steel beams of the WTC to the video recordings at the Pentagon. He was also responsible for the quick repatriation of all Israeli spies, as well as the "dancing Israelis"(see below). In 2003, he was appointed to the newly created ministerial position of Secretary of Homeland Security, which allowed him to control dissenting citizens and restrain access to the evidence under the pretext of Sensitive Security Information.

---

[399] Original *Florida Sun-Sentinel* article by Jody Benjamin. See Griffin, *9/11 Contradictions, op. cit.,* p. 142-156, quoting *The Daily Mail, The Boston Herald, The San Francisco Chronicle* and *The Wall Street Journal.*
[400] Robert Worth, "Lebanese in Shock Over Arrest of an Accused Spy": www.nytimes.com/2009/02/19/world/middleeast/19lebanon.html?_r=0

25. Dancing Israelis and Mini-Nukes

One event in particular makes the connection between Mossad and 9/11 hard to dismiss. It was reported the day after the attacks by the journalist Paulo Lima in the regional newspaper of Bergen County, New Jersey, *The Record*, based on "sources close to the investigation." Immediately after the first impact on the North Tower, three individuals were seen on the roof of a van parked at Liberty State Park in Jersey City, "celebrating," and "jumping up and down," taking pictures with the twin towers in the background. The suspects then moved their van to another parking spot in Jersey City, where other witnesses saw them in the same ostentatious celebrations. The police soon issued a BOLO alert (be-on-the-look-out): "Vehicle possibly related to New York terrorist attack. White, 2000 Chevrolet van with New Jersey registration with 'Urban Moving Systems' sign on back seen at Liberty State Park, Jersey City, NJ, at the time of first impact of jetliner into World Trade Center. Three individuals with van were seen celebrating after initial impact and subsequent explosion."[401]

The van was intercepted around 4 pm, with five young men inside. The news soon reached TV viewers that they were Middle Eastern. Middle-Eastern they were, but only in the sense of being Israeli citizens. They are named Sivan and Paul Kurzberg, Yaron Shmuel, Oded Ellner and Omer Marmari. While being reluctantly pulled out of his driver's seat, Sivan Kurzberg burst out strangely: "We are Israelis. We are not your problem. Your problems are our problems. The Palestinians are your problem." The Kurzberg brothers were formally identified as Mossad agents. Police sources interviewed by Paulo Lima said they were convinced of these Israelis' involvement in the morning's attacks: "There are maps of the city in the car with certain places highlighted. It looked like they're hooked in with this. It looked like they knew what was going to happen when they were at Liberty State Park." They were carrying passports of different nationalities, $6,000 in cash, and open plane tickets for abroad.

---

[401] Raimondo, *The Terror Enigma, op. cit.*, p. xi.

The five Israelis officially worked for a moving company (a classic cover for espionage) named Urban Moving Systems. An employee of the company told *The Record* that the majority of his colleagues were Israeli and that they were happy upon hearing of the attacks: "I was in tears. These guys were joking and that bothered me." On September 14th, after a visit from the police, the business owner, Israeli-American Dominik Otto Suter, fled the country for Tel Aviv.[402]

The information disclosed by *The Record* was verified and taken up by investigative sites like *The Wayne Madsen Report* (September 14, 2005) and *Counterpunch* (February 7, 2007). It was also reported in some mainstream media, but in a curtailed way that minimized its significance: *The New York Times* (November 21, 2001) forgot to mention the nationality of the five suspects, as did *Fox News* and *Associated Press*. *The Washington Post* (November 23, 2001) did mention it, but not their apparent foreknowledge of the event. Only *The Forward* (March 15, 2002) revealed their Mossad connection, quoting an anonymous U.S. Intelligence source to the effect that Urban Moving Systems was a front company for the Mossad.

Omer Marmari, Oded Ellner, and Yaron Shmuel, three of the five "dancing Israelis," were invited on an Israeli TV talk show after their return home in November 2001. "Our purpose was simply to document the event," ingenuously declared Ellner (middle), while implicitly denying any Mossad connection.[403] Yaron Shmuel (right) has a LinkedIn profile that boasts his "explosives" and "secret services" expertise and experience. His Facebook account mentions that he got married on September 11, 2002[404]—the first anniversary of the "Big Wedding," as 9/11 has been code-named by the perpetrators (in a fake "Al Qaeda communication" intercepted in late summer of 2001 by Jordanian King Abdallah's men).[405]

The 579-page FBI report on the investigation that followed (partially declassified in 2005, fully in 2035), reveals several important elements.[406] First, once developed, the photos taken by the suspects with the North Tower on fire in

---

[402] Raimondo, *The Terror Enigma, op. cit.,* p. xi, 19.

[403] YouTube, "Israel and September 11 9/11":
www.youtube.com/watch?v=8OyUoGUV7b8&feature=youtu.be

[404] il.linkedin.com/in/yaronshmuel; www.facebook.com/shmuel.yaron?fref=ts

[405] John Colley, "Other unheeded warnings before 9/11?" *The Christian Science Monitor,* May 23, 2002: www.csmonitor.com/2002/0523/p11s01-coop.html

[406] This report is available at: www.takeourworldback.com/dancingisraelisfbireport.htm

the background confirm their attitudes of celebration: "They smiled, they hugged each other and they appeared to 'high five' one another." To explain their contentment, the suspects said they were simply happy that, thanks to these terrorist attacks, "the United States will take steps to stop terrorism in the world." Yet at this point, everyone believed the crash was an accident. Besides, at least one witness saw them positioned to watch the scene at 8 am, *before* the first plane hit the WTC, while others confirmed seeing them immediately after. A former employee of Urban Moving Systems testified about the anti-American mentality prevailing in the company, quoting one Israeli employee as telling non-Israelis: "Give us twenty years and we'll take over your media and destroy your country." The FBI investigation also revealed that the five Israelis from the van had contacts with another moving company called Classic International Movers, which employed five other Israelis arrested for their contacts with the nineteen presumed suicide hijackers. In addition, one of the five suspects had called "an individual in South America with authentic ties to Islamic militants in the middle east." Finally, the FBI report states that the "The vehicle was also searched by a trained bomb-sniffing dog which yielded a positive result for the presence of explosive traces."

After all this incriminating evidence comes the most unexpected conclusion of the report: "the FBI no longer has any investigative interests in the detainees and they should proceed with the appropriate immigration proceedings." In fact, a letter dated September 25, 2001 proves that, less than two weeks after the events, the FBI federal headquarter had already decided to close the investigation, asking that: "The U.S. Immigration and Naturalization Service should proceed with the appropriate immigration proceedings."[407] The five "dancing Israelis," also known as "the high-fivers," were detained 71 days in a Brooklyn prison, where they first refused, then failed, lie detector tests, before being quietly returned to Israel under the minimal charge of "visa violation."

What remains the most puzzling aspect of this whole story is the recklessly ostentatious behavior of these young Israelis undercover agents, high-fiving on top of their van. One possible explanation is suggested by their first being reported as being or looking Middle-Eastern. One anonymous call to the police in Jersey City, reported the same day by *NBC News,* mentioned "a white van, 2 or 3 guys in there. They look like Palestinians and going around a building. [...] I see the guy by Newark Airport mixing some junk and he has those sheikh uniforms. [...] He's dressed like an Arab."[408] It was this call that led to the interception of the van and the arrest of the five Israelis. Two hypotheses come to mind, here. Either they were indeed dressed up as Arab/Palestinian/Muslim, or the anonymous witness was an accomplice. The

---

[407] Letter partially declassified and reproduced by Hamza, *Le Grand Tabou, op. cit.,* ch. 2.
[408] whatreallyhappened.com/WRHARTICLES/fiveisraelis.html

second hypothesis seems more likely for two reasons: first, neither the police nor the FBI report mention any Middle-Eastern clothes found in the van. Second, the anonymous caller falsely said that the van was heading toward Holland Tunnel, whereas it was intercepted on Lincoln Tunnel, only because the police decided to block all access between New York and New Jersey. In either case, there is the obvious intention to start a rumor that Arabs had been seen rejoicing at the attacks and behaving suspiciously. If police hadn't spotted the van, the story may have circulated worldwide on mainstream TVs under the headline: "The Dancing Arabs." After all, television news coverage didn't refrain from the most blatant fakery by repeatedly showing on 9/11, to a wounded nation, images of Palestinians rejoicing over the 9/11 attack: Mark Crispin Miller, a professor of media studies at New York University, has shown that the footage was filmed during the funeral of nine people killed the day before by Israeli authorities.[409]

Ehud Barak, former chief of the Israeli military Intelligence (*Sayeret Matkal*) was Prime Minister from July 1999 to March 2001. When replaced by Sharon, he took a job as advisor for Electronic Data Systems and for SCP Partners, a front company specialized in security, known as a front for Mossad. SCP Partners had an office in the town of Englewood, New Jersey, less than 7 miles from Urban Moving Systems. One hour after the explosion of the North Tower, Barak was on BBC World to point the finger at bin Laden as prime suspect, and to demand immediate retaliation against Afghanistan.[410]

All the facts mentioned in the present chapter give new meaning to the words of Bob Graham, pseudo-whistleblower of the 9/11 Commission, in an interview with PBS in December 2002, that there was "evidence that there were foreign governments involved in facilitating the activities of at least some of the terrorists in the United States."[411] Graham, of course, was referring to Saudi Arabia. Why would the Saud family help Osama bin Laden after stripping him of his Saudi nationality and putting price on his head for his attacks on their soil? Graham's response, given in July 2011, is "the threat of civil unrest against the monarchy, led by Al-Qaeda."[412] This ridiculous theory

---

[409] On History Commons: www.historycommons.org/entity.jsp?entity=mark_crispin_miller
[410] Bollyn, *Solving 9-11, op. cit.,* p. 278-80.
[411] Raimondo, *The Terror Enigma, op., cit.,* p. 64.
[412] "Saudi Arabia: Friend or Foe?", *op. cit.*

(which Graham, lacking arguments, developed in a novel)[413] has only one purpose: to divert suspicion away from the only "foreign government" whose links with terrorist suspects are out in the open: Israel (an enemy of Saudi Arabia, as it happens). In asserting further that the Saudi connection was stifled because of the friendship between the Bushes and the Saudis, Graham and his neoconservative friends use George W. Bush as a fuse or a lightning rod. The strategy has worked, since the 9/11 Truth movement hardly breathes a word on Israel but pursues the Bush clan with hostility—exaggerating, for example, the part played in the WTC security (until 1998) by the company Securacom/Stratesec, co-directed by the President's brother Marvin Bush (until June 2000).[414] Here we see Machiavelli at work: accomplish your dirty ends (war in the Middle-East) through the actions of another, and then turn popular vengeance against him. When, under mounting pressure from public opinion, the mainstream media will be forced to abandon the official story, the protest movement will have been already well infiltrated, and the slogan "9/11 was an inside job" will have prepared the public to turn against Bush, Cheney and Rumsfeld, while the neocons will remain legally untouchable. As for Israel's implication, if it can no longer be hidden, it will be minimized according to Noam Chomsky's good old sophistry: after all, Israel is only the 51st American State, controlled from Washington, so that, whatever evil Israel does, it can always claim that "America made me do it."

Noam Chomsky, a militant Zionist in his youth, has been the most conspicuous spokesman of the the radical left for fourty years, ever since pseudo-trotskists like Irving Kristol moved to the other far end of the political spectrum. Chomsky has always been hostile to any questionning of the official 9/11 story—as well as, curiously, to the quest for truth on the Kennedy assassination (in 1993, he published *Rethinking Camelot* to defend the official story).[415] Howard Zinn has taken a similar view of 9/11, known as the "blowback theory": the important question, for him, is not who did 9/11, but "why the Arab world hate us so much."[416]

A very revealing effort to direct popular suspicion toward the WASP faction of Wall Street (symbolized by the name Rockefeller, as opposed, implicitly, to the name Rothschild associated to both Jewish finance and Zionism) has been made by film producer Aaron Russo who, six months before passing away

---

[413] *The Keys to the Kingdom,* Vanguard Press, 2011.

[414] Read the debunking of this point on : www.911myths.com/html/stratesec.html

[415] Read Jeffrey Blankfort's articles on Chomsky on:
www.voltairenet.org/auteur123803.html?lang=en

[416] See Zinn's interview on YouTube: www.youtube.com/watch?v=EISJTXHELd8invstigating

from cancer in 2007, may have wanted to "do something for Israel," as American influential Jews are constantly pressured to do. In an interview with Alex Jones of Infowars.com, he pretended to have been befriended by Nicholas Rockefeller (having only a photograph to substantiate his claim). Nick Rockefeller, Russo said, forwarned him of 9/11 eleven months in advance and explained it as part of the Wall Street elite's plan for a New World Order based on worldwide enslavement. Nick Rockefeller is a very minor and and very distant member in the dynasty, already dead by the time of Russo's interview. The probability that he would know such a secret, let alone share it with a Hollywood figure, is totally preposterous. Yet Russo's claim has had tremendous success on the net, all the more so that his subsequent death by cancer can be claimed as assassination.[417] To the same kind of make-believe belongs the widespread fake quote of David Rockefeller, grandson of John D. Rockefeller, thanking the *Washington Post*, the *New York Times* and other publications for having "respected the promises of discretion for almost forty years" on the Trilateral Commission's project for a "supranational sover-eignty of an intellectual elite and world bankers." More credible would be a descendant of Lord Lionel Walter Rothschild of the *English Zionist Federation* (who laid the first stone of the Jewish State through bargaining for the Balfour Declaration with the British Government)[418] congratulating the Sulzbergers and the Grahams (hereditary directors of the *Times* and *Post* respectively) for their discretion of forty years on the crimes and deceptions of Israel.

We should not, however, oversimplify the issue and seek to blame only Israel for 9/11. As said earlier, a complex operation like 9/11 necessarily involves a broad range of intertwined interests, and it is most likely that the Bushes, like many other key players within the deep state, are held hostages of the Israelis by their own involvement in the plot, and kept in line by both retribution and blackmail. The Bushes, perhaps only interested in invading Afghanistan at the start, may have found themselves forced into the invasion of Iraq that the first Bush had resisted in 1991.

The notion that Bush has fallen under the control of "a rogue network or in-visible government faction" through blackmail or threat has been convincingly argued by Webster Tarpley in his *9/11 Synthetic Terror.* Tarpley quotes an article published on the Internet journal *Debka* eleven days after 9/11, which reveals that a message of threat against the presidential plane had been re-ceived at 9 am on September 11, using coded terminology which proved that "the terrorists had obtained the White House code and a whole set of top-secret signals." That raised the question, writes the author in *Debka*: "How did the

[417] www.prisonplanet.com/articles/january2007/290107rockefellergoal.htm
[418] For an insider's view of this deal, read Benjamin Freedman on rense.com/general34/amaz.htm

terrorists access top-secret White House codes and procedures? Is there a mole, or more than one enemy spy in the White House, the Secret Service, the FBI, the CIA or the Federal Aviation Administration?" The author of the article concludes that Al-Qaeda must have received help from ... Iraq. That is not surprising, says Tarpley, since *Debka* often reflects the view of the Mossad. What Tarpley fails to notice, however, is that the neoconservatives fully qualify as moles operating for a foreign government within the White House; rather, Tarpley believes that "The foreign intelligence service which contributed the most indirect support to 9/11 was unquestionably the British MI-6."[419]

Perhaps the question of the ultimate culprit of the 9/11 terror bombings can be solved if approached through the technical means used to destroy the Twin Towers. The murder weapon classically leads to the murderer. A scientific confirmation of the use of explosives came in February 2009, when an international team of chemists led by professors Niels Harrit of Copenhagen University and Steven Jones of Brigham Young University (Utah), after having examined wreckage dust materials from the WTC, published an article in the scholarly journal *Open Chemical Physics Journal*, entitled: "Active Thermitic Material Discovered in Dust from the 9-11 World Trade Center Catastrophe." The thermite (a high-tech incendiary capable of cutting through steel beams) found in the WTC dust is the product of sophisticated nanotechnology. The media felt compelled to report such indisputable scientific evidence, but in such a way as to minimize its importance. For example, on the French governmental TV channel France 5, December 2, 2009, the reporter commented: "And so what does this mean? It changes little in regards to the facts on the towers' collapse. Obviously, there is no point denying that two planes hit the towers. But it means that the explosive may have been put there previously before the impact of the planes into the WTC, and the shock of the planes' impact collapsed [sic] and detonated the thermite. And it would mean that the WTC security was perhaps much worse than what we were led to believe at the time."[420] The repetitive "it means," here, is intended to divert the listener from conceptualizing what this stunning piece of information really does mean: the collapse of the Al-Qaeda theory. Nanothermite is a sophisticated explosive that only a high-tech industry is capable of producing. The media's misrepresentation of evidence such as above works like a vaccine: a small dose of devitalized information injected once, and only once, immunizes against the conspiracy fever, all the while protecting against accusations of media censorship.

---

[419] Debka, "Digital moles in White House? Terrorists had top-secret presidential codes", WorldNetDaily.com, September 22, 2001, quoted in Tarpley, *9/11 Synthetic Terror, op. cit.,* p. 295-6; Tarpley, *9/11 Synthetic Terror, op. cit.,* p. 324
[420] Watch on DailyMotion, "11 sept: France5 traite des explosifs du WTC", www.dailymotion.com/video/xkzy1h_11-sept-france5-traite-des-explosifs-du-wtc_webcam

But there may be another reason why the media chose to report the presence of nanothermite in the WTC dust anyway. A number of scientists claim that nanothermite, an incendiary rather than an explosive, cannot by itself account for the force of the explosions in the Twin Towers. It may have been enough to "pull" WTC7, which has been classically destroyed from bottom to top with no horizontal projection and little dust produced, but it fails to explain the very different destruction of the Twin Towers, from top to bottom, and the pulverization into very fine dust of almost all their concrete—not to mention the eleven hundred bodies never recovered. Thermite also leaves unexplained the deep craters found in the basements of the towers. It doesn't explain the temperatures of 600 to 1,500 °F at Ground Zero for 6 months after 9/11.[421] It doesn't explain the high percentage of some residuals of nuclear fusion/fission reactions in the rubble (barium, strontium, thorium, uranium, lithium, lanthanum, yttrium, chromium, tritium), and neither does thermite explain the high rate of rare cancers (thyroid cancer, leukemia, and multiple myeloma) among Ground Zero workers, typical of radiation exposure. For these reasons and more, a growing number of scientists are now rejecting the nanothermite thesis and believe that mini-neutron bombs (perhaps no bigger than apples) had been planted in the core columns of the buildings.[422]

WTC6, an eight-story building that stood north of the North Tower and housed federal government agencies, was severely damaged on September 11, with two holes that extend the height of the building. The multicolored glass-like smooth bedrock in the deep crater at the center of the building is the signature of a fusion-fission reaction.[423]

The use of such mini-nuclear bombs, or "micro-nukes," is fully consistent with other evidence implicating Israel: contrary to the United States, Israel has

---

[421] See for example: gcn.com/articles/2002/09/09/handheld-app-eased-recovery-tasks.aspx
[422] Read Jeff Prager, *9/11 America Nuked,* freely downloadable on: 911scholars.ning.com/profiles/blogs/jeff-prager-9-11-america-nuked-free-downloadable-ebook. Read also on Veterans Today the article by Don Fox, Jeff Prager and Ed Ward, "Mystery Solved: The WTC was Nuked on 9/11": www.veteranstoday.com/2013/05/01/mystery-solved-the-wtc-was-nuked-on-911/
[423] Jeff Prager, *9/11 America Nuked, op. cit.,* p. 85. See also p. 138.

never signed the Non-Proliferation Treaty, and its nuclear arsenal is not subject to inspection or control of any kind.[424] Moreover, this is not the only case where Israel is suspected to have used mini-neutron bombs in a false flag bombing. On October 12, 2003, an extremely powerful explosive device destroyed an Australian nightclub in Bali, Indonesia, killing 187 people and injuring more than 300 others. The bombing, blamed on Islamists, stopped a movement of protest in Australia against the Iraq war. The device was planted in a monsoon drain approximately five feet under the road nearby. According to Australian investigator Joe Vialls, the force of the blast, which set some 27 buildings in the neighborhood on fire, is indicative of a micronuclear device. So is the fact that 30 people were totally vaporized by the explosion, while many around the blast received severe flash burns of a kind which Australian surgeons declared having "never seen before." Vialls concludes to the use of a plutonium fission bomb, which leaves behind only alpha radiation "invisible" to a standard Geiger counter. And he points the finger at Israeli secret services.[425]

In the case of the WTC, just a few individuals working two or three days would have been needed to place easily disguised micro-nukes no bigger than apples within the buildings, every five to ten floors, and the same people could have detonated the explosive sequence. In contrast, to plan the demolition of the Twin Towers with nanothermite would have required hundreds of people, months of work and a lot of highly visible masonry work to reach the steel column. Professor Neils Harrit has actually estimated the amount of nanothermite needed to blow the Twin Towers between 29,000 and 144,000 metric tons. Just to unload the lowest estimate would have needed 1,500 tractor trailer loads with a crew working 24 hours a day for 300 days non-stop. That seems inconceivable for a foreign power. In fact, it is inconceivable altogether.

Yet the nanothermite theory remains the most widely accepted explanation for the destruction of the Twin Towers. This raises disturbing questions. Jim Fetzer, a Veteran in 9/11 research and founder of "Scholars for 9/11 Truth," has been unfairly attacked or ostracized by influential 9/11 Truth groups since he has endorsed the mini-nuke theory and pointed the finger at Israel,[426] while Steven Jones, co-founder of the same organization, has received the broadest support after parting from Fetzer and founding the competing "Scholars for

---

[424] See Jim Fetzer on YouTube, "Midwest 9/11 Truth Conference Part 2": www.youtube.com/watch?feature=player_embedded&v=ZAEvw2CjAYQ#t=2611, and his article with Don Fox's article, "2 + 2 = Israel nuked the WTC on 9/11": www.veteranstoday.com/2013/08/28/2-2-israel-nuked-the-wtc-on-911/

[425] Joe Vialls, "Bali Micro Nuke – Lack of Radiation Confuses 'Experts'": web.archive.org/web/20030210220533/http://homepage.ntlworld.com/steveseymour/nuke/bali_micro_nuke.htm

[426] See his article co-authored by Don Fox, "2 + 2 = Israel nuked the WTC on 9/11": www.veteranstoday.com/2013/08/28/2-2-israel-nuked-the-wtc-on-911/

9/11 Truth and Justice," which support the nanothermite theory. Moreover, as the shortcomings of that theory are becoming increasingly known, a new theory has recently appeared, which circumvents the simple mini-nuke theory with an extremely complicated alternative which points back to the U.S. military-industrial complex rather than to Israel: according to professor Judy Wood, the most zealous exponent of this new theory, the "dustification" of the Twin Towers can only be explained by the use of as yet unknown "directed energy weapons," possibly "Star Wars beam weapons" shooting from orbital stations.[427] Wood can offer no evidence of the existence of such weapons.[428]

---

[427] Judy Woods, *Where Did the Towers Go ? Evidence of Directed Free-Energy Technology on 9/11,* The New Investigation, 2010.
[428] For a harsh critic of Wood as a "gatekeeper" of 9/11, see: donaldfox.wordpress.com/2013/01/20/dr-judy-wood-911-gatekeeper-extraordinaire/

26. The Israeli False-Flag Tradition

Americans have a long history of manufacturing false pretenses for war. We could go back to 1845 with the expansionist war against Mexico, triggered by U.S. provocations on the disputed border area with Texas (the Nueces River according to Mexico, the Rio Grande according to the Texans); skirmishes eventually gave President James Polk (a Texan) the opportunity to declare that the Mexicans "invaded our territory and shed American blood on American soil" (after the war, a congressman by the name of Abraham Lincoln argued the falsity of the *casus belli*). Thereafter, all the wars waged by the United States have been under false pretenses: the explosion of the USS Maine in the war against Spain, the sinking of the Lusitania for entry into the First World War, Pearl Harbor for the Second, and the Gulf of Tonkin for the bombing of North Vietnam. However, only the explosion of the USS Maine can properly be called a false flag operation, and still it is unclear.

It is a fact, however, that Israel has a long history and grand expertise in false flag terror. A world history of false flag operations would need to dedicate at least half of its pages to modern Israel, a nation less than a century old. The pattern was formed even before the creation of the Jewish State, with the bombing of the King David Hotel, headquarter of the British authorities in Jerusalem: the morning of July 22, 1946, six terrorists of the Irgun (the terrorist militia commanded by Menachem Begin, future Prime Minister) dressed as Arabs entered the building, and around the central pillar placed 225 kg of explosives hidden in milk churns, while others spread explosives along the access roads to the hotel to prevent emergency aid. When a British officer manifested his suspicion a gunfight broke out and the Irgun members fled, but not before igniting the explosives. The explosion killed 91 people, mostly British, but also 15 Jews.

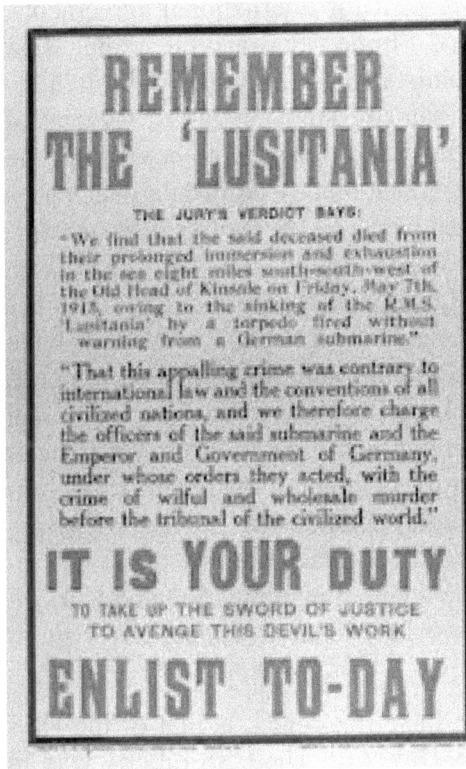

REMEMBER
THE 'LUSITANIA'

THE JURY'S VERDICT SAYS:

"We find that the said deceased died from their prolonged immersion and exhaustion in the sea eight miles south-south-west of the Old Head of Kinsale on Friday, May 7th, 1915, owing to the sinking of the R.M.S. 'Lusitania' by a torpedo fired without warning from a German submarine."

"That this appalling crime was contrary to international law and the conventions of all civilized nations, and we therefore charge the officers of the said submarine and the Emperor and Government of Germany, under whose orders they acted, with the crime of wilful and wholesale murder before the tribunal of the civilized world."

IT IS YOUR DUTY

TO TAKE UP THE SWORD OF JUSTICE
TO AVENGE THIS DEVIL'S WORK

ENLIST TO-DAY

The transatlantic ferry RMS Lusitania was torpedoed on May 7, 1915 by the Germans, while sailing in a war zone forbidden by the Germans. The slogan "Remember the Lusitania" was later used to mobilize public opinion in favor of entering the war. The fact that one torpedo was enough to sink the ship in fifteen minutes raised questions. In his *Intimate Papers* published posthumously, Colonel Mendel Edward House, Woodrow Wilson's advisor, reports a conversation he had shortly before with British Foreign Secretary Edward Grey (who would become ambassador in Washington in 1919). "What will Americans do if Germans sink an ocean liner with American passengers on board?" asked Grey, to which House answered: "I believe that a flame of indignation would sweep the United States and that by itself would be sufficient to carry us into war."[429]

The strategy was repeated in Egypt during the summer of 1954, with Operation Susannah. The goal was to compromise the Brit's withdrawal from the Suez Canal, demanded by Colonel Abdul Gamal Nasser with support from President Eisenhower. Egyptian Jews trained in Israel bombed several British targets, then placed the blame on the Muslim Brotherhood, so as to discredit Nasser in the eyes of the British and the Americans, and to generate antipathy against Egypt. The accidental detonation of an explosive device allowed the exposure of the conspiracy. The Defense Minister Pinhas Lavon was held responsible, even though he placed the blame on Colonel Benjamin Givli, Director of Military Intelligence (Aman). The scandal, known as the "Lavon Affair," was largely overlooked in the Israeli and American media, and it was not until more than fifty years later in 2005, that the State of Israel publicly acknowledged its responsibility.

At the time, Ben Gurion had temporarily withdrawn from his two positions as Prime Minister and Minister of Defense. While still pulling the ropes behind the scenes, he had handed the Prime Ministry to Moshe Sharett, who was already serving as Minister of Foreign Affairs, and the Ministry of Defense to

---

[429] Charles Seymour, ed., *The Intimate Papers of Colonel House,* 1926.

Pinhas Lavon. These two men embodied two conflicting visions of Israel. Sharett stood for a moderate Zionism and a respect for international agreements, while Lavon, much like Moshe Dayan and Shimon Peres, other protégés of Ben Gurion, embraced a dangerously extremist Zionism. Sharett, writing in his diary in 1955, regretted that "Lavon [...] has constantly preached for acts of madness and taught the army leadership the diabolic lesson of how to set the Middle East on fire, how to cause friction, cause bloody confrontations, sabotage targets and property of the Powers [and performs] acts of despair and suicide." Sharett included Shimon Peres in the same verdict: "he wants to frighten the West into supporting Israel's aims." Of this man who would finally become President of Israel at 84 years old, Sharett wrote again in 1957, "I have stated that I totally and utterly reject Peres and consider his rise to prominence a malignant, immoral disgrace." Livia Rokach, daughter of the mayor of Tel Aviv Israel Rokach, who printed these remarks from Sharett's diary in *Israel's Sacred Terrorism* (1980), criticizes Sharett for having not made public his sentiments; had he alerted Israeli citizens through public debate, he may have very well been able to prevent the final takeover of the Israel State by the most violent brand of Zionism, this breed become so adept at manipulation and betrayal in international relations, and who, in the words of Sharett, "raises terrorism to the level of a sacred principle."[430]

The most infamous and calamitous Israeli false flag attack is that of the USS Liberty, two days before the end of the Six Day War. The USS Liberty was an unarmed American vessel of the NSA stationed in international waters and easily recognizable. On that sunny day of June 8, 1967, three unmarked Mirage bombers and three torpedo boats carrying Israeli flag bombed, strafed and torpedoed it for 75 minutes—even strafing the lifeboats—with the obvious intention of leaving no survivors. They stopped the carnage only at the approach of a Soviet ship, after killing and severely wounding more than 200 crewmembers, mostly engineers, technicians and translators. When the attack was first reported on American television and radio, people were led to believe that it was an Egyptian act of war, and some elected officials immediately called for retaliation against Egypt. When it was finally revealed to be an Israeli attack, it was excused as a targeting error and the story was quietly dropped. The Israeli government offered a discreet apology along with financial compensation. Lyndon Johnson accepted this ridiculous excuse, under the pretext that "I will not embarrass our ally." Oliver Kirby, Deputy Director for Operations at the NSA at the time, reported to journalist John Crewdson of the *Chicago Tribune* (October 2, 2007) that the transcripts of the communications intercepted from the Israeli planes and immediately sent to Washington by the

---

[430] Livia Rokach, *Israel's Sacred Terrorism: A Study Based on Moshe Sharett's Personal Diary and Other Documents,* Association of Arab-American University Graduates, 1986, p. 42-9.

NSA, left no doubt that the Israeli pilots had identified their target as American before attacking it: "I'm willing to swear on a stack of Bibles that we knew they knew [that the ship was American]."[431] According to Peter Hounam, author of *Operation Cyanide: Why the Bombing of the USS Liberty Nearly Caused World War III* (2003), the attack on the Liberty had been secretly authorized by the White House as part of the project Frontlet 615, "a secret political agreement in 1966 by which Israel and the U.S. had vowed to destroy Nasser." It has been reported that, on learning that the Sixth Fleet had sent fighter jets to rescue the USS Liberty, Johnson personally called Admiral Geiss to order him: "I want that goddamn ship going to the bottom. No help. Recall the wings."[432] If the Israelis had been able to sink the ship without survivors and witnesses, the attack would have been blamed on Egypt, and the United States would have had a pretext to come alongside Israel. Egypt being then an ally of the USSR, world war was clearly on the program.

In 1986, Israel tried to make it seem that a series of terrorist orders were transmitted from Libya to various Libyan embassies around the world. According to former agent Victor Ostrovsky (*By Way of Deception*, 1990), the Mossad was using a special communication system named "Trojan Horse" hidden inside enemy territory by Mossad commandos. The system acted as a relay station for faked transmissions originating from an Israeli ship, immediately retransmitted on a radio frequency used by the Libyan state. As the Mossad had hoped, the NSA intercepted and deciphered the transmissions, which were then interpreted as evidence that the Libyans were supporting terrorism, evidence that the Mossad would reinforce by providing the U.S. more faked intelligence of their own. Israel's strategy relied on Reagan's promise for retaliation against any country caught in the act of supporting terrorism. As expected, the Americans fell into the trap, dragging with them their British and German NATO allies: April 14, 1986, 160 American aircrafts dropped over sixty tons of bombs on Libya, targeting mainly airports and military bases. Among the civilian casualties on the Libyan side was Gaddafi's four-year-old adopted daughter.

---

[431] Bollyn, *Solving 9-11, op. cit.*, p. 60.
[432] Robert Allen, *Beyond Treason: Reflections on the Cover-up of the June 1967 Israeli Attack on the USS Liberty, an American Spy Ship*, CreateSpace, 2012.

Isser Harel, founder of Israeli secret services (*Shai* in 1944, *Shin Bet* in 1948, Mossad since 1963) predicted in 1980, in a conversation with the Christian Zionist Michael Evans, that Islamic terrorism would end up hitting America. "In Islamic theology, the phallic symbol is very important. Your biggest phallic symbol is New York City and your tallest building will be the phallic symbol they will hit."[433] When repeating these words in 2004 (in an interview with Deborah Caldwell and in his book *The American Prophecies: Terrorism and Mid-East Conflict Reveal a Nation's Destiny*), Evans hoped to pass Harel as a prophet. It seems more rational to conclude that 9/11 was an idea born thirty years earlier within the Israeli Deep State.

The manipulative capacity of the Mossad during that time can be further illustrated by two stories analyzed by Gordon Thomas in *Gideon's Spies: the Secret History of the Mossad* (2009). On April 17, 1986, a young Irish woman named Ann-Marie Murphy boarded a flight from London to Tel Aviv, unknowingly carrying 1.5 pounds of Semtex. The man who had given her the bag was her fiancé, a Pakistani named Nezar Hindaoui, who was then arrested while trying to find refuge at the Syrian Embassy. He had himself been manipulated by the Mossad, who would achieve their desired result: the Thatcher government broke off diplomatic relations with Syria.[434] In January 1987, the Palestinian Ismail Sowan, a Mossad mole who had infiltrated the PLO (Palestinian Liberation Organization) in London, was entrusted, by someone claiming to work for Sowan's PLO superior, with two suitcases packed with weapons and explosives. Sowan immediately called his Mossad contact, who instructed him to take the next flight to Tel Aviv, only to fly him back to London the next day. What he didn't know is that the Mossad simultaneously denounced him to Scotland Yard as a suspect in a potential Islamist attack in London. He was picked up on his return to Heathrow Airport and charged on the basis of the weapons found at his home. As a result, the Mossad found favor with the Thatcher government again.[435]

A third story will make the pattern even clearer. After the attack of February 26, 1993, against the WTC, the FBI arrested the Palestinian Ahmed Ajaj and identified him as a terrorist linked to Hamas, but the Israeli newspaper *Kol Ha'ir* showed that Ajaj had never been involved with Hamas or the PLO. According to the journalist Robert Friedman, author of an article in *The Village*

---

[433] Bollyn, *The 9/11 Deception, op. cit.,* p. 71.
[434] Gordon Thomas, *Gideon's Spies, op. cit.,* p. 384-5.
[435] Gordon Thomas, *Gideon's Spies, op. cit.,* p. 410-41.

Voice (August 3, 1993), Ajaj was actually nothing more than a petty crook arrested in 1988 for forging currency, sentenced to two and a half years in prison and released a year later thanks to a deal made with the Mossad, for whom he would then infiltrate Palestinian groups. Upon his release, Ajaj underwent a classic *sheep-dipping* by being once again briefly imprisoned, this time under the fake charge of trying to smuggle weapons for the Fatah into the West Bank. We have, therefore, with the bombing of the WTC in 1993, a prototype and precedent for September 11th, in which is demonstrated the deep involvement of Israel in false flag terrorism.[436]

It is worth noting that, in December 1993, Philip Zelikow and John Deutch wrote an article entitled "Catastrophic Terrorism" in *Foreign Affairs,* where they speculated on what would have happened in the 1993 WTC bombing had been done with a nuclear bomb: "An act of catastrophic terrorism that killed thousands or tens of thousands of people and/or disrupted the necessities of life for hundreds of thousands, or even millions, would be a watershed event in America's history. It could involve loss of life and property unprecedented for peacetime and undermine Americans' fundamental sense of security within their own borders in a manner akin to the 1949 Soviet atomic bomb test, or perhaps even worse. [...] Like Pearl Harbor, the event would divide our past and future into a before and after. The United States might respond with draconian measures scaling back civil liberties, allowing wider surveillance of citizens, detention of suspects and use of deadly force."[437]

The list of Israeli false flag operations goes on, and it must be remembered that only the failed ones can be documented. For the successful ones, the deep historians can only point out suspicions. That is the case for the crash of Egyptair Flight 990 on October 31, 1999. After this Boeing 767 bound from New York to Cairo crashed into the sea, the National Transportation Safety Board blamed co-pilot Gameel al-Batouti, portraying him as the first Islamic suicide pilot, despite the fact that this 60-year old *bon vivant*, married with five children, who was bringing back home a new tire and Viagra samples to distribute to his friends, didn't match the profile of a suicide jihadist. If we look at the victims, on the other hand, we get a better idea of the probable suspect: the flight was carrying a group of Egyptian military officers who had just been trained in the United States to fly Apache helicopters, despite objections on the part of the Israeli government.[438]

---

[436] Robert Friedman, "Mossad Linked to WTC Bomb Suspect", *The Village Voice,* August 3 1993: www.fromthewilderness.com/timeline/1990s/villagevoice080393.html.
[437] Griffin, *9/11 Contradictions, op. cit.,* p. 295-6.
[438] Tarpley, *9/11 Synthetic Terror, op. cit.,* p. 169

On March 17, 1992, the bombing of Israel's Embassy in Buenos Aires killed 29 and wounded 242. It was immediately blamed on Hezbollah using a truck bomb. But the judge in charge concluded that the explosives had been placed inside the building, and revealed pressures and false testimonies from American Jews and Israelis in order to contradict him. When the Argentine Supreme Court confirmed his thesis, Israeli diplomats accused all of the judges of anti-Semitism. On July 18, 1994, a new bomb killed 85 and wounded 300 in another Jewish center in Buenos Aires, the AMIA (*Asociación Mutual Israelita Argentina*). Again, the judges complained of pressures and false testimonies from the Jewish community, and expressed the same suspicions of an Israeli false flag terror attack meant to damage the blooming economic relationship between Iran and Argentina.[439]

And there are all the failed operations, some of them purposefully failed. On January 12, 2000, according to the Indian magazine *The Week*, officers of Indian Intelligence arrested at Calcutta airport eleven Islamist preachers who were preparing to board a flight to Bangladesh. They were suspected of belonging to Al-Qaeda and of intending to hijack the plane. They presented themselves as Afghans who had stayed in Iran before spending two months in India to preach Islam. Unfortunately for their story, they all had Israeli passports. The officer of the Indian Intelligence services told *The Week* that Tel Aviv "exerted considerable pressure" on Delhi to secure their release.[440] Here we have already, eight months before the "dancing Israelis" of 9/11, Israelis posturing as Arabs terrorists. Other failed (perhaps on purpose) plane hijacking include the case of shoe-bomber Richard Reid, who was arrested in December 2001, after attempting to blow up a transatlantic Paris-Miami airliner with explosives planted in the soles of his shoes. Reid, clearly mentally deficient, had travelled from London to Tel Aviv in the summer of 2001, and the Israeli visa in his passport was interpreted positively at the pre-board security screening.[441]

On October 12, 2000, in the final weeks of Clinton's presidency, the destroyer USS Cole en route to the Persian Gulf, was ordered from its homeport of Nor-

---

[439] Thierry Meyssan, *L'Effroyable imposture II. Manipulations et désinformations,* Alphée, 2007, p. 31-8.

[440] Subir Bhaumik, "Aborted Mission: Did Mossad attempt to infiltrate Islamic radical outfits in south Asia?" *The Week,* February 6, 2000. The article disappeared from the website of *The Week,* but can be found on: whatreallyhappened.com/WRHARTICLES/mossad_india.html

[441] Tarpley, *9/11 Synthetic Terror, op. cit.,* p. 74, quoting *New York Times* and *Washington Post,* December 29, 2001.

folk to refuel in the port of Aden in Yemen—a rather unusual procedure since these destroyers are generally supplied by a Navy tanker at sea. The captain of the ship expressed his surprise and concern: the USS Cole had recently filled up at the entrance of the Suez Canal, not to mention the fact that Yemen is a hostile zone. The USS Cole was in a docking maneuver when it was approached by a garbage disposal dinghy, which then exploded against the hull, killing 17 sailors and wounding 50. The two "suicide bombers" driving the dinghy also perished. The attack was immediately blamed on Al-Qaeda, even though bin Laden did not take responsibility and the Taliban denied that he could have been involved. The accusation gave the United States a pretext to force the Yemeni President Ali Abdullah Saleh to cooperate in the fight against anti-imperialist Islamism, by closing three paramilitary camps on its territory. What's more, a few weeks before the elections, the attack would become the "October Surprise" that brought Bush to power.

John O'Neill was put in charge of the investigation. An experienced counter-terrorism specialist at the FBI for twenty years, he had already investigated the WTC bombing in 1993. His team came to suspect that Israel had fired a missile from a submarine: the hole in the USS Cole was indeed indicative of that type of munitions and inexplicable by the explosion of one dinghy. O'Neill and his team suffered the hostility of the U.S. Ambassador Barbara Bodine and were forbidden to dive to fully inspect the damage. Finally, taking advantage of their trip home for Thanksgiving, Bodine refused them reentry to Yemen. The crew of the USS Cole was forbidden to speak about the attack except to Naval Criminal Investigative Service (NCIS). In July 2001, O'Neill resigned from the FBI. He was then hired as head of security at the WTC, by Kroll Associates' managing director Jerome Hauer; September 11 was his first day on the job. His remains were recovered from the World Trade Center site on September 28 and identified by Hauer. As for Barbara Bodine, in 2003 she would join the corrupt team of the Coalition Provisional Authority (CPA) in Baghdad, under Lewis Paul Bremer.[442]

To conclude, it cannot be disputed that Israel is the master deceiver on the international stage, and has a long experience of false flag operations. That is consistent with the Machiavellian principles guiding its leaders, openly advertised by Obadiah Shoher in *Samson Blinded: A Machiavellian Perspective on the Middle East Conflict* (2006). Of course, the U.S. National Security State is also used to fabricating false pretexts for imperialistic wars, and Operation Northwoods proves that it is capable of false flag terror attacks not unlike 9/11, in the absence of a moral President determined to stand in the way. In 2005, Jason Bermas and Dylan Avery made the Northwoods project the opening

---

[442] On the USS Cole and John O'Neill, watch on YouTube, "Zionists Exposed 911 USS Cole Link to War with Iran", www.youtube.com/watch?v=2sO2adojI58

argument of their *Loose Change* film, which did more than anything to stir the 9/11 Truth movement toward the drone hypothesis and the culpability of the U.S. military industrial complex. The timeliness of the Northwoods revelation in James Bamford's *Body of Secret* four months before 9/11, and its immediate coverage by ABC News, actually raise disturbing questions. Random House informs us that, to write his book, Bamford—an ex-Navy employee gone into journalism after Watergate, just like Bob Woodward—was granted, "unprecedented access to Crypto City (the NSA campus in Ft. Meade, MD), senior NSA officials, and thousands of NSA documents," by none other than NSA director Michael Hayden.[443] In view of the fact that Hayden, after moving to the CIA, has retired as a principal at the Chertoff Group, the security consultancy founded by Michael Chertoff, there is a good possibility that the Northwoods revelation was calculated to predispose truth seekers toward the hypothesis of a U.S. rather than Israeli false flag operation.[444] There are even some who believe that the document is a forgery, pointing out a few anachronistic British colloquialisms.[445] After all, the National Security Archive team of scholars and activists had never heard of Operation Northwoods until Bamford provided them with the memo. And, when asked about it by David Talbot, Robert McNamara, the supposed recipient of this outrageous memo, declared: "I have absolutely zero recollection of it."[446]

---

[443] Bamford's profile on Random House's website: www.randomhouse.com/features/bamford/author.html

[444] Seamus Coogan, "Who is James Bamford and what was he doing with ARRB?" August, 2010, on the *Citizens for Truth about the Kennedy Assassination* website: www.ctka.net/2010/OpNorthwoods.html. Read also Jim DiEugenio on Bamford's editor Robert Loomis: www.ctka.net/posner_jd4.html

[445] Carol Valentine on: www.public-action.com/911/northwds.html

[446] Talbot, *Brothers, op. cit.,* p. 107.

27. Toward World War IV

In April 2003, only weeks after the Anglo-American attack of Iraq, the House of Representatives introduced the Syria Accountability and Lebanese Sovereignty Restoration Act, which grants power to President Bush to act against Syria in order to force it to "halt support for terrorism," "cease the development and production of biological and chemical weapons," and make peace with Israel.[447] A war against Syria is secretly planned in the Pentagon for 2004, while, under the auspices of the National Endowment for Democracy, a puppet government in exile is created, the Syrian Democratic Coalition. Thanks to French President Jacques Chirac, who has close ties in Lebanon, the war is temporarily avoided by the UN Resolution 1559 (adopted on September 2, 2004), which demands simultaneous withdrawal of Israel and Syria from Lebanon. But on February 2, 2005, former Prime Minister Rafik Hariri, a leading figure of Lebanon and a personal friend of Chirac, is torn apart in his car by an explosion. The assassination is immediately blamed on Syrian leader Bachar el-Assad, but the Commissioner of the UN investigation, Detlev Mehlis, is soon forced to resign after his accusation of Syria is proven biased and ill-founded. In May 2006 it is the turn of Mahmoud Al-Majzoub, a leader of the Palestinian Islamic Jihad, to fall victim of an explosion in South-Lebanon. The involvement of an Israeli terrorist network is, this time, clearly established, when a former Lebanese officer named Mahmoud Radeh confesses working for the Mossad since 1994. The Lebanese investigation revealed that "the network members have followed training sessions inside and outside Israel," and that the Mossad provided them "with secret and sophisticated communication and surveillance equipment, along with precise maps of the targeted places and other locations in Lebanon." Suspicion arises that Israel is also behind Hariri's assassination, as well as fourteen other bomb attacks de-

---

[447] Library of Congress : www.congress.gov/cgi-bin/query/F?c108:1:./temp/~c108NN5Rpq:e2206:

signed to rekindle the civil war between Maronites, Sunnis and Shiites, and hostility between Lebanon and Syria.[448]

This is the moment Israel chose to invade Lebanon, after Netanyahu's meeting with Dick Cheney and Donald Rumsfeld on June 18, 2006, and under the pretext of trying to liberate two Israeli soldiers captured in Lebanon on July 12. Lasting thirty-four days, the war transforms South-Lebanon into a field of ruins, and causes the temporary exodus of one million people. Secretary of State Condoleezza Rice, speaking at a press conference on July 21, welcomes here "the birth pangs of a new Middle East." But the Israeli army (Tsahal) is ultimately unable to stand its ground and must retreat before Hezbollah resistance. This setback provokes a severe political crisis in Israel. From then on, the Jewish State will make sure to use U.S. and NATO forces to fight its own imperialistic wars.[449]

Despite having pulled its troops from Lebanon in compliance to UN Resolution 1559, Syria continues to be the target of incessant accusations from the U.S. and Israel. In 2003, Ariel Sharon turned the failure to recover Saddam's "weapons of mass destruction" into a pretext to accuse Syria, claiming that Iraq had secretly transferred them to Syria, along with its nuclear scientists. The actual aggression against Syria didn't begin until 2012, under the guise of a civil war, but it had been premeditated since February 2000 at the latest, when David Wurmser, in an article for the American Enterprise Institute entitled "Let's Defeat Syria, Not Appease It," was calling for a conflict through which "Syria will slowly bleed to death."[450] Not without irony, we will learn in 2013 that among the "rebels" armed by NATO to overthrow Bachar el-Assad are Al-Qaeda jihadists, which further confirms the real nature and function of Al-Qaeda. These mercenary "rebels" film their massacres and the Western media blame these very killings on the Syrian army.[451] We know what happened next: on August 21, 2013, Bashar al-Assad is accused of having "crossed the red line" by using chemical weapons against civilians—stupidly, just after having allowed UN inspectors into his country. Despite blatant inconsistencies in the accusation, American and European mass media unanimously accepted it. There is every evidence that the chemical attacks were, in fact, perpetrated by the "rebels" against loyalist Alawite families, with deadly gas provided by their Western sponsors; and evidence is presented that the

---

[448] Nicholas Blanford, "Lebanon exposes deadly Israeli spy ring", *The Times,* June 15, 2006: www.thetimes.co.uk/tto/news/world/middleeast/article2605183.ece. See also Cook, *Israel and the Clash, op. cit.,* p. 141-2.

[449] Meyssan, *L'Effroyable imposture II, op. cit.,* p. 131-6, 227-78.

[450] February 25, 2000, on AEI: www.aei.org/article/foreign-and-defense-policy/regional/middle-east-and-north-africa/lets-defeat-syria-not-appease-it/

[451] Watch John-Paul Leonard's film on YouTube, "The Big Lie & Dirty War on Syria": www.youtube.com/watch?v=_6YAOJ35yMk&feature=youtu.be

dead children shown on the videos broadcast around the world had been abducted two weeks prior by these "rebels."[452]

Since September 2001, Iran, like Iraq, has been placed in the crosshairs of the neoconservatives. They seem to echo the sentiments of Israeli Prime Minister Ariel Sharon, who, in the London *Times* on November 2, 2002 called Iran the "center of world terror" and called for threats against Iran "the day after the U.S. invades Iraq."[453] The invasion of Iraq proved to be more time consuming and costly than expected, causing the aggression against Iran to be delayed but not canceled. The public is kept at the doorstep of war by a series of accusations: a leading member of JINSA, Kenneth Timmerman, claim that Iran has sheltered bin Laden and worked with Al-Qaeda (*Countdown to Crisis: The Coming Nuclear Showdown With Iran*, 2005); on October 25, 2007, the Senate voted for the Kyle-Lieberman amendment that placed the *Pasdaran* ("Guardians of the Revolution"), an elite unit of the Iranian regime, on the black list of terrorist organizations, as part of a ploy to justify a preemptive war.

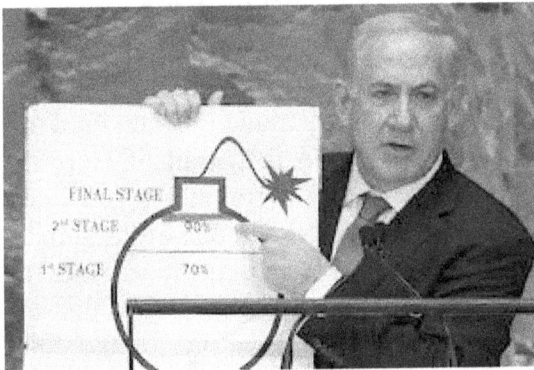

Netanyahu's subtle rhetoric against Iran was met with little enthusiasm in the United Nations on September 27, 2012.

The failure of U.S. troops to silence the resistance in Iraq has forced the postponement of the attack on Iran. But Daniel Pipes took the bad news in good spirits, cheerfully stating in the *New York Sun* (February 28, 2006) that the Iraqi civil war will invite "Syrian and Iranian participation, hastening the possibility of an American confrontation with those two states."[454] In spring 2008, President Bush took up this new neoconservative chorus: "The regime of Tehran has a choice to make. [...] If Iran makes the wrong choice, America will act to protect our interests and our troops and our Iraqi partners."[455] Unbe-

---

[452] Read Stephen Lendman, "False Flag Chemical Weapons Attack on Syria" on *Veterans News Now*: http://www.veteransnewsnow.com/2013/08/24/226407false-flag-chemical-weapons-attack-on-syria/, or Thierry Meyssan's articles on Voltairenet: http://www.voltairenet.org/article180149.html

[453] Sniegoski, *Transparent Cabal, op. cit.*, p. 199.

[454] "Civil War in Iraq?", *New York Sun*, February 28, 2006: www.nysun.com/foreign/civil-war-in-iraq-2006-02-28/28267/)

[455] April 10, 2008, on: www.presidentialrhetoric.com/speeches/04.10.08.html.

knownst to the American public, in May 2003, the Iranian government had sent to Washington, through the Swiss ambassador in Tehran, a proposal known as the "Grand Bargain," by which, in exchange for the lifting of economic sanctions, Iran promised cooperation with the United States to stabilize Iraq and establish there a secular democracy. Iran was prepared to make further concessions, including peace with Israel. Bush and Cheney, however, prevented Powell from responding positively to the gesture, so that, in the words of his Chief of Staff Lawrence Wilkerson, "the secret cabal got what it wanted: no negotiations with Tehran."[456]

In parallel to this kind of diplomatic obstinacy, false pretenses of war have been regularly created. We know from Gwyneth Todd, advisor to the Bahrain-based U.S. Navy's Fifth Fleet, that just after his appointment as commander of the fleet in 2007, Vice Admiral Kevin Cosgriff ordered his aircraft carriers and other ships into aggressive maneuvers in the Persian Gulf in order to strike panic into the Iranians, hoping for them to fire the first shot, which would start the war the Israel lobby was hoping for. Cosgriff wanted to "put a virtual armada, unannounced, on Iran's doorstep," without even informing Washington, according to the *Washington Post,* August 21, 2012.

On January 6, 2008, the Pentagon announced that Iranian boats fired on American ships USS Hooper and USS Port Royal in the Strait of Hormuz, while broadcasting threatening messages such as: "I am coming to you," and "you will explode after two minutes." The television showed one of the Iranian boats dumping small white objects into the water, presenting the situation as one of hostility, as though the white objects were mines. Referring to this exceptionally "provocative and dramatic" incident, the Chairman of the Joint Chiefs of Staff Mike Mullen expressed concern about "the threat posed by Iran," including "the threat of mining those straits," and affirmed his willingness to use "deadly force" if necessary. In reality, the situation presented by the media and Mullen was completely untrue. The Iranian boats that patrolled the area and passed American ships on a daily basis, had issued no threat whatsoever. Vice Admiral Cosgriff admitted that American crews had, in fact, noted that there was nothing to worry about, since the Iranian boats carried "neither anti-ship missiles nor torpedoes."[457] Nor did the threatening radio messages come from these vessels: "We don't know for sure where they came from," admitted the spokesman for the Fifth Fleet Lydia Robertson.[458]

---

[456] Sniegoski, *Transparent Cabal, op. cit.,* p. 258.

[457] Matthew Abbot, "Why was a Navy advisor stripped of her career", *The Washington Post,* August 21, 2012: www.washingtonpost.com/lifestyle/magazine/sunk/2012/08/21/96209788-cebd-11e1-aa14-708bac2c7ee9_story.html)

[458] Petras, *Zionism, Militarism and the Decline of US Power, op. cit.,* p. 58-82; Peter Dale Scott, *The War Conspiracy: JFK, 9/11, and the Deep Politics of War,* Mary Ferrell Foundation Press, 2008 p. 111-3.

Gwyneth Todd, who opposed and denounced the provocative strategy of Admiral Cosgriff, fled Bahrain out of fear for her life and now lives in Australia.

The 2009 Iranian elections and the ensuing protests in Tehran presented an occasion for a new tactic of psychological warfare, this time using Internet-based social networks and relays in the American media. Within a few days, the death of a young woman during the protests was appropriated as a horrifying symbol of the oppression taking place in the Islamic regime. Neda Agha-Soltan, the world was told, was killed June 20, 2009 by a sniper from the government militia, while exiting her car with her music teacher. A video of her agony, filmed live by mobile phone, was transmitted almost instantly around the world on Facebook and YouTube. Several rallies were held in her honor in Europe and America. There was talk of her being awarded the Nobel Peace Prize. Her fiancé, a photographer named Caspian Makan, met Shimon Peres in Israel and said: "I come to Israel as an ambassador of the Iranian people, a messenger of peace," adding, "I have no doubt that the spirit and soul of Neda was with us during the presidential meeting." Unfortunately, blatant inconsistencies started to emerge. First, there are actually three videos of Neda's agonizing death, which resemble several "takes" of the same scene. Second, a BBC interview with the doctor who attended her death is rife with contradictions. Third, the autopsy concluded that Neda was killed at point blank range. Fourth, Nedas's face that became a global icon is actually that of another young girl, Neda Soltani. Many surmised that Neda Agha-Soltan, an apprentice actress, agreed to act her own death in exchange for a promising career abroad, but was shot for real immediately after.[459]

---

[459] See the documentary by PressTV on YouTube, "Press TV-Cross Road – A closer look to the death of Neda Agha-Soltan »: www.youtube.com/watch?v=N6DO9bo4HeI

The stolen face of Neda Soltani, who tried in vain to suppress her picture from the web. Fearing for her life, she settled in Germany, where she published her story under the title, *My Stolen Face.*

Iran has also been accused, since the beginning of the first Bush presidency, of using its civilian nuclear research program as a front for secret military operations. The 2005 publication of a first National Intelligence Estimate (NIE) report regarding Iran and its supposed nuclear interests was the subject of intense media attention, but its contrary conclusions in 2007 were largely ignored, as was the fact that Iran's Supreme Leaders since Ayatollah Khomeini have issued fatwas banning nuclear weapons. Meanwhile, nothing is whispered regarding the illegal Israeli program that operates still unacknowledged, one that has allowed Israel to stockpile an estimated 200 atomic bombs to date.

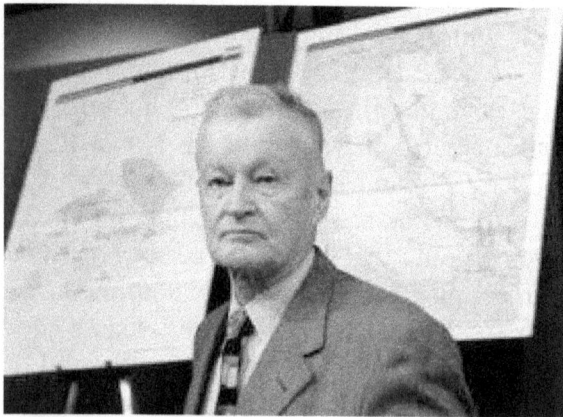

On the 1st of February 2007, in front of the Senate Foreign Relations Committee, Brzezinski denounced the Iraq war as "a historic, strategic, and moral calamity [...] driven by Manichean impulses and imperial hubris." As a veteran of deep politics, he can see what is coming next: "some provocation in Iraq or a terrorist act in the U.S. blamed on Iran; culminating in a 'defensive' U.S. military action against Iran that plunges a lonely America into a spreading and deepening quagmire eventually ranging across Iraq, Iran, Afghanistan, and Pakistan." Correctly seeing a war against Iran as part of a Zionist agenda, Brzezinski has recently warned the Obama administration against following Israel "like a stupid mule."[460] This dramatic backtracking by a major imperialist ideologist serves to demonstrate the loss of control by the U.S. of its own foreign and military policies.

---

[460] Sniegoski, *Transparent Cabal, op. cit.,* p. 301. YouTube, "Brzezinski: US won't follow Israel like a stupid mule":
www.youtube.com/watch?feature=player_embedded&v=ifEGiJ2ZxDM#at=41

The war against Iraq under the pretext of non-existent weapons of mass destruction, and then the threat of a war with Iran, again under the pretext of a non-existent nuclear armament program, both betray a desire to inflame conflicts in the Middle East rather than to control resources, let alone encourage stability. Michael Ledeen himself declares in his article "The War on Terror will not end in Baghdad" in the Wall Street Journal, on September 4, 2002: "We do not want stability in Iran, Iraq, Syria, Lebanon, and even Saudi Arabia: we want things to change. The real issue is not whether, but how to destabilize."[461]

What can possibly be the motivation for these incessant accusations and threats, and the destabilization of the Middle East? It follows a plan designed by a group of exceptionally intelligent men, with precise and realistic goals; but to what greater purpose? Osama bin Laden replied to this question in an article published by the London Arabic newspaper *Al-Quds al-Arabi* on February 23, 1998. Referring to "the Crusader-Jewish alliance," bin Laden writes of "their attempts to dismember all the states of the region, such as Iraq and Saudi Arabia and Egypt and Sudan, into petty states, whose division and weakness would ensure the survival of Israel."[462] Indeed, it appears that a Zionist cabal is interested in a new kind of world war, one that would weaken and fragment all the enemies of Israel for decades to come, putting Israel in a position to surpass even the United States, who would be ruined by their relentless military spending (just like the USSR in the 80s) and hated across the globe. Little, it would seem, stands in the way of the final phase of the Zionist plan: a thorough ethnic cleansing and the annexation of the whole of Palestine. Not without some irony, the neoconservative Stephen Schwartz, in *The Two Faces of Islam: The House of Saud, from Tradition to Terror* (2003), attributed to Saudi Arabia a plan that would spread terror throughout the world (while admitting it "incapable of defending its own territory"). "The war against terrorist Wahhabism is therefore a war to the death, as the Second World War was a war to the death against fascism."

In an article in the *Wall Street Journal* dated November 20, 2001, the neoconservative Eliot Cohen speaks about the war against terrorism as "World War IV," a framing soon echoed by other Americano-Zionists. In September 2004, at a conference in Washington attended by Norman Podhoretz and Paul Wolfowitz entitled "World War IV: Why We Fight, Whom We Fight, How We Fight," Cohen said: "The enemy in this war is not 'terrorism' [...] but militant Islam." Like the Cold War (considered to be WWIII), this imminent Fourth World War, according to Cohen's vision, has ideological roots, will

---

[461] Cook, *Israel and the Clash, op. cit.,* p. 118-9.

[462] Translation from Bernard Lewis, "License to Kill: Osama bin Ladin's Declaration of Jihad", *Foreign Affairs,* Nov-Dec 1998: www.foreignaffairs.com/articles/54594/bernard-lewis/license-to-kill-usama-bin-ladins-declaration-of-jihad.

have global implications and will last a long time, involving a whole range of conflicts. The self-fulfilling prophecy of a new World War centered in the Middle East has also been popularized by Norman Podhoretz, in "How to Win World War IV" (*Commentary,* February 2002), followed by a second article in September 2004, "World War IV: How It Started, What It Means, and Why We Have to Win," and finally in 2007 in a book called *World War IV: The Long Struggle Against Islamofascism.*[463] Meanwhile, the Israeli-Zionists are beating on their own drums of war. Less than two hours after the London bombings of July 7, 2005, the *Jerusalem Post* printed an article by Efraim Halevi, ex-Mossad chief and Director of Israel's National Security Council, entitled "Rules of Conflict for a World War": "We are in the throes of a world war, raging over the entire globe" and winnable only by "the destruction, the complete destruction, of the enemy."[464]

Iran has the largest Jewish population in the Middle East after Israel. Despite generous offers from Israel, most of these 30,000 Iranian Jews have refused to emigrate and remain loyal to their country. This fact does not fit with the repeated accusation that the Iranian government is consumed by anti-Semitism, and "preparing another Holocaust of the Jewish state," as written in Israeli newspaper *Haaretz* (November 14, 2006).[465]

---

[463] Sniegoski, *Transparent Cabal, op. cit.,* p. 193.

[464] Kollerstrom, *Terror on the Tube, op. cit.,* p. 73.

[465] Peter Hirschberg, "Netanyahu: It's 1938 and Iran is Germany; Ahmadinejad is preparing another Holocaust", *Haaretz,* November 14, 2006: www.haaretz.com/news/netanyahu-it-s-1938-and-iran-is-germany-ahmadinejad-is-preparing-another-holocaust-1.205137

28. The Bible and The Empire

Clearly, the strategists of Likud and their neoconservative allies intend to forge their legacy as those who waged and won the global annihilation of the Islamic civilization. How does one account for such hubris? We can search for an explanation in the very nature of the State of Israel, and the leadership role held by its military since day one. David Ben Gurion, who combined the functions of Prime Minister and Defense Minister, saw the whole fate of Israel integrally intertwined with its failure or success in the defeat of Arab enemies: "Why should the Arabs make peace? If I were an Arab leader I would never make terms with Israel. That is natural: [...] we have come here and stolen their country. Why should they accept that? They may perhaps forget in one or two generations' time, but for the moment there is no chance. So, it's simple: we have to stay strong and maintain a powerful army. Our whole policy is there. Otherwise the Arabs will wipe us out."[466] Thus, circumstances decree that Israel is and will be a security state.

It is primarily, of course, an expansionist and colonizing state, whose diplomatic tricks can no longer deceive anyone. The "partition of Palestine," Ben Gurion stated in 1948, "does not commit us to renounce Transjordan; one does not demand from anybody to give up his vision. We shall accept a state in the boundaries fixed today, but the boundaries of Zionist aspirations are the concern of the Jewish people and no external factor will limit them." Menachem Begin was even more straightforward: "Eretz Israel will be restored to the people of Israel. All of it. And forever."[467] In 1956, three days after Israel's invasion of Suez, Ben Gurion declared before the Knesset that the stake was no less than "the restoration of the kingdom of David and Solomon," that is, Israel's "Biblical borders" ("from the Euphrates to the Nile," as another saying

[466] Nahum Goldmann, *The Jewish Paradox: A Personal Memoir*, 1978.
[467] Quoted in Chomsky, *The Fateful Triangle: The United States, Israel and the Palestinians*, South End Press, 1983, p. 161.

goes).[468] Plans for the Israeli invasion and the French-British intervention which supported it, had been finalized in a secret meeting near Paris on October 24, 1956, attended by Ben Gurion, Patrick Dean of the British secret services, and Christian Pineau, French Minister of Foreign Affairs. The agreement, known as the Sèvres Protocol, aimed at overthrowing Nasser and taking control of the Canal.[469] That attempt failed because of Eisenhower's intervention, but the next one, a decade later, would partially succeed thanks to the non-intervention and secret help of Lyndon Johnson. Although Americans and Europeans have been led to believe that Israel's conquest of new land in 1967 had been a response to an Egyptian attack, historians today know better. Israeli Prime Minister Menachem Begin admitted himself, in a speech on August 8, 1982 before the National Defense College in Jerusalem, that the Six Day War was not a "war of necessity," but rather a "war of choice... Nasser did not attack us. We decided to attack him."[470] Ariel Sharon, who won renown in taking the Sinai, summed up the power gained at that time by Israel's National Security complex when declaring shortly after the Six Day War: "We could have locked the ministers in the room and gone off with the key. We would have taken the appropriate decisions and no one would have known that the events taking place were the result of decisions by major generals."[471]

Sharon is the man who, in the eyes of Israel and the world, most aptly embodies the spirit of the Israeli military and its security apparatus. He commanded Unit 101, which, on October 14, 1953, razed the village of Qibya, Jordan, with dynamite, killing 69 civilians in their homes. In 1956, during the Suez Canal crisis, a unit under his command executed more than 200 Egyptian prisoners and Sudanese civilians. In 1971, charged with putting an end to ongoing resistance in the Gaza Strip, his troops killed more than 100 Palestinian civilians. And in September 1982, after overseeing the slaughter of more than 1,500 women, children, and elderly in two Palestinian camps in West Beirut, he earned the nickname, "the butcher of Sabra and Chatila."

While Foreign Minister to Netanyahu from 1996 to 1999, Sharon described the Oslo Accords as "national suicide" and rather advocated the "Biblical borders," thereby encouraging illegal settlements: "Everybody has to move, run and grab as many hilltops as they can to enlarge the settlements because everything we take now will stay ours," he said on November 15, 1998.[472] When he

---

[468] Israel Shahak, *Jewish History, Jewish Religion,* Pluto Press, 1994, p. 10.

[469] *Nouvel Observateur*, October 17-23, 1996.

[470] George and Douglass Ball, *The Passionate Attachment: America's Involvement With Israel, 1947 to the Present,* WW Norton & Co, 1992, p. 22.

[471] Ze'ev Schiff, "Surprising conversations", *Haaretz*, June 1st, 2007, in Cook, *Israel and the Clash, op. cit.,* p. 105.

[472] Lela Gilbert, "An outpost carved in bedrock", *The Jerusalem Post,* February 25, 2010: www.jpost.com/Features/In-Thespotlight/An-outpost-carved-in-bedrock

came to power in February 2001, with Netanyahu in turn becoming Foreign Minister, Sharon deliberately sabotaged the peace process and ignited the second *Intifada* through a series of calculated provocations. On March 28, 2001, twenty-two nations gathered in Beirut under the auspices of the Arab League and agreed to recognize Israel if it only complied with Resolution 242. The next day, the Israeli army invaded and besieged Yasser Arafat in his Ramallah headquarters. Six months later, September 11th brought the fatal blow to any hope of peace.

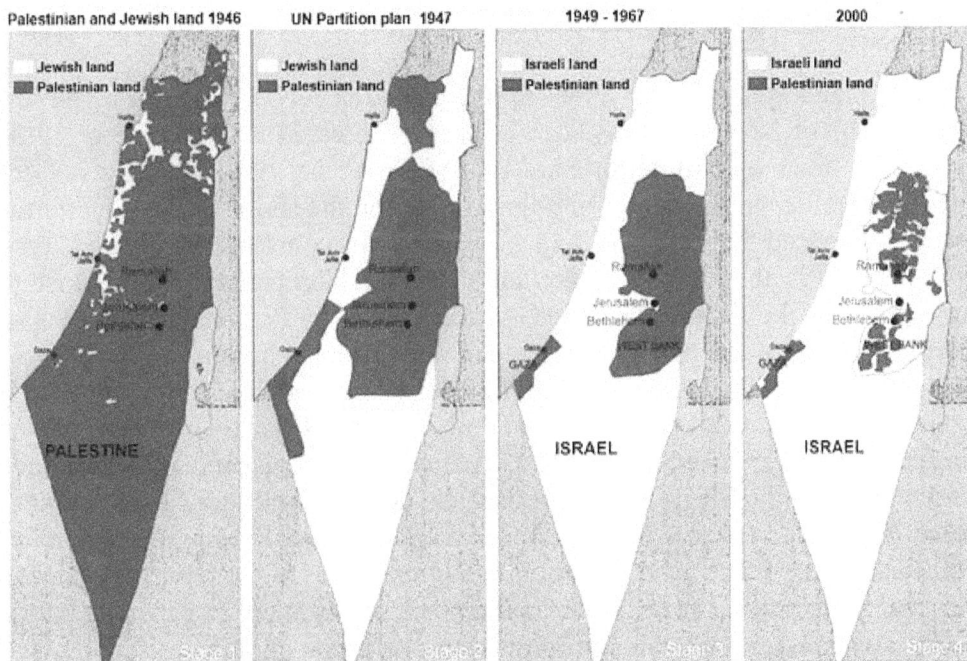

Sharon and Netanyahu's Likud have ceaselessly worked for a Greater Israel and against a Palestinian state. The Israel of their dream, soon to be realized, will include all of "Judea and Samaria."

More recently, the prevailing state of mind within Israel's National Security State seems accurately reflected by Martin van Creveld, renowned military expert and historian at the Hebrew University in Jerusalem, when he declared to *The Guardian* that the Palestinians' recurrent *Intifadas* will ultimately find only one solution: the "transfer" of all Palestinians out of Palestine, that is, the completion of the ethnic cleansing started in 1947-48. Concerning the risk of opposition by the International community, he added: "We possess several hundred atomic warheads and rockets and can launch them at targets in all directions, perhaps even at Rome. Most European capitals are targets for our air force. Let me quote General Moshe Dayan: 'Israel must be like a mad dog, too dangerous to bother.' [...] We have the capability to take the world down with us. And I can assure you that that will happen before Israel goes under."[473] Ron Rosenbaum, in *How the End Begins: The Road to a Nuclear World War III,* 2012, warns against taking such threats lightly, for "Abandonment of proportionality is the essence of the so-called Samson Option in all its variants. A Samson Option is made possible by the fact that even if Israel has been obliterated, it can be sure that its Dolphin-class nuclear missile submarines cruising the Red Sea, the Indian Ocean, and the Persian Gulf at depths impervious to detection, can carry out a genocidal-scale retaliation virtually anywhere in the world." Israel could easily "bring down the pillars of the world (attack Moscow and European capitals, for instance)" as well of the "holy places of Islam."[474]

The Likud and their political allies among orthodox Jews are driven by an imperial vision of Israel's destiny. Ariel Sharon expressed it in December 1981, in a speech for the Institute for Strategic Affairs at Tel Aviv University: "Beyond the Arab countries in the Middle East and on the shores of the Mediterranean and the Red Sea, we must expand the field of Israel's strategic and security concerns in the eighties to include countries like Turkey, Iran, Pakistan, and areas like the Persian Gulf and Africa, and in particular the countries of North and Central Africa."[475] This speech was canceled because of the controversy over the annexation of the Syrian territories at Golan Heights, but it would be published shortly after the in daily *Maariv.* This "Sharon doctrine" is consistent with a number of other texts written in Hebrew, some of which have been translated by Israeli scholar and peace activist Israel Shahak (*Open Secrets: Israeli Nuclear and Foreign Policies,* 1997), as well as by the *Journal of Palestine Studies.* For example, in an essay entitled "A Strategy for Israel in the Eighties," written for the World Zionist Organization in February 1982, Oded Yinon, a former senior official in the Ministry of Foreign Affairs, put forward a strategy to exert control over the Middle East through the fragmentation of Israel's neighbors, beginning with Lebanon: "The total disintegration of Lebanon into five regional localized governments is the precedent for the entire Arab world including Egypt, Syria, Iraq, and the Arab peninsula, in a similar fashion. The dissolution of Egypt and later Iraq into districts of ethnic and religious minorities following the example of Lebanon is the main long-range objective of Israel on the Eastern Front. The present military weakening of these states is the short-term objective. Syria will disintegrate into several states along the lines of its ethnic and sectarian structure, as is happening in

---

[473] David Hirst, "The War Game", *The Guardian,* September 21, 2003: www.guardian.co.uk/world/2003/sep/21/israelandthepalestinians.bookextracts
[474] Ron Rosenbaum, in *How the End Begins: The Road to a Nuclear World War III,* Simon & Schuster, 2012
p. 141-2, 21-2.
[475] Translated from Hebrew in *The Journal of Palestine Studies,* Spring 1982, quoted in Cook, *Israel and the Clash, op. cit.,* p. 101-2.

Lebanon today."[476] In September 1982, Ariel Sharon, acting as Minister of Defense, launched the invasion of Lebanon, and the carpet bombing of Beirut (using jet fighters and bombs supplied by the United States), which killed 10,000 civilians and drove half a million people from their homes. According to Moshe Sharett's dairy, Israel's plan to destabilize Lebanon by first fomenting a civil war and then using it as an excuse to annex land was first elaborated in May 1955 by Defense Minister Moshe Dayan.[477]

The ideology underlying the strategy of the Likud Party and of its neocon moles in the U.S. is a radical, intransigent brand of Zionism. As the label coined by its founders suggests, Zionism is essentially a biblical dream; Zion is the name given to Jerusalem 152 times in the Hebrew Bible. "The Bible is our mandate," proclaimed Chaim Weisman, the future first President of Israel, at the Versailles Conference in 1919. In Germany in the late 19th century, the biblical notion of a "chosen people" was translated by the founding fathers of Zionism into a racial ideology, totally consistent with the racial ideology of the Nazis and their fantasy of a superior Aryan race. Zionism, like Nazism, opposed the assimilationist leanings of the majority of European Jews. Zeev Jabotinsky, one of Zionism's founding figures, wrote in 1923, two years before Hitler's *Mein Kampf*: "A Jew raised in the midst of Germans [...] can become totally immersed in this German milieu, but he will always be a Jew, because his blood, his body and his racial type, his entire organic system, is Jewish."[478] Such claims of racial purity are today rightly regarded as unscientific: the settlers from Eastern Europe who massively populated modern Israel cannot claim descent from among the ancient Hebrews in Judea or Samaria, unlike the Palestinians they have evicted from their ancestral lands—and perhaps the Sephardic Jews from North Africa, once called "human garbage" by the Prime Minister Levi Eshkol, and subjected to eugenic policies in the 1950s (Haim Malka, *Selection and Discrimination in the Aliya and Absorption of Moroccan and North African Jewry, 1948-1956,* 1998).[479]

The "Revisionist Zionism" of Zeev Jabotinsky is as important a key as the Machiavellianism of Leo Strauss in decrypting the mentality of the men who, in Israel and in the United States, are trying to reshape the Middle East. It is, at least, a key to understand the ultimate goals of Benjamin Netanyahu, whose father, Ben Zion Netanyahu (born Mileikowsky in Warsaw), was the personal

---

[476] Quoted in Cook, *Israel and the Clash, op. cit.,* p. 109, in the translation by *The Journal of Palestine Studies,* Spring 1982.

[477] Rokach, *Israel's Sacred Terrorism, op. cit.,* p. 41.

[478] Text on the website of the Jabotinsky Institute: jabotinsky.org/multimedia/upl_doc/doc_191207_49117.pdf.

[479] Lital Levin, "Jewish Agency: We discriminated against North Africans", *Haaretz,* September 2, 2012: www.haaretz.com/print-edition/features/jewish-agency-we-discriminated-against-north-africans-1.382046

secretary of Jabotinsky. March 31, 2009, Netanyahu appointed Foreign Minister Avigdor Lieberman, from the *Yisrael Beiteinu* Party that presents itself as "a national movement with the clear vision to follow in the brave path of Zeev Jabotinsky."[480] Lieberman is intent upon "fighting Hamas just as the United States fought the Japanese during the Second World War."[481]

Zeev Jabotinsky writes in *The Iron Wall: We and the Arabs*: "All colonization, even the most restricted, must continue in defiance of the will of the native population. Therefore, it can continue and develop only under the shield of force, comprising an Iron Wall that the local population can never break through. This is our Arab policy. To formulate it any other way would be hypocrisy. [...] Zionism is a colonizing adventure and therefore it stands or it falls by the question of armed force."

Zionism has outlived Nazism because, after the war, it was able to shamelessly capitalize on the terrible persecution of Jews in Europe, and usurp the representation of the Jewish community.[482] To do that, it had to erase the memory of its active cooperation with the Nazi regime throughout the 30s, which have been thoroughly documented by Jewish anti-Zionist authors Ralph Schoenman (*The Hidden History of Zionism*, 1988) and Lenni Brenner (*Zionism in the Age of Dictators*, 1983; *51 Documents: Zionist Collaboration with the Nazis*, 2002). The Zionists supported Hitler's racial laws forbidding mixed marriages, while the Nazis saw the massive immigration of Jews from Germany to Palestine as the best "solution to the Jewish question." Writing in Berlin in 1934, Joachim Prinz, who would later become President of the American Jewish Congress (1958-1966) and a founding member of the Conference of Presidents of Major American Jewish Organizations, celebrated the Nuremberg Laws in his book *Wir Juden*: "A state built upon the principle of the purity of nation and race can only be honored and respected by a Jew who declares his belonging to his own kind."[483] Discrimination against assimilationist Jews would help their conversion to the Zionist ideal, Theodore Herzl had surmised: "The anti-Semites will become

---

[480] On the home page of the official website: www.yisraelbeytenu.com/.

[481] "Lieberman : Do to Hamas what the US did to Japan", *The Jerusalem Post*, January, 13 2009: www.jpost.com/Israel/Lieberman-Do-to-Hamas-what-the-US-did-to-Japan

[482] Read Norman Finkelstein, *The Holocaust Industry: Reflections on the Exploitation of Jewish Suffering*, Verso, 2000.

[483] Lenni Brenner, *Zionism in the Age of Dictators*, Lawrence Hill & Co, 1983.

our most dependable friends, the anti-Semitic countries our allies."[484] While in 1933 the American Jewish Congress organized the boycott of German goods, the World Zionist Organization signed with the Nazi government the Haavara Agreement which allowed the transfer of Jewish wealth to Palestine. In 1941, the terrorist group known as "Lehi," a dissident branch of the Irgun once headed by future Prime Minister Yitzhak Shamir (born Yzernitsky), formally offered "to actively take part in the war on the side of Germany" against the British, who were restricting Jewish immigration in Palestine.[485]

Because Zionism is the founding ideology of a "Jewish State" which treats its non-Jews as second-rate citizens and forbids interracial marriages, the General Assembly of the United Nations has declared in 1975 "that Zionism is a form of racism and racial discrimination" (Resolution 3379, revoked in 1991). Israel is an apartheid state like South Africa was until 1990, and it is no surprise that the two countries had established close economic and military ties (in violation of UN anti-apartheid sanctions); their cooperation included research on "ethno-specific" bacteriological weapons, meant to contaminate selectively undesirable populations, under Project Coast in South Africa (headed by the infamous Dr Wouter Basson), and the Institute of Biological Research in Israel (a department of the Ministry of Defense).[486] Israel pursued this secret research at least until the end of the 1990s, while sending out worldwide disinformation on the imaginary danger of Saddam Hussein's chemical and bacteriological weapons.[487]

Besides its racist ideology, Zionism has relied heavily upon its biblical roots to build its legitimacy. Despite being agnostic, David Ben Gurion (born Grün in Poland) was indoctrinated by "Ancient Israel," to the point of adopting the name of a Judean general who fought the Romans. "There can be no worthwhile political or military education about Israel without profound knowledge of the Bible," he is quoted stating.[488] While envisioning an attack against Egypt in 1948, he wrote in his diary: "This will be our revenge for what they did to our ancestors in Biblical times."[489] Ben Gurion, and most Zionists to this day, believe the Torah to be historically accurate and shun the growing archeological evidence that Solomon's Kingdom, like most of "biblical history," be-

---

[484] *The Complete Diaries of Theodor Herzl*, Vol. 1, ed. Raphael Patai, trans. Harry Zohn, Herzl Press and Thomas Yoseloff, 1960, p. 83-4.

[485] Klaus Polkhen, "The Secret Contacts", *Journal of Palestine Studies*, Spring-Summer 1976, p.78-80.

[486] Cockburn (ed.), *The Politics of Anti-Semitism, op. cit.*, p. 112; Gordon Thomas, *Gideon's Spies, op. cit.*, p. 502-3.

[487] Uzi Mahnaimi and Marie Colvin, "Israel planning 'ethnic' bomb as Saddam caves in", *The Sunday Times*, November 15, 1998.

[488] Dan Kurzman, *Ben-Gurion, Prophet of fire*, Olympic Marketing Corp, 1984.

[489] Ilan Pappe, *The Ethnic Cleansing of Palestine*, 2008, Oneworld Publications, p. 195.

longs to the realm of myths and propaganda.[490] Bible stories and prophecies are for them a model and a program. The ethnic cleansing planned by Ben Gurion in 1947-48, which forced the fleeing of 750,000 Palestinians (more than half of the native population), was deeply reminiscent of that which was ordained by Yahweh against the Canaanites: "dispossess them of their towns and houses," and, in the towns that resist, "not leave alive anything that breathes" (Deuteronomy 19:1, 20:16-17). What makes the biblical concept of a "chosen people" so much more toxic than secular forms of racism—besides its complete immunity to rational arguments—is that it is inseparable from the idea that other peoples are "doomed" unless they serve the chosen people. Descending upon "the people he has doomed," the biblical God has a sword "sated with blood and gorged with fat" (Isaiah 34:5-6, Jeremiah 46:10).

This dream instilled by the biblical Yahweh to his chosen people is not only racist; it is militarist and imperialist. The following verses from the second chapter of Isaiah (reproduced in Micah 4:1-3) are often held up to show the pacifist trend of the biblical prophecy: "they shall beat their swords into plowshares, their spears into pruning hooks. Nation will not take up sword against nation, nor will they train for war anymore" (Isaiah 2:4); but taken in context, we see that such *Pax Judaica* will come only when "all the nations shall flow" to the Jerusalem temple, from where "shall go forth the law" (Isaiah 2:1-3). This prophetic vision was appropriated by Ben Gurion, who predicted in 1962 in *Look* magazine, for the next twenty-five years (a few decades too early): "All armies will be abolished, and there will be no more wars. In Jerusalem, the United Nations (a truly United Nations) will build a Shrine of the Prophets to serve the federated union of all continents; this will be the seat of the Supreme Court of Mankind, to settle all controversies among the federated continents, as prophesied by Isaiah."[491]

This vision of a new world order with Jerusalem at its center resonates more than ever within Likudnik and neoconservative circles. At the Jerusalem Summit, held from October 12 to 14, 2003 in the symbolically significant King David Hotel, an alliance was forged between Zionist Jews and Evangelical Christians around a "theopolitical" project, one that would consider Israel, in the words of the "Jerusalem Declaration" signed by its participants, "the key to the harmony of civilizations," replacing the United Nations that's become "a tribalized confederation hijacked by Third World dictatorships": "Jerusalem's spiritual and historical importance endows it with a special authority to become a center of world's unity. [...] We believe that one of the objectives of Israel's divinely-inspired rebirth is to make it the center of the new unity of the

---

[490] See for example Keith Whitelam, *The Invention of Ancient Israel. The Silencing of Palestinian History*, Rutledge, 1996, or the classic by Philip Davies, *In Search of "Ancient Israel": A Study in Biblical Origins*, Journal of the Study of the Old Testament, 1992.

[491] *Look*, January 16, 1962.

nations, which will lead to an era of peace and prosperity, foretold by the Prophets." Three acting Israeli ministers spoke at the summit, including Benjamin Netanyahu; and Richard Perle, the guest of honor, received on this occasion the Henry Scoop Jackson Prize.[492]

With more than 50 million members, Christians United for Israel is a major political force in the U.S. Its Chairman, pastor John Hagee, declared: "The United States must join Israel in a preemptive military strike against Iran to fulfill God's plan for both Israel and the West, [...] a biblically prophesied end-time confrontation with Iran, which will lead to the Rapture, Tribulation, and Second Coming of Christ."

Will the "New World Order" finally prove to be the Empire of Zion? Let us recall that, long before being hailed by President Bush senior, the phrase had been coined in 1957 by geopolitician Robert Strausz-Hupé, in the first issue of his review *Orbis*, to define the agenda of his Foreign Policy Research Institute (FPRI), one of the early crucibles of neo-conservatism. Strausz-Hupé identifies the coming New World Order as "the American universal empire," destined to "to bury the Nation-States": "The American empire and mankind will not be opposites but merely two names for the universal order under peace and happiness. *Novus orbis terrarum* (New World Order)."[493] Strausz-Hupé's pupil Henry Kissinger may have given the appearance of following this vision. But not Daniel Pipes, ultra-Zionist son of neocon Richard Pipes, whom Strausz-Hupé named editor in chief of *Orbis* in 1986, and head of the Middle East Forum (MEF, originally a branch of FPRI) in 1990.[494] Has the disciple betrayed the master? It rather seems that the Americans have been fooled into thinking this New World Order would be American: it will be Israelo-American.

Americans had not been told either that the price for this New World Order would be a New World War. But that, too, was part of the Zionist program from the start, for it is the preliminary nightmare of the Biblical dream. The prophet Zechariah, often cited on Zionist forums, predicted that the Lord would fight "all nations" allied against Israel. In a single day, the whole earth

---

[492] The "Jerusalem Declaration" is on the Jerusalem Summit's official website: www.jerusalemsummit.org/eng/declaration.php
[493] Robert Strausz-Hupé, "The Balance of Tomorrow", *Orbis,* 1957, quoted in Meyssan, *L'Effroyable imposture II, op. cit.,* p. 217-8.
[494] Voltairenet, "Daniel Pipes, the expert of hate": www.voltairenet.org/article136260.html

will become a desert, with the exception of Jerusalem, who "shall remain aloft upon its site" (14:10). Zechariah seems to have envisioned what God could do with nuclear weapons: "And this shall be the plague with which the Lord will smite all the peoples that waged war against Jerusalem: their flesh shall rot while they are still on their feet, their eyes shall rot in their sockets, and their tongues shall rot in their mouths" (14:12). It is only after the carnage that the world will finally find peace, providing their worship of "the Lord Almighty": "Then everyone that survives of all the nations that have come against Jerusalem shall go up year after year to worship the King, the Lord of hosts, and to keep the feast of booths. And if any of the families of the earth do not go up to Jerusalem to worship the King, the Lord of hosts, there will be no rain upon them..." (14:16-17).

Is it possible that such a biblical dream, mixed with the neo-Machiavellianism of Leo Strauss and the militarism of Likud, be quietly animating a determined and organized ultra-Zionist clan? General Wesley Clark testified on numerous occasions before the cameras, that one month after September 11, 2001 a Pentagon general showed him a memo from neoconservative strategists "that describes how we're gonna take out seven countries in five years, starting with Iraq, and then Syria, Lebanon, Libya, Somalia and Sudan and finishing off with Iran."[495] Is it just a coincidence that the motif of the "Seven Nations" doomed by God form part of the biblical myths instilled in Israeli schoolchildren? According to Deuteronomy, Yahweh says that he will deliver to Israel "seven nations greater and mightier than [it]," adding: "you must utterly destroy them; you shall make no covenant with them, and show no mercy to them. You shall not make marriages with them..." (7:1-2). It is further prophesied to Israel: "And he will give their kings into your hand, and you shall make their name perish from under heaven" (7:24).

Evangelical Christians, who see the coming End of the World as good news, find in the *Book of Revelation* plenty of material to feed their fantasy, especially with the Angel Faithful and True of chapter 19, coming with "the armies of heaven," with eyes "like a flame of fire," "a robe dipped in blood," and in his mouth "a sharp sword with which to smite the nations."

---

[495] Listen for example to Clark at the Commonwealth Club of California in San Francisco, October 3, 2007, on YouTube, "Retired General of USA: America taking out 7 countries in 5 years": www.youtube.com/watch?v=iY96Z5Mqn40

CONCLUSION

29. Looking Back at Dallas

On the 22nd of November 1963, American democracy was assassinated in Dallas, Texas, by a demon calling itself National Security, who took possession of its body. Since then, that animated corpse roams the earth, sowing deception and terror everywhere, with only the appearance of humanity. Soon it became possessed by another demon, the Machiavellian soul of a paranoid petty state, which now controls its nerve system and its heavily armed limbs; the U.S. Deep State has become virtually an extension of Israel's fanatic, rightist Likud party. We have tried to tell, in as few words as we possibly could, this unfinished macabre tragedy. Let's now return to the opening scene, and look back to the genesis of this "special relationship" ("eternal," keep repeating U.S. presidents since Reagan), and from which many observers fear the U.S. may never recover.

Harry Truman, father of the monstrous CIA and first nuclear mass murderer, was also the U.S. president who recognized the State of Israel ten minutes after its proclamation, on May 15, 1948. "Truman's historic act of recognition will remain forever inscribed in golden letters in the 4000-year history of the Jewish people," the Israeli ambassador would proclaim soon afterward. Truman shed tears, it's been said, when in Washington in 1949 the Chief Rabbi of Israel told him: "God put you in your mother's womb so you would be the instrument to bring the rebirth of Israel after two thousand years."[496]

Truman's support for Zionism not only assured him a place in the biblical story as a new Cyrus, it also earned him "two million dollars in cash, in a suitcase" to revive his campaign, if we are to believe a knowledgeable young journalist of the time, John Kennedy.[497] What we know for certain is that Truman's "act of recognition" was strongly encouraged by his campaign manager

---

[496] Ronald Radosh, *A Safe Haven: Harry S. Truman and the Founding of Israel,* Harper Perennial, 2010.
[497] Kennedy quoted by Gore Vidal in his preface to Israel Shahak, *Jewish History, Jewish Religion, op. cit.,* p. vi.

Clark Clifford, while strongly opposed by his Secretary of State George Marshall, his Secretary of Defense James Forrestal, as well as by British Foreign Minister Ernest Benin. In addition, Truman betrayed the promise made by Franklin Roosevelt to King Ibn Saud during their lengthy meeting in February 1945—a promise that Roosevelt confirmed in a letter dated April 5th to his "Great and good friend," that "no decision be taken with respect to the basic situation in that country without full consultation with both Arabs and Jews"; "I would take no action, in my capacity as Chief of the Executive Branch of this Government, which might prove hostile to the Arab people."[498]

Truman (here offered a Torah scroll by Israeli President Chaim Weizmann) declared on the 3rd of April 1951, six years after Hiroshima: "Divine Providence has played a great part in our history. I have the feeling that God has created us and brought us to our present position of power and strength for some great purpose. [...] It is given to us to defend the spiritual values—the moral code—against the vast forces of evil that seek to destroy them."[499] Thus speaks Power in the guise of Virtue.

In 1960, presidential candidate John Kennedy himself received an offer of financial aid from the Israeli lobby, represented by Abraham Feinberg. He summed it up to his friend and journalist Charles Bartlett: "We know your campaign is in trouble. We're willing to pay your bills if you'll let us have control of your Middle East policy"; Bartlett recalls that Kennedy was deeply upset and swore that, "if he ever did get to be President, he was going to do something about it."[500] From 1962 to 1963, he submitted seven bills in an effort to reform the Congressional campaign finance system; all of them were defeated by the influential groups they sought to curtail. Meanwhile, with the support of the Attorney General Robert Kennedy, Senator William Fulbright, Chairman of the Committee on Foreign Relations, conducted an audit regarding "an increasing number of incidents involving attempts by foreign govern-

---

[498] Text on Crethi Plethi, www.crethiplethi.com/letter-from-president-roosevelt-to-king-ibn-saud-april-5-1945/usa/2010/

[499] Truman Library: www.trumanlibrary.org/publicpapers/index.php?pid=280

[500] Thomas, *Gideon's Spies, op. cit.*, p. 135.

ments, or their agents, to influence the conduct of American foreign policy by techniques outside normal diplomatic channels."[501] The Committee insisted that by virtue of its funding coming in through the State of Israel, the American Zionist Council be registered as a "foreign agent" and therefore subject to the obligations defined by the Foreign Agents Registration Act of 1938. The investigation would be brought to a halt by the Kennedy assassination and the replacement of his brother by Nicholas Katzenbach as Attorney General. The American Zionist Council escaped foreign agent status by renaming itself the American Israel Public Affairs Committee (AIPAC). Fulbright drew the conclusion on CBS (April 15, 1973): "Israel controls the U.S. Senate. [...] The great majority of the Senate of the U.S.—somewhere around 80 percent—are completely in support of Israel; anything Israel wants, Israel gets."[502]

If there was any doubt that Israel controls the American Congress, Benjamin Netanyahu proved it on May 24, 2011 by receiving 29 standing ovations from a full assembly, including at each of the following sentences: "in Judea and Samaria, the Jewish people are not foreign occupiers"; "No distortion of history could deny the 4,000-year-old bond between the Jewish people and the Jewish land"; "Israel will not return to the indefensible boundaries of 1967"; "Jerusalem must never again be divided. Jerusalem must remain the united capital of Israel."[503]

In an early chapter of this book, we have learned how Kennedy, being determined to prevent Israel from completing its nuclear weapons program, had firmly warned Prime Ministers David Ben Gurion and Levi Eshkol that, without immediate international inspection of the Dimona complex, "This [U.S.] Government's commitment to and support of Israel could be seriously jeopardized." Kennedy's death freed Israel from these pressures and restrictions. Instead, within ten years, without hindrance or control, in total illegality and impunity, Israel would build up enough nuclear bombs to start implementing its own aggressive brand of nuclear deterrence, known as "the Samson Option": the paranoid threat of reducing the Middle East and Europe to ashes rather than let the Jews be the victims of a new "Holocaust"—by which is meant any military defeat of Israel. This is exactly how Golda Meir blackmailed Nixon into sending military support to save Israel from an inevitable defeat by Egypt and

---

[501] The Israel Lobby Archive: www.irmep.org/ila/forrel/

[502] Quoted in Jeff Gates, *Guilt by Association: How Deception and Self-Deceit Took American to War,* State Street Publications, 2008.

[503] Watch on YouTube, "Netanyahu Addresses US Congress (5.24.11)": www.youtube.com/watch?v=9tqBYzWhcjQ

Syria in the 1973 Yom Kippur War, as journalist Seymour Hersh has documented.[504]

Kennedy was also committed to the right of return for the nearly 800,000 Palestinian refugees expelled from their neighborhoods and villages in 1947-48, that is, for the implementation of 1948 UN Resolution 194. Former Undersecretary of State George Ball notes in his book, *The Passionate Attachment* (1992), that "In the fall of 1962, Ben-Gurion conveyed his own views in a letter to the Israeli ambassador in Washington, intended to be circulated among Jewish American leaders, in which he stated: 'Israel will regard this plan as a more serious danger to her existence than all the threats of the Arab dictators and Kings, than all the Arab armies, than all of Nasser's missiles and his Soviet MIGs. [...] Israel will fight against this implementation down to the last man.'"[505] On November 20, 1963, Kennedy's delegation to the United Nations was calling again Israel to implement Resolution 194. Kennedy never read the outraged reactions in the *London Jewish Chronicle* of November 22: "Prime Minister Levi Eshkol summoned the U.S. ambassador [...] and told him that Israel was 'shocked' by the pro-Arab attitude adopted by the U.S. delegation." Golda Meir, for her part, "expressed Israel's 'astonishment and anger' at the attitude of the U.S."[506]

No wonder the coming to power of Johnson was greeted with relief in Tel Aviv, as evidenced in the Israeli newspaper *Yedio Ahoronot*: "There is no doubt that, with the accession of Lyndon Johnson, we shall have more opportunity to approach the President directly if we should feel that U.S. policy militates against our vital interests."[507] By contrast, the mourning was deep in the Arab world, where the portrait of Kennedy graced many homes. With his disappearance from the world stage, said Nasser, "De Gaulle is the only Western State leader on whose friendship the Arabs can now depend."[508] Kennedy had reduced financial aid to Israel, and sent grain to Egypt under the Food for Peace program. In 1965, Johnson would cut aid to Egypt and multiply aid to Israel, which went from $40 million to $71 million, reaching $130 million the following year. Under Johnson more than 70% of U.S. aid to Israel financed the purchase of military equipment. Conversely, by denying Egypt and Algeria U.S. aid, Johnson forced them to turn to the USSR in their effort to keep up with Israel's militarization.

In 1956, Americans under Eisenhower had opposed the invasion of the Suez Canal by Israel, France and Britain. In contrast, in June 1967, Johnson would

---

[504] Hersh, *The Samson Option, op. cit.,* p. 207-15.

[505] Quoted in Ball, *The Passionate Attachment, op. cit.,* p. 51.

[506] Quoted in Piper, *Final Judgment, op. cit.,* p. 115.

[507] Stephen Green, *Taking Sides: America's Secret Relations With a Militant Israel*, William Morrow & Co, 1984, p. 186.

[508] Jean Lacouture, *De Gaulle: Tome 3, le souverain (1959-1970)*, Seuil, 2010.

give Israel a green light for its "preemptive" war against Egypt, waged under a false pretext for the purpose of territorial expansion, as is now well documented.[509] In a letter dated June 3rd, Johnson assured Israeli Prime Minister Levi Eshkol: "I want to protect the territorial integrity of Israel [...] and will provide as effective American support as possible to preserve the peace and freedom of your nation and of the area."[510] Two days earlier, in a Washington meeting on May 30th, the CIA provided Mossad chief Meir Amit photos taken from satellites and spy planes, which enabled Israel to precisely locate the Egyptian armaments and destroy them within six days. That was the beginning of a longstanding cooperation between CIA and Mossad, under the supervision of James Jesus Angleton, the "Israel Office" man in Langley.

James Jesus Angleton directed the Counter-intelligence Division of the CIA since his nomination by Allen Dulles in 1954 until his dismissal by William Colby in 1974. Having survived the 1961 purge like Helms, he played an important role in the cover-up after Kennedy's assassination, as the CIA liaison officer to the Warren Commission investigators. His biographer Tom Mangold (*Cold Warrior*) states: "Angleton's closest professional friends overseas [...] came from the Mossad and [...] he was held in immense esteem by his Israeli colleagues and by the state of Israel, which was to award him profound honors after his death."[511]

Two days before the end of the 1967 war, on June 8th, Israel launched its treacherous attack on the weaponless NSA ship USS Liberty, with the obvious intention of leaving no one alive and blaming Egypt for the raid. Johnson accepted Israel's spurious "targeting error" explanation. In January 1968 he invited the Israeli Prime Minister, Levi Eshkol, to Washington, and warmly welcomed him to his Texas ranch.[512] The lesson would not be lost on Israel: the price for failure in a false flag attack against the United States is non-existent. In fact, failure is impossible, since the Americans will take it upon themselves to cover up the crime. Better yet, Johnson rewarded Israel by lifting the embargo on military offensive equipment: U.S.-made tanks and aircrafts immediately flowed to Tel Aviv. Under Nixon, military sales would reach $600 million in 1971 and $3 billion two years later, making Israel the first customer of the U.S. defense industry.

---

[509] Andrew and Leslie Cockburn, *Dangerous Liaison, op. cit.,* p. 140-7.
[510] U.S. Department of State Archive: 2001-
2009.state.gov/r/pa/ho/frus/johnsonlb/xix/28057.htm
[511] Tom Mangold, *Cold Warrior: James Jesus Angleton: the CIA's Master Spy Hunter,* Simon & Schuster, 1991.
[512] Andrew and Leslie Cockburn, *Dangerous Liaison, op. cit.,* p. 163.

In view of the tremendous advantages that Israel has reaped from John Kennedy's assassination, should we consider Israel's guilt in the assassination as a reasonable hypothesis? Some authors have done so, most notably Michael Collins Piper in *Final Judgment* (1993). The case rests in part on the mysterious personality of James Jesus Angleton, who rendered great services to Israel as chief of CIA's Israel Office from 1954 to 1974, and was actively involved in covering up the JFK assassination, including by stealing the diary of his sister-in-law Mary Pinchot after her death.[513] The case against Israel rests more strongly still on Jack Ruby, the man who killed the man who killed (allegedly) Kennedy, after having introduced himself in the Dallas Police station as a translator for Israeli reporters. As Collins Piper makes abundantly clear, the common wisdom that connects Ruby to the "Mafia" is misleading: rather, Jacob Rubenstein, as his real name was, was closely associated to a Jewish international crime syndicate led by Meyer Suchowljansky, alias Lansky, a generous contributor to the Zionist cause who would flee to Israel in 1970. This "Yiddish Connection" or "Kosher Nostra," as it is sometimes referred to, included the famous Benjamin "Bugsy" Siegel (romanticized by Hollywood in 1991, played by Warren Beatty), one of the leaders of Murder Incorporated. Ruby was a close friend of Siegel's successor as Lansky's West Coast Henchman, Mickey Cohen, who claims in his memoirs to have been "engrossed with Israel" and boasts of his financial contributions and arms smuggling in favor of the cause. Ruby himself, after having travelled to Israel in 1955, became involved in an international arms smuggling operation from Dallas, that involved a Mossad agent (Texas being then a major center of fundraising and arms smuggling on behalf of the Zionist cause). Gary Wean, a detective sergeant for the Los Angeles Police Department, reveals in his book *There's a Fish in the Courthouse* (1987) that Cohen had frequent contacts with Menachem Begin. Incidentally, Wean also believes that Cohen, who specialized in sexually compromising Hollywood stars for the purpose of blackmail, was responsible for arranging John Kennedy's encounter with Marilyn Monroe, from whom he would then try to extract information regarding Kennedy's intention on Israel.[514]

As told earlier (end of chapter 7), Gary Wean raised the possibility, based on Senator John Tower's testimony, that the Dallas coup was "a double-cross of fantastic dimensions," in which a failed assassination attempt staged by the CIA had been transformed into a successful one by another force. According to Piper, Frank Sturgis, who reportedly boasted of the Dallas assassination, is the likely mole who introduced the real snipers into the CIA's staged assassination—a bit like when actor Brandon Lee was killed on set by a gun that should have been loaded with a blank cartridge, to borrow Nick Kollerstrom's meta-

---

[513] Janney, *Mary's Mosaïc, op. cit.*
[514] Piper, *Final Judgment, op. cit.,* p. 219-27, 232-7.

phor.[515] Besides being involved with the Cuban exiles, Sturgis is known to have served in the Hagannah in 1948 and to have kept intimate ties with Israeli intelligence. This double-cross scenario is comparable to a drill exercise being diverted into a real attack, as 9/11 was in part.[516]

Among the likely *sayanim* who orchestrated the Warren Commission cover-up Piper mentions Arlen Specter, assistant counsel to the Warren Commission, who came up with the "single bullet theory" and stubbornly defended it against common sense (sticking to it in his 2000 book, *Passion for Truth*). As wrote journalist Jefferson Morley: "Specter's theory remains the keystone on which the edifice of Oswald's sole guilt rests."[517] At his death in 2012, Specter, the son of Russian Jewish immigrants, was officially mourned by the Israeli government as "an unswerving defender of the Jewish State," and by AIPAC, as "a leading architect of the congressional bond between our country and Israel," while the Committee to Free Jonathan Pollard reminded that he was "among the first to join the call for Pollard's release."[518]

All this and a few other things—such as Yitzhak Rabin's presence in Dallas "hours before" Kennedy's death (a "mere coincidence" revealed by his wife in her biography)[519]—may not seem enough to implicate Israel in Kennedy's assassination, unless we are ready to consider as Israel's tools not only Ruby, Sturgis and maybe Angleton, but Lyndon Johnson himself. It is hardly remembered today that during the Suez Crisis in 1957, Johnson wrote a letter to Secretary of State John Foster Dulles urging the Eisenhower Administration not to support UN sanctions aimed at forcing Israel to retreat. Johnson's letter (which, as the Senate Majority Leader, he got endorsed by the Senate Democratic Policy Committee) appeared in the *New York Times* on February 20, 1957.[520] Johnson's passionate attachment to Israel is an ancient story: he is hailed by some in the Israeli fan club as a "righteous gentile" for having facilitated the illegal immigration in Texas of German Jews in 1938.[521] Johnson himself attributed his philo-Semitism to a family heritage, in remembrance of his grandfather's advice to "Take care of the Jews, God's chosen people. Consider them your friends and help them any way you can."[522] As Johnson's wife Lady Bird would later testify, "Jews have been woven into the warp and woof

---

[515] Kollerstrom, *Terror on the Tube, op. cit.,* p. 28.

[516] Piper, *Final Judgment, op. cit.,* p. 290-7.

[517] www.spartacus.schoolnet.co.uk/JFKspecter.htm

[518] www.haaretz.com/jewish-world/jewish-world-news/prominent-jewish-american-politician-arlen-specter-dies-at-82-1.469977

[519] Lea Rabin, *Rabin: Our Life, His Legacy,* Putnam, 1997, p. 119. Read on Education Forum: educationforum.ipbhost.com/index.php?showtopic=19206&page=8

[520] Louis Bloomfield, *Egypt, Israel, and the Gulf of Aqaba,* Carswell, 1957, p. 152.

[521] See for example "Lyndon B. Johnson – A Righteous Gentile": lyndonjohnsonandisrael.blogspot.fr

[522] James Smallwood, quoted in Wikipedia, "Operation Texas."

of all his years." And is not Johnson the only American President ever to have inaugurated a synagogue—in Austin, a month after becoming President?[523] Some authors have therefore speculated that Lyndon, son of Samuel and Rebekah, belonged to a lineage of Crypto-Jews or *Conversos*. Originating from Spain and Portugal where they had been forced to baptize, then cruelly persecuted by the infamous Inquisition, *Conversos* or *Marranos* were numerous in Texas; most had kept their Christian cover under Mexican rule, where the Inquisition was still tracking them until the middle of the 18th century, and some families maintained some form of attachment to Judaism well into the 20th century.[524] Such speculation, however, add little to our subject: Johnson's friendship with Jews, whatever its origin, does not constitute evidence of his collusion with Israeli elements in Kennedy's assassination.

A clue, however, can be found in Ruby's own words regarding his role in the Dallas coup. Questioned by the Warren Commission, Ruby insisted to be taken to Washington, since, he said, "I am the only one that can bring out the truth to our President." "If you don't take me back to Washington tonight to give me a chance to prove to the President that I am not guilty, then you will see the most tragic thing that will ever happen." Ruby did not detail this "tragic thing," but made it clear that it had to do with the fate of the Jewish people: "there will be a certain tragic occurrence happening if you don't take my testimony and somehow vindicate me so my people don't suffer because of what I have done." He feared that his act would be used "to create some falsehood about some of the Jewish faith," but added that "maybe something can be saved [...], if our President, Lyndon Johnson, knew the truth from me."[525] Ruby seems to have wanted to send a message to Johnson, through the Commission members, a message containing a warning that he may spill the beans about Israel's involvement if Johnson did not intervene in his favor. That impression gets reinforced when we compare the respect he shows Johnson, referred to as "our President, who believes in righteousness and justice," to the accusation he would make in 1967 against that same Johnson, whom he would now call "a Nazi in the worst order" in a handwritten letter.[526] Ruby's violent resentment suggests a sense of betrayal; perhaps Ruby was hoping that Johnson would get him out of jail, just as, in 1952, Johnson had managed, through corruption of the judge and threat to the jury, to keep his personal hitman Mac Wallace out of jail, with only a five-year suspended sentence despite his being found guilty

---

[523] Hersh, *The Samson Option, op. cit.,* p. 127.
[524] Richard Santos, *Silent Heritage: The Sephardim and the Colonization of the Spanish North American Frontier, 1492-1600,* New Sepharade Press, 2000. The hypothesis of Johnson's crypto-judaism is explored in Salvador Astucia, *Opium Lords: Israel, the Golden Triangle, and the Kennedy Assassination,* Dsharpwriter, 2002, p. 170-5.
[525] Read Ruby's deposition on: jfkmurdersolved.com/ruby.htm
[526] Nelson, *LBJ: The Mastermind, op. cit.,* p. 604-7.

of first degree murder (a sure ticket for the death row in Texas, normally).[527]

Ruby's statement to the Warren Commission was obtained from an unknown source and published by journalist Dorothy Kilgallen in the *New York Journal American,* August 18-20, 1964. Kilgallen also interviewed Jack Ruby during his court case and boasted afterwards of being about to "break the real story" and publish "the biggest scoop of the century." She was found dead by an overdose of barbiturate and alcohol on November 8, 1965. Her last published line said about the Kennedy assassination: "That story isn't going to die as long as there's a real reporter alive, and there are a lot of them alive."[528] There has been indeed many reporters investigating Kennedy's assassination, but none has paid sufficient attention to Ruby, his Israeli connections, and his bizarre statements about "his people" or people "of the Jewish faith." Even his real name has been lost in footnotes. That is remarkable, if we pose for a moment and think about it: shouldn't the search for Kennedy's assassin begin with investigating the known assassin of his presumed assassin, that is, the man who made sure the patsy played fully his role? Logic has it that Ruby acted on behalf of Kennedy's real assassin, and that by following his trail, we could get to the heart of the plot. In fact, before dying, Ruby repeatedly told his defense lawyer William Kunstler that he killed Oswald "for the Jews," repeating on several occasions: "I did this that they wouldn't implicate Jews." During Kunstler's last visit Ruby handed him a note in which he reiterated that his motive was to "protect American Jews from a pogrom that could occur because of anger over the assassination."[529] He must have been out of his mind.

Your Jewish Community

Those who find offensive any suspicions of Israel in the assassination of an Amer ican president, should be reminded of the editorial published in *The Atlanta Jewish Times* by its owner and editor in chief Andrew Adler, January 13, 2012, under the heading "What would you do?" Adler calls on Israeli Prime Minister Netanyahu to "give the go-ahead for U.S.-based Mossad agents to take out a president deemed unfriendly to Israel in order for the current Vice-President to take his place and forcefully dictate that the United States' policy includes its helping the Jewish state obliterate its enemies."[530]

---

[527] Nelson, *LBJ: The Mastermind, op. cit.,* p. 271-80.

[528] Talbot, *Brothers, op. cit.,* p. 262-3.

[529] William Kunstler, *My Life as a Radical Lawyer,* Carol Publishing, 1994, p. 158

[530] Joe Sterling, "Jewish paper's column catches Secret Service's eye »", CNN, January 22, 2012: edition.cnn.com/2012/01/21/us/jewish-president-threat

All of the above elements may still fall short of prosecuting Israel in John Kennedy's assassination. But there are also suspicions of Israel's guilt in the assassination of John Kennedy's brother Robert on June 6, 1968. How else can we explain the fact that the hypnotized patsy accused of the crime was, this time, a Palestinian young man allegedly motivated by hatred of Israel? Pages in Sirhan Sirhan's diary (of which he would claim no memory) were filled with repetitive expressions of anger at RFK for his promise to sell military armament to Israel, if elected: "RFK must die, RFK must be killed." The assassination of Robert Kennedy is therefore remembered in "superficial history" (as opposed to "deep history") as the first act of international terrorism carried out on American soil and motivated by the Palestinians' hatred for Israel. Once we recognize it as a false flag scenario, Robert's assassination bears the stamp of Israel.

Could Robert's assassination have something to do with the attack on the USS Liberty by the Israeli army a year earlier, almost to the day, and with Johnson's willingness to cover it up? The question will probably remain forever unanswered, but what we know of Johnson's unbridled psychopathy makes it conceivable that he bargained the impunity of Israel for the near sinking of the USS Liberty in exchange for the murder of his mortal enemy. What we know of Johnson's key role in linking the destinies of Israel and the U.S. makes it even possible that the deal was only part of a secret pact.

There may be, after all, some mundane truth behind the mystical rumor (widespread on Zionist blogs) of a "curse" brought upon the Kennedys by patriarch Joe Kennedy's anti-Semitism.[531] Ten years after John Kennedy Jr's tragic death on July 16, 1999 (his private plane exploded in mid-air, seconds after he had announced that he was preparing to land at an airport near Martha's Vineyard, Massachusetts), Israel's prominent journalist Barry Chamish wrote: "Yes, I'm sure he was murdered. And yes, the Israeli political establishment had a motive for involvement. The latest Kennedy to die violently was the only American editor to expose (in the March 1997 issue of his magazine *George*) the conspiracy behind Rabin's assassination. And he had every intention of continuing his exposes' until he got to the bottom of the matter. We don't know what drove him to stand alone in seeking the truth, but it may have had much to do with the information contained within Michael Piper's (2004) book the *Final Judgment*."[532]

---

[531] See for example: lifeinisrael.blogspot.fr/2012/05/frum-version-of-kennedy-curse.html. Nothing is mentioned of this "jewish curse" in literature destined for the *goyim*, such as Edward Klein, *The Kennedy Curse: Why Tragedy Has Haunted America's First Family for 150 Years*, St. Martin Press, 2003, which places the blame on the Kennedys' own hubris.

[532] Barry Chamish, "The Murder of JFK Jr – Ten Years Later," BarryChamish.com, reproduced on: www.rense.com/general87/tenyrs.htm

The assassination of Robert Kennedy bears some resemblance with the assassination of King Faisal of Saudi Arabia on March 25, 1975. Faisal, who was much loved for having modernized his country and saved it from bankruptcy and corruption, was assassinated by his nephew Faisal bin Musaid, a psychologically disturbed young man addicted to LSD, who had just come back from California via Beirut, where he had received psychiatric treatment. He was quickly beheaded before explaining his motivation. King Faisal had been the first and the last Saudi King to really support the Palestinian cause and the Pan-Arabic project. He had provoked the first oil crisis in the attempt to change U.S. pro-Israel foreign policy.

The collaboration between the American and Israeli deep states would only be strengthened throughout the 1970s and 80s. Israeli intelligence services played a decisive role in the secret negotiations with Iran that deprived Carter of his October Surprise and allowed the Republicans the win in 1980. The Israeli Prime Minister Menachem Begin wanted to eliminate Carter, who was pressuring Israel for the restitution of Sinai to Egypt and the creation of a Palestinian state, as Ari Ben-Menashe, one Israeli officer involved in the secret deal, explained to investigative journalist Robert Parry.[533] The proceeds from the illegal arms sales to Iran were used to illegally arm the Contras, again with the help of the Israelis, who found advantage in having Iran and Iraq destroy each other. This secret collaboration between Israel and the U.S. under Bush Sr., and its concomitant manipulation of American democracy, would be reactivated again under Bush Jr. in 2001.

---

[533] Robert Parry, *America's Stolen Narrative, op. cit.,* pos. 3293-3309.

30. JFK-9/11

Ultimately, there is an undeniable causal link between the assassination of John F. Kennedy and September 11th: the conditions for the second would not have materialized if President Kennedy had survived and continued his policy. The Cold War could not have been exploited for Israel's purely nationalist ends, and imperialist militarism would likely have been restrained. The main perpetrators of the Kennedy assassination and September 11th are not the same; but it is likely that the involvement of George Bush Sr. in the Dallas crime, however limited, created the conditions for a complex blackmail of his son and family, forcing George Bush Jr. to take the brunt of the responsibility for the September 11th plot and to pursue a pro-Israeli policy of which his father disapproved. The Bush clan was beaten at their own game, albeit by players of a higher league.

From the point of view of social psychology, there are also reasons to believe that the handling and cover-up of September 11th could not have taken place without the mechanisms of propaganda designed to keep the truth about November 22nd hidden. To use a psychoanalytic concept, the Kennedy lie constitutes a kind of "crypt," a dark and repressed secret working deep within America's unconscious that made, and makes it vulnerable to other lies. Every lie told creates a further predisposition to lie, not least due to all the lies required to keep the first one from exposure, and the crypt deepens as each lie is buried into another. Conversely, the unveiling of a lie threatens to unveil other lies. That is why we still see a fierce desire to perpetuate the lie about the death of Kennedy, which if once ever fully exposed would inevitably lead to the unearthing of the truths about September 11th.

There are structural parallels between the two cases. The role of the Vice-President is one: Johnson and Cheney were both key players in conspiracies. Though Kennedy had to be murdered for Johnson to take his place, Bush didn't have to die to let Cheney rule: he was merely a dummy from the beginning. Another parallel is the role played by a foreign power. Even if we exonerate Israel from any direct involvement in Kennedy's assassination, it can still be regarded as a partially aborted false flag terror operation involving three powers: a foreign government "F" (the anti-Castro Cubans in exile) organizes an attack against its powerful ally (the United States) under the false flag of a enemy power "E" (the Castro government), in hopes of duping the United States to fight E in its place. From this point of view, the Kennedy assassination is the blueprint for September 11th, a much more successful operation whose triangular structure is even more clearly marked: "F" is this time Israel, and the enemy "E" to be fought includes all of Israel's hostile neighbors. In both cases, the project was developed through a close relationship between the secret services of the United States and its ally: in the 1960s, Cuban exiles had woven a fine relationship with the CIA, and beginning with the Johnson Presidency, the Mossad has done much, if not more, of the same.

There are many commonalities between American policies vis-à-vis Cuba and Israel, as shown by Lawrence Davidson in *Foreign Policy, Inc.: Privatizing America's National Interest* (2009).[534] U.S. policy regarding Cuba is largely due to the powerful lobby, Cuban American National Foundation (CANF), founded in 1981 by Jorge Mas Canosa. Canosa explained that he had modeled his organization on AIPAC: "We realized pretty soon that to influence the U.S. political system we must copy [...] the Jewish model, and we became very closely allied with the Jewish lobby and the Jewish movement in Washington." Canosa was a veteran of the Bay of Pigs motivated by a visceral hatred of Castro and, according to Davidson, had "institutionalized that hatred when he founded the Cuban American National Foundation." Florida has always been a "swing state" because of a million Cuban exiles, whose votes the CANF can rally relatively at will. Consequently, after Kennedy, without exception all American presidents have maintained the political embargo against Cuba. Clinton, for example, felt obliged to promise during his campaign to "put the hammer down on Fidel Castro and Cuba," and his successor Bush Jr., to "see the end of the Castro régime." Lawrence Wilkerson, Colin Powell's Chief of Staff at the State Department, called the embargo "the dumbest policy on the face of the earth," because it serves the interests of neither the Americans nor the Cubans, and is rather merely the obsession of a powerful lobby. The U.S. policy towards Israel is the exact opposite of the unconditional hostility towards Cuba, but shows the same rigid permanence, and for many of the same electoral reasons. Both policies are as absurd as the other, which is why they are kept mired in convoluted rhetoric and perpetual propaganda. They involve criminal behaviors of secret services, which inevitably degenerate into staging fake or real attacks carried out under false flags. On the side of the Cuban diaspora, the criminal transformation is embodied in Mas Canosa himself, who,

---

[534] Lawrence Davidson, *Foreign Policy, Inc.: Privatizing America's National Interest,* The University Press of Kentucky, 2009.

according to an investigation by the *New York Times* based on a hundred sources, was at the origin of the attack on Flight 455 of the Cuban national company *Cubana de Aviacion*, on October 6, 1976, killing 73 Cuban and Venezuelan passengers. Among those involved was Cuban exile Luis Posada Carriles, also formerly of Operation 40 and the assault on the Bay of Pigs, but the U.S. has refused to extradite him to Venezuela for judgment, in violation of the extradition treaty between the two countries.[535] Thus the United States government, which has recently threatened any country harboring terrorists, falls under its own judgment.

"The nation which indulges towards another a habitual hatred or a habitual fondness is in some degree a slave. It is a slave to its animosity or to its affection, either of which is sufficient to lead it astray from its duty and its interest. [...] Sympathy for the favorite nation, facilitating the illusion of an imaginary common interest in cases where no real common interest exists, and infusing into one the enmities of the other, betrays the former into a participation in the quarrels and wars of the latter without adequate inducement or justification. [...] And it gives to ambitious, corrupted, or deluded citizens (who devote themselves to the favorite nation), facility to betray or sacrifice the interests of their own country, without odium, sometimes even with popularity" (George Washington, *Farewell Address*, 1796).[536]

The abusive power of pressure groups is merely a symptom of a deeper disease in American democracy. How is it that American institutions, originally designed to allow citizens to be governed by those they deem worthy, have become the opposite: a system that encourages the most corrupt to claw their way to the summit of power, and permits anti-democratic forces to govern from behind a shroud? The short answer was given by Iranian President Ahmadinejad on September 26, 2012, in the form of a rhetorical question: "Can anybody believe that those spending hundreds of millions of dollars on electoral campaigns have the people's interests at heart?" The power of lobbies is essentially

---

[535] Lawrence Davidson, *Foreign Policy, Inc., op. cit.,* p. 92-3.
[536] From this speech, former Undersecretary of State George Ball borrows the title of his book, *The Passionate Attachment* (1992), dealing with America's involvement with Israel from 1947. It is also quoted by Glen Stanish in his "Foreword" to Christopher Bollyn, *Solving 9-11,* p. xxxii-xxxiv.

financial, and results from a U.S. electoral system that imposes no limit on campaign financing; writ large, it means that anyone elected, unless benefitting from a huge personal fortune (as was the case with Kennedy), has been bought before setting foot in the Oval Office.

But the disease is not only institutional. Though it's said that the fish rots from the head, to a large extent, a democracy gets the leaders it deserves. The Americans' submissiveness to Israeli propaganda is rooted in a civilizational affinity of the two peoples; that is to say in their national mythologies. Is not American patriotism rooted in the myth of the puritan "pilgrim fathers" fleeing religious persecution and settling in a new "promised land" like a new "chosen people"? Lyndon Johnson once summarized it well when, speaking before a Jewish audience, he compared "the Jewish pioneers building a home in the desert" to his own ancestors colonizing the New World.[537] What he emphasized, perhaps unintentionally, is the equivalence between the Zionist lie of "a land without a people for a people without a land," which has been used by every denier of the ethnic cleansing of the Palestinians, and the Americans' denial of their own genocidal history. Are not the Palestinians Israel's Indians? This shared denial rooted in the national unconscious is accompanied by the same arrogant belief in divine election, summarized in American mythology by Manifest Destiny, so eloquently expressed by President Woodrow Wilson in 1912: "We are chosen and prominently chosen to show the way to the nations of the world how they shall walk in the path of liberty."[538] Such ideas are potentially paranoid, for placing oneself above common humanity easily leads to seeing others as less than human.

"The more cruel we are towards others, the more devastated we are by the possibility that the subjects of our brutality may also be as nasty as we happen to be." Thus Israeli musician Gilad Atzmon denounces the paranoid spiral in which his country has fallen.[539]

---

[537] Lawrence Davidson, *Foreign Policy, Inc., op. cit.,* p. 112.

[538] Wilson Center: www.wilsoncenter.org/about-woodrow-wilson

[539] Gilad Atzmon, *The Wandering Who: A Study of Jewish Identity Politics,* Zero Books, 2011.

Empathy, which is the experience of human brotherhood, and the only path toward peace, comes not from one who believes himself superior by virtue of his race, nationality, ideology, religion or divine election. Empathy is the ability to put oneself into another's shoes. It is the ability to say, after visiting a coal mine in Chile where miners belonged to a communist union, "If I worked in this mine, I'd be a Communist too," as did Robert Kennedy in November 1965.[540] The rhetoric of the "clash of civilizations," invented today as an ideological tool and replacement for anti-communism, spreads Islamophobic propaganda and seeds a culture of antipathy and fear, inevitably leading to hatred and war. The neoconservatives, who have crafted this myth, like to paint the world in a brutal portrait, calling our human relationships relentless fights to the death, and conclude that therefore the first responsibility of any civilization wanting to survive is to construct the highest capability for defense, for aggression, and for maximum destruction. "Creative destruction is our middle name," said Michael Ledeen in *The War against the Terror Masters*. "Our enemies have always hated this whirlwind of energy and creativity, which menaces their traditions (whatever they may be) and shames them for their inability to keep pace. [...] They must attack us to survive, just like we must destroy them to advance our historic mission."[541]

It is urgent that we think differently if we hold out hope to build upon these ruins of Empire a "civilization of empathy"; perhaps to begin, should we not admit that the whole of humanity is together a "chosen people"? "For, in the final analysis, our most basic common link is that we all inhabit this small planet. We all breathe the same air. We all cherish our children's future. And we are all mortal."[542]

---

[540] Newfield, *RFK, a Memoir, op. cit.,* p. 46.
[541] Quoted in Cook, *Israel and the Clash, op. cit.,* p. 92.
[542] Kennedy's *Peace Speech,* quoted in Douglass, *JFK and the Unspeakable, op. cit.,* p. 390-2.

Essential Bibliography

The books are listed by order of importance.

Book I

James Douglass, *JFK and the Unspeakable: Why He Died and Why it Matters,* Touchstone, 2008. Douglass not only covers the most important evidence accumulated throughout the years, but tells Kennedy's story with such passion as to raise it to mythic dimension.

David Talbot, *Brothers: The Hidden History of the Kennedy Years*, Simon & Schuster, 2007. The second most important source of my Book I, which also covers Robert Kennedy's attempt to conquer the White House.

Mark Lane, *Last Word: My Indictment of the CIA in the Murder of JFK*, Skyhorse Publishing, 2011. Lane, a lawyer, is one of the earliest JFK investigators, and built the strongest case against the CIA.

Peter Janney, *Mary's Mosaic: the CIA Conspiracy to Murder John F. Kennedy, Mary Pinchot Meyer, and Their Vision for World Peace,* Skyhorse Publishing, 2012. Written by the son of a CIA officer, this book focuses on Kennedy's close relationship with Mary Pinchot, until her assassination one year after Kennedy.

Phillip Nelson, *LBJ: The Mastermind of JFK's Assassination,* XLibris, 2010. The most thorough analysis of Lyndon Johnson's implication in the Dallas coup (I have not been able to consult Roger Stone's *The Man Who Killed Kennedy: The Case Against LBJ,* Skyhorse, 2013).

Michael Collins Piper, *Final Judgment: The Missing Link in the JFK Assassination Conspiracy,* American Free Press, 6th ed., 2005. The unique representant of the "third kind of JFK book," exploring the Israeli trail.

Anthony Summers, *The Arrogance of Power: The Secret World of Richard Nixon,* Penguin Books, 2001. A highly critical biography of Richard Nixon.

Russ Baker, *Family of Secrets: The Bush Dynasty, America's Invisible Government, and the Hidden History of the Last Fifty Years,* Bloomsbury Press, 2009. The deep story of the Bushs' rise into politics, covering the JFK assassination and the Watergate scandal.

www.spartacus.schoolnet.co.uk/ The indispensable encyclopedic website on JFK chaired by John Simkins. The most important entries are included in his e-book (Kindle), containing 600 entries: *Assassination of J. F. Kennedy Encyclopedia,* Spartacus Educational, 2012.

www.gwu.edu/~nsarchiv/ : the site of the *National Security Archive Project* of the George Washington University, where most declassified documents of the *National Security Council* can be found.

www.jfklibrary.org/: The site of the John F. Kennedy Presidential Library and Museum, where most of Kennedy's speeches can be read or listened to.

Among the many documentaries on Kennedy and his time, I recommend:

Murder of JFK, a Revisionist History (2006), directed by Matthew White.

JFK 3 Shots That Changed America, 2009, produced by The History Channel directed by Nicole Rittenmeyer and Seth Skundrick.

Virtual JFK: Vietnam if Kennedy Had Lived, by Koji Masutani, 2008.

Dark Legacy, 2009. John Hankey's investigation into George H. W. Bush's role in the Kennedy assassination. Watch it on www.youtube.com/watch?v=YYmombA4WwE

Fog of War, 2003. Errol Morris's acclaimed film based on an interview of Robert McNamara, covering his years as Defense Secretary under Kennedy and Johnson.

Book II

Stephen Sniegoski, *The Transparent Cabal: The Neoconservative Agenda, War in the Middle East, and the National Interest of Israel,* Enigma Edition, 2008.

Jonathan Cook, *Israel and the Clash of Civilizations: Iraq, Iran and the Plan to Remake the Middle East,* Pluto Press, 2008.

James Petras, *Zionism, Militarism and the Decline of US Power,* Clarity Press, 2008. These are my three major sources for chapters 21 to 23.

Webster Griffin Tarpley, *9/11 Synthetic Terror Made in USA,* Progressive Press, 2008. A great and indispensable classic on 9/11, focusing on the rogue network inside the U.S.

David Ray Griffin, *9/11 Contradictions,* Arris Books, 2008. Griffin is one of the earliest and most respected scholars on September 11th, and has authored many other books on the subject.

Christopher Bollyn, *Solving 9-11: The Deception that Changed the World,* 2012. This book summarizes ten years of research and articles by Bollyn, who has built the strongest case for Israel's role in 9/11.

Justin Raimondo, *The Terror Enigma: 9/11 and the Israeli Connection,* iUniversal, 2003.

Gordon Thomas, *Gideon's Spies: the Secret History of the Mossad,* St. Martin's Griffin, 2009. Thomas, perhaps the best historian of the Mossad, has also authored important books on the CIA.

www.voltairenet.org/en. A web of non-aligned press groups founded by Thierry Meyssan, and dedicated to the analysis of international relations, yielding precious insight into the deep and Machiavellian politics underlying contemporary wars.

www.911research.com and www.911review.com. Two scholarly sites providing a wealth of information and analyses.

www.consensus911.org/ While there are still many disagreements among 9/11 researchers, the 9/11 Consensus Panel, comprising engineers, pilots, lawyers and journalists, focuses on the most recognized 32 factual elements which contradict the government's theory.

The following documentaries are recommended:

Loose Change 2, Dylan Avery's famous film, in the 2006 version, the best in my judgment.

September Clues, Simon Shack's systematic and thorough analysis of all films of the crashes on the WTC broadcast on mainstream TVs. The associated forum cluesforum.info/ is also a precious source of information.

Solving the Mystery of WTC7, a 15-minute documentary focusing on WTC7, by Architects & Engineers for 9/11 Truth, which produced other highly convincing films, available on its website: www.ae911truth.org

The Power of Nightmares, 2005, one of Adam Curtis's great BBC documentaries, awarded at the Cannes Festival.

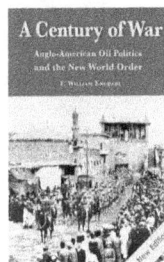

History

Two by George Seldes: *1,000 Americans Who Rule the USA* (1947, 324 pp, $18.95) and *Facts and Fascism* (1943, 292 pp., $15.95) by the great muckraking journalist, whistleblower on the plutocrats who keep the media in lockstep, and finance fascism.

Afghanistan: A Window on the Tragedy. 98 full-page black and white photos. 110 pp, $9.95.

Battling Wall Street: The Kennedy Presidency, by Prof. Donald Gibson. JFK, a martyr who strove mightily for social and economic justice. 208 pp, $14.95.

Enemies by Design: Inventing the War on Terrorism. A century of Middle East imperialism. Biography of Osama bin Laden; Zionization of America; PNAC, Afghanistan, Palestine, Iraq; 416 pp, $17.95.

Global Predator: US Wars for Empire. A damning account of the atrocities committed by US armed forces over two centuries. Also by Stewart H. Ross: *Propaganda for War: How the US was Conditioned to Fight the Great War*. Propaganda by Britain and her agents like Teddy Roosevelt sucked the USA into the war to smash the old world order. 350 pp and $18.95 each.

Inside the Gestapo: Hitler's Shadow over the World. Intimate, fascinating Nazi defector's tale of ruthlessness, intrigue, and geopolitics. 287 pp, $17.95.

The Iraq Lie: How the White House Sold the War, the full inside story, by Congressman Joseph Hoeffel. 268 pp, $14.95

The Nazi Hydra in America: Suppressed History of a Century by Glen Yeadon. US plutocrats launched Hitler, then recouped Nazi assets to erect today's police state. Fascists won WWII because they ran both sides. "Shocking and sobering." – Howard Zinn. 700 pp, $19.95.

Sunk: The Story of the Japanese Submarine Fleet, 1941-1945. The bravery of doomed men in a lost cause, against impossible odds. 300 pp, $15.95.

Troublesome Country: Why we Need to Live Up to Our Creed: A History. 148 pp, $12.95.

Psychology: Brainwashing

The Telescreen: An Empirical Study of the Destruction of Consciousness, by Prof. Jeffrey Grupp. How mass media brainwash us with consumerism and war propaganda. Fake history, news, issues, and reality steal our souls. 199 pp, $14.95. Also by Grupp: *Telementation: Cosmic Feeling and the Law of Attraction*. Deep feeling rather than thought or faith is our secret nature and key to self-realization. 124 pp, $12.95.

Conspiracy, NWO

Corporatism: the Secret Government of the New World Order by Prof. Jeffrey Grupp. Corporations control all world resources. Their New World Order is a "prison planet". 408 pp, $16.95.

Descent into Slavery by Des Griffin. How the banksters took over America and the world. The Founding Fathers, Rothschilds, the Crown and the City, the world wars, and globalization. 310 pp, $16.

Dope Inc.: Britain's Opium War against the United States. "The Book that Drove Kissinger Crazy." Underground Classic, new edition. 320 pp, $19.95.

Final Warning: A History of the New World Order by D. A. Rivera. Classic, in-depth research into the Great Conspiracy: the Fed, the CFR, Trilateral Commission, Illuminati. 360 pp, $19.95.

In Search of the Truth: An Exposure of the Conspiracy, by Azar Mirza-Beg. A portrait of our times, society and religion, and the threat that faces us .208 pp, $15.95

How the World Really Works by A.B. Jones. Crash course in conspiracy offers digests of 11 classics like *Tragedy and Hope, Creature from Jekyll Island*. 336 pp, $15.

Killing Us Softly: Causes and Consequences of the Global Depopulation Policy. The covert agenda to sterilize us with GMO's, vaccines, social influences. 148 pp, $16.95.

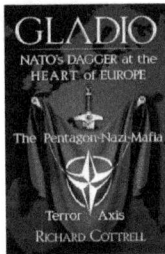